WITHDRAWN

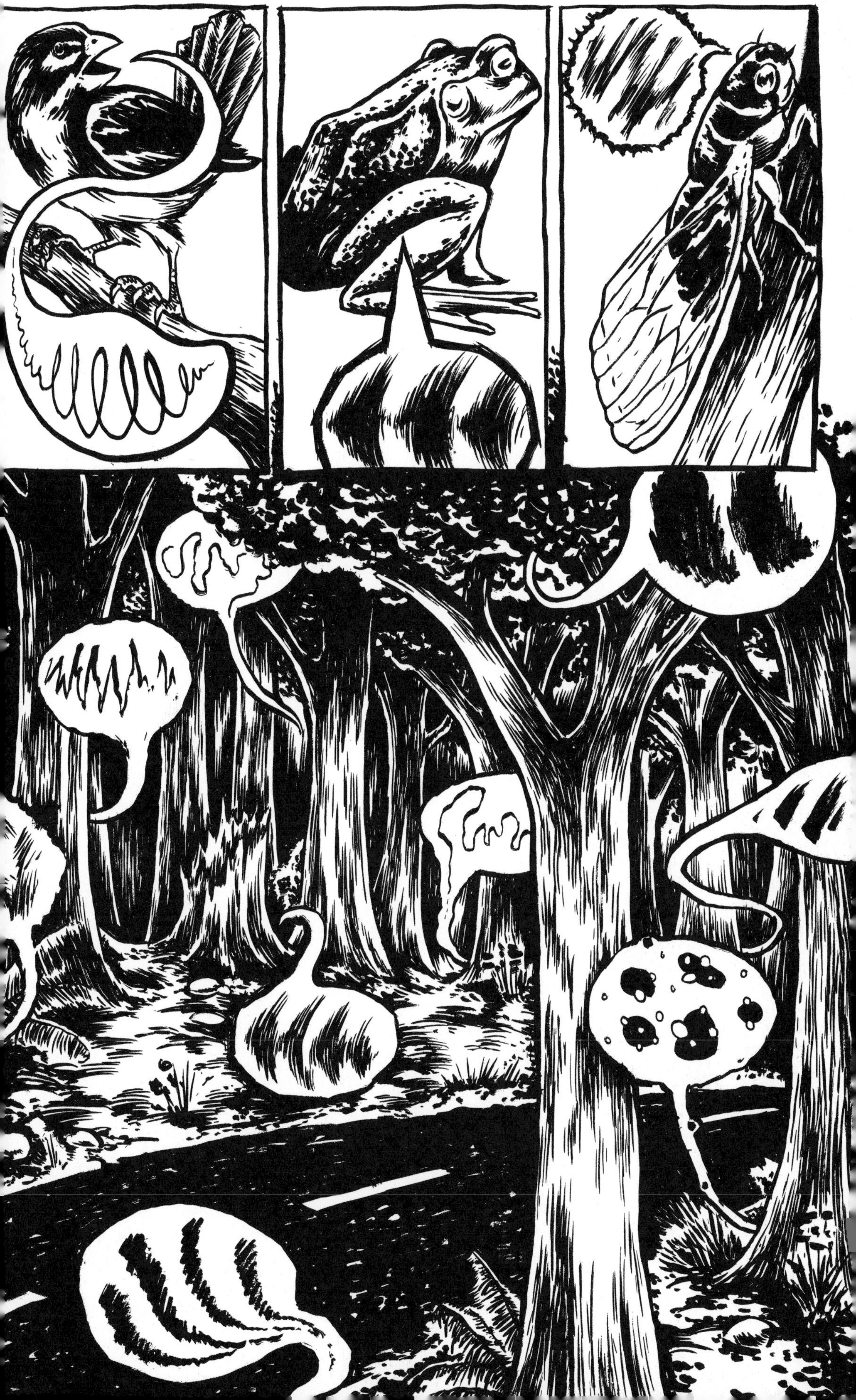

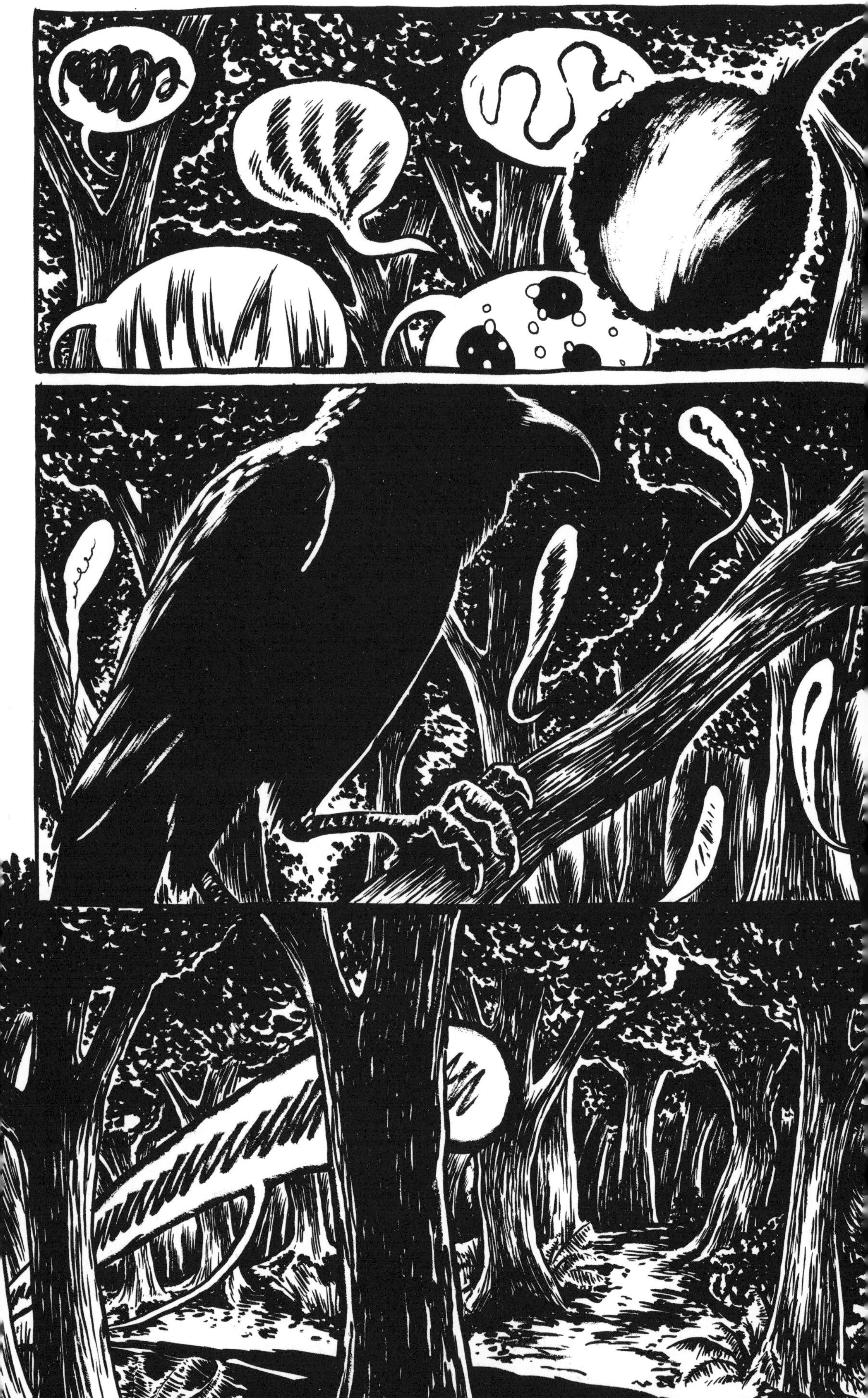

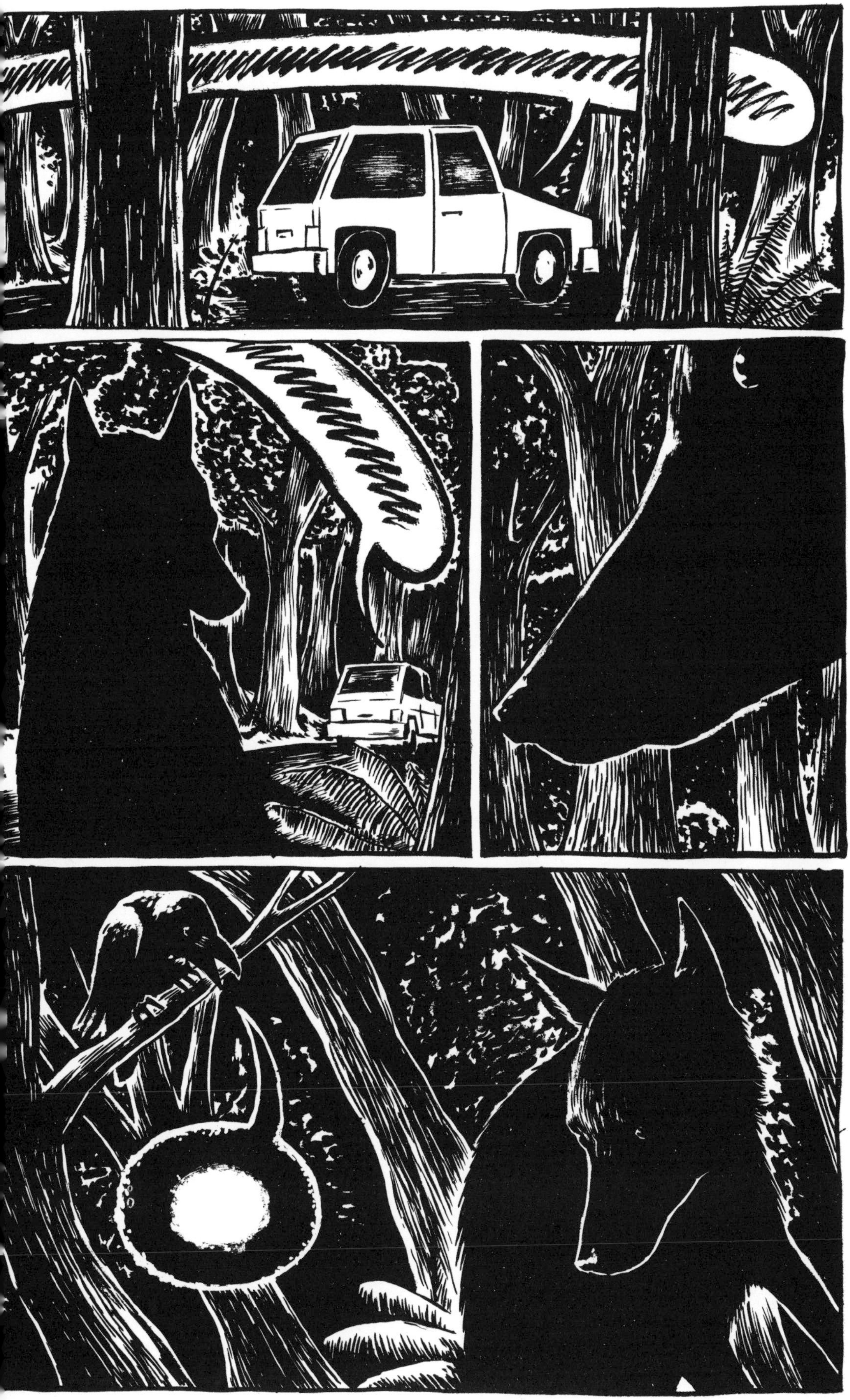

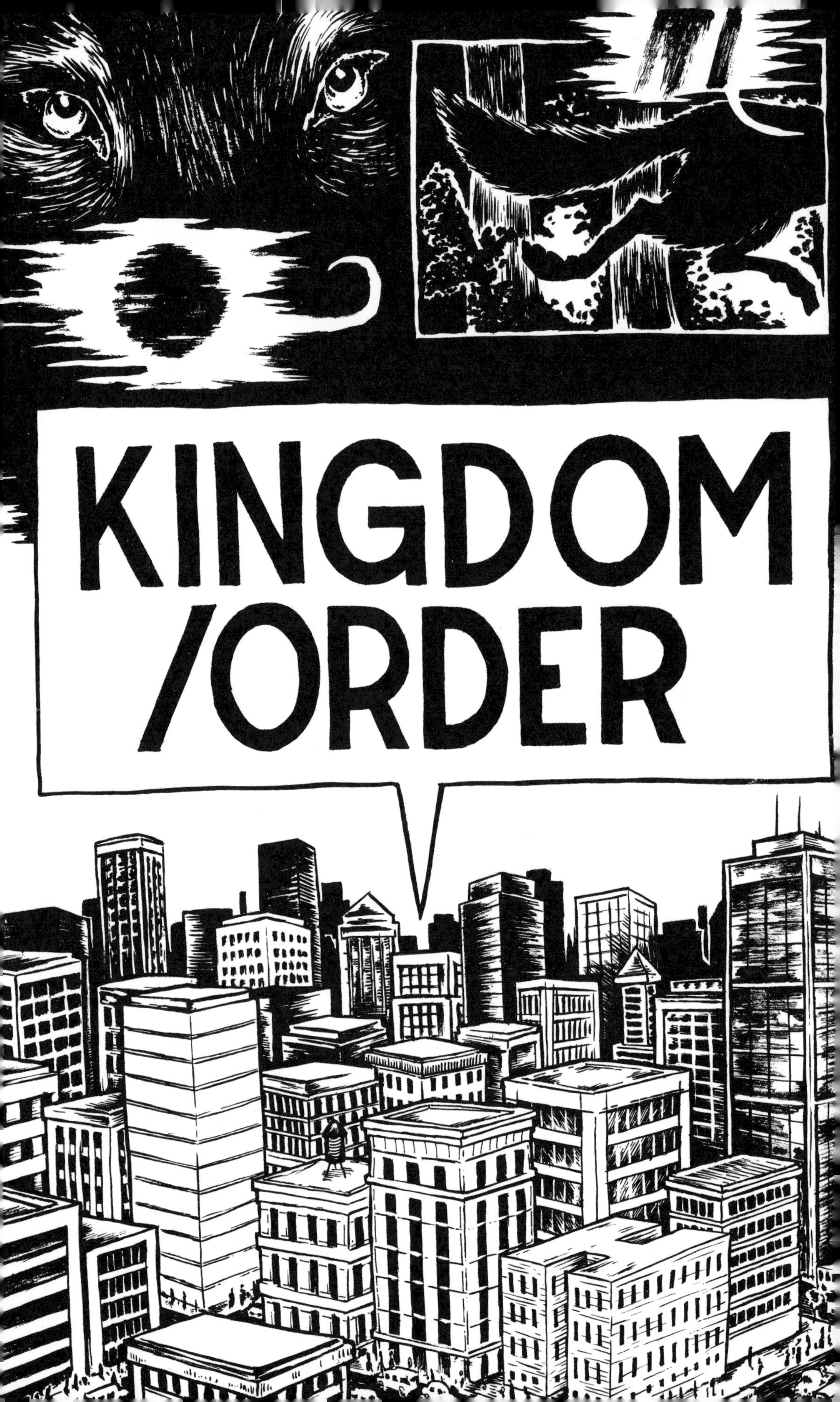
KINGDOM
/ORDER

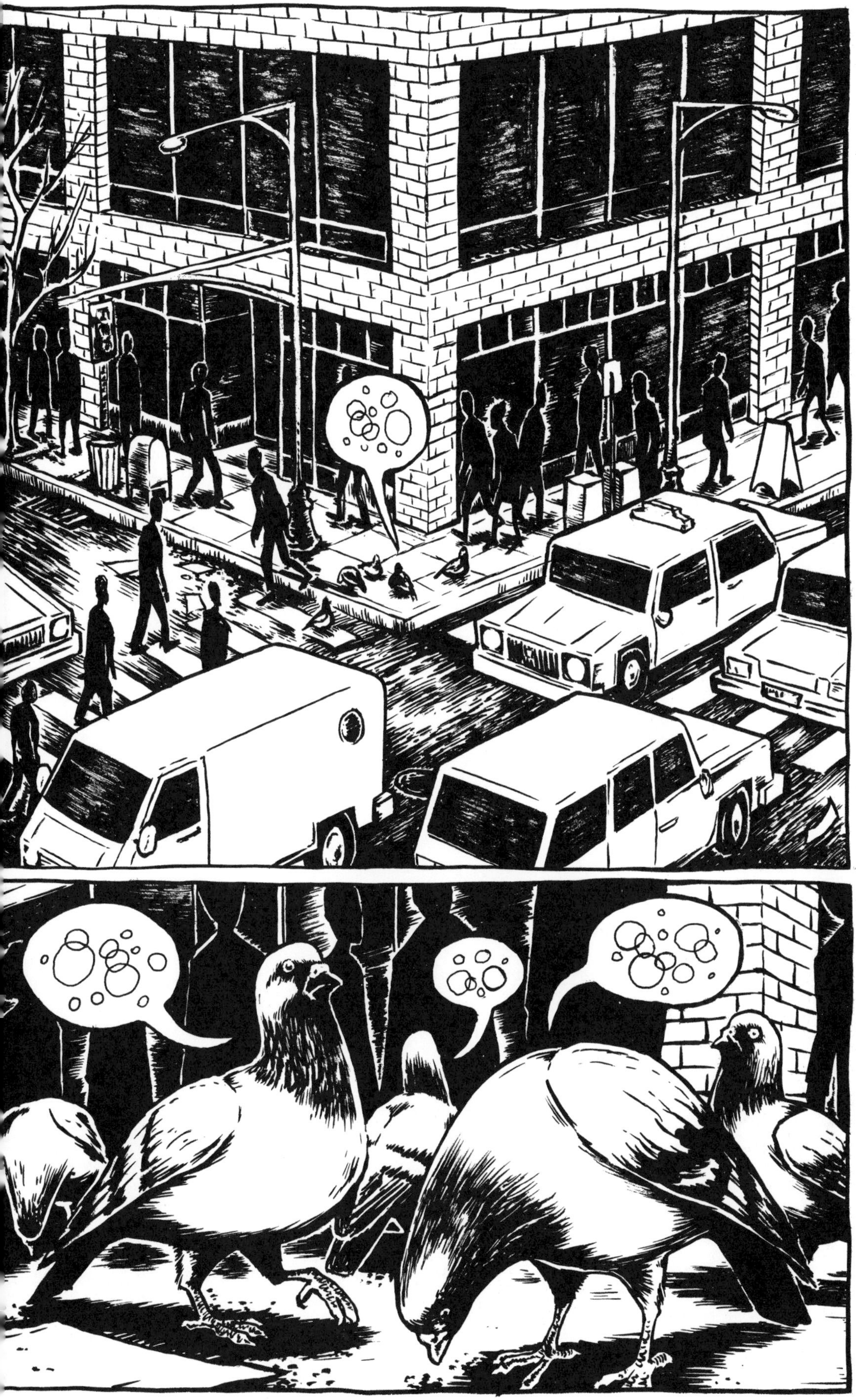

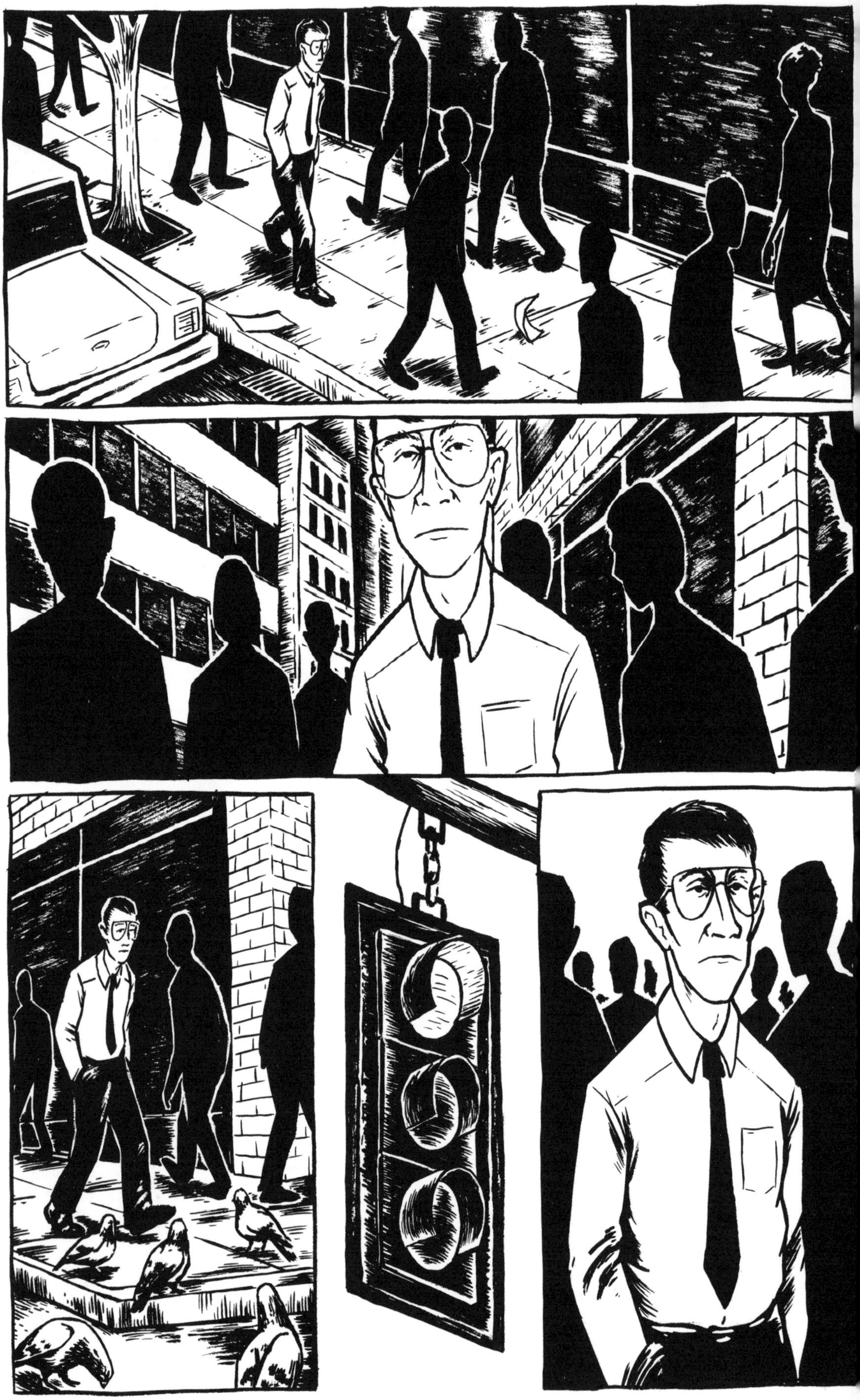

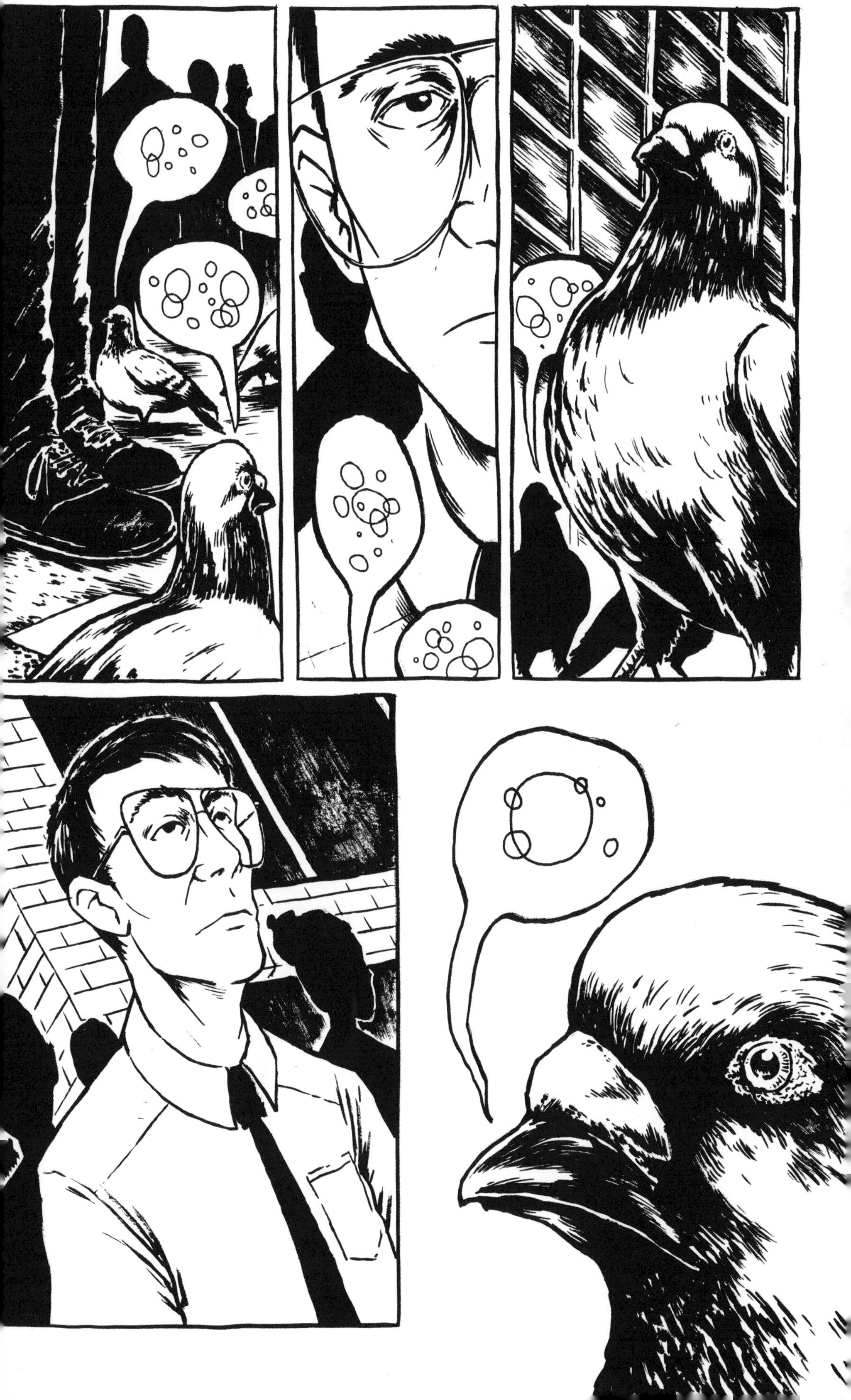

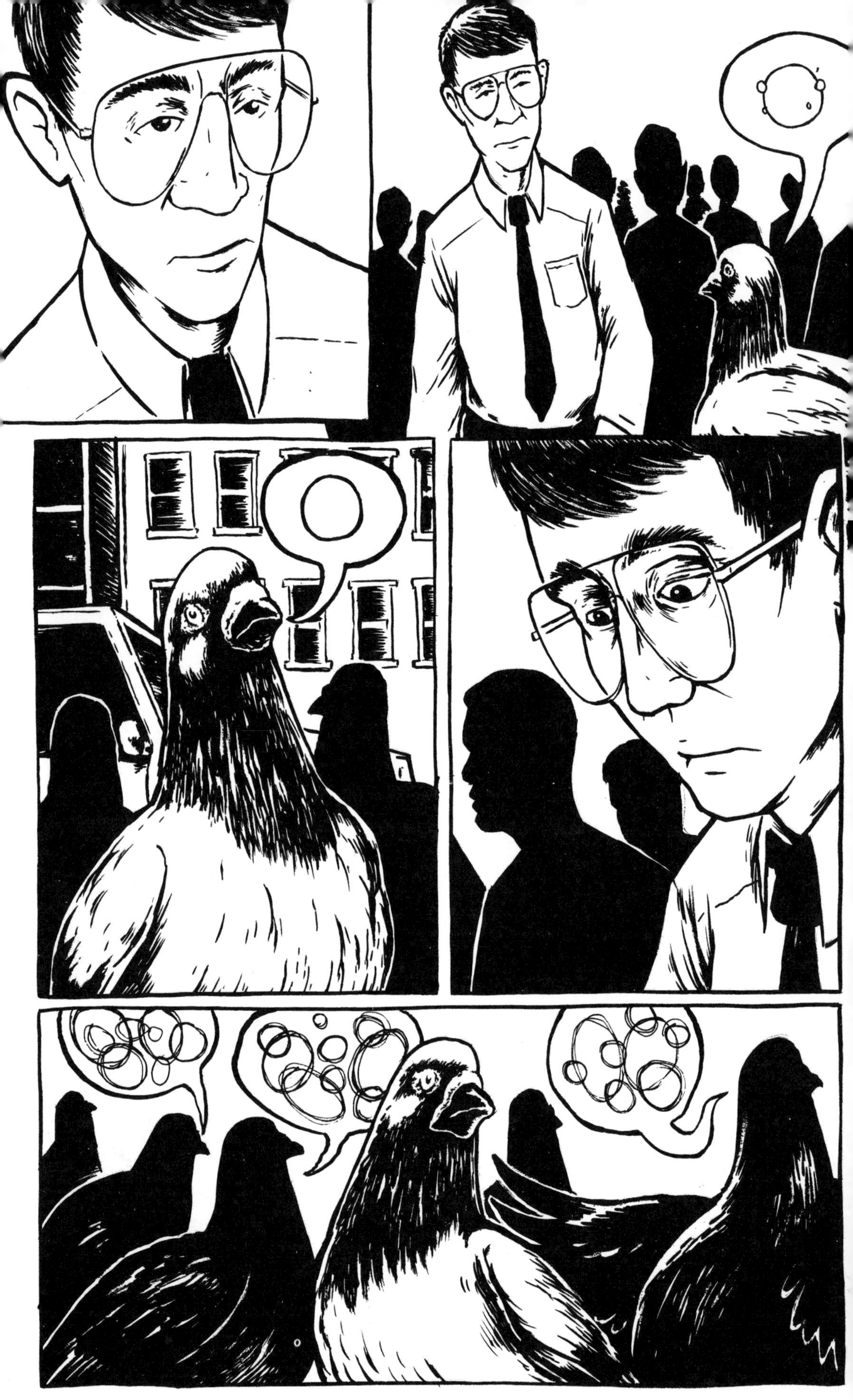

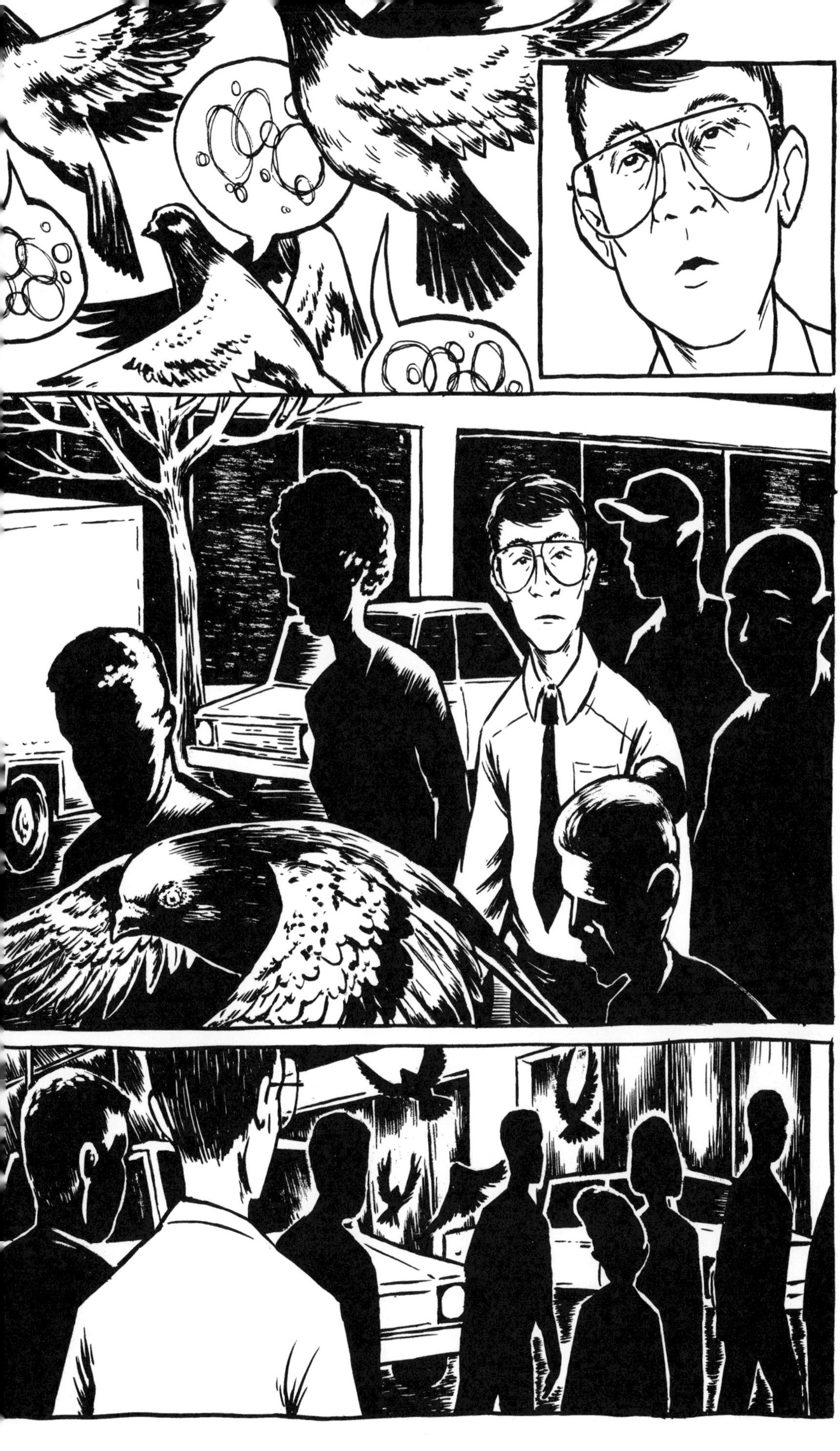

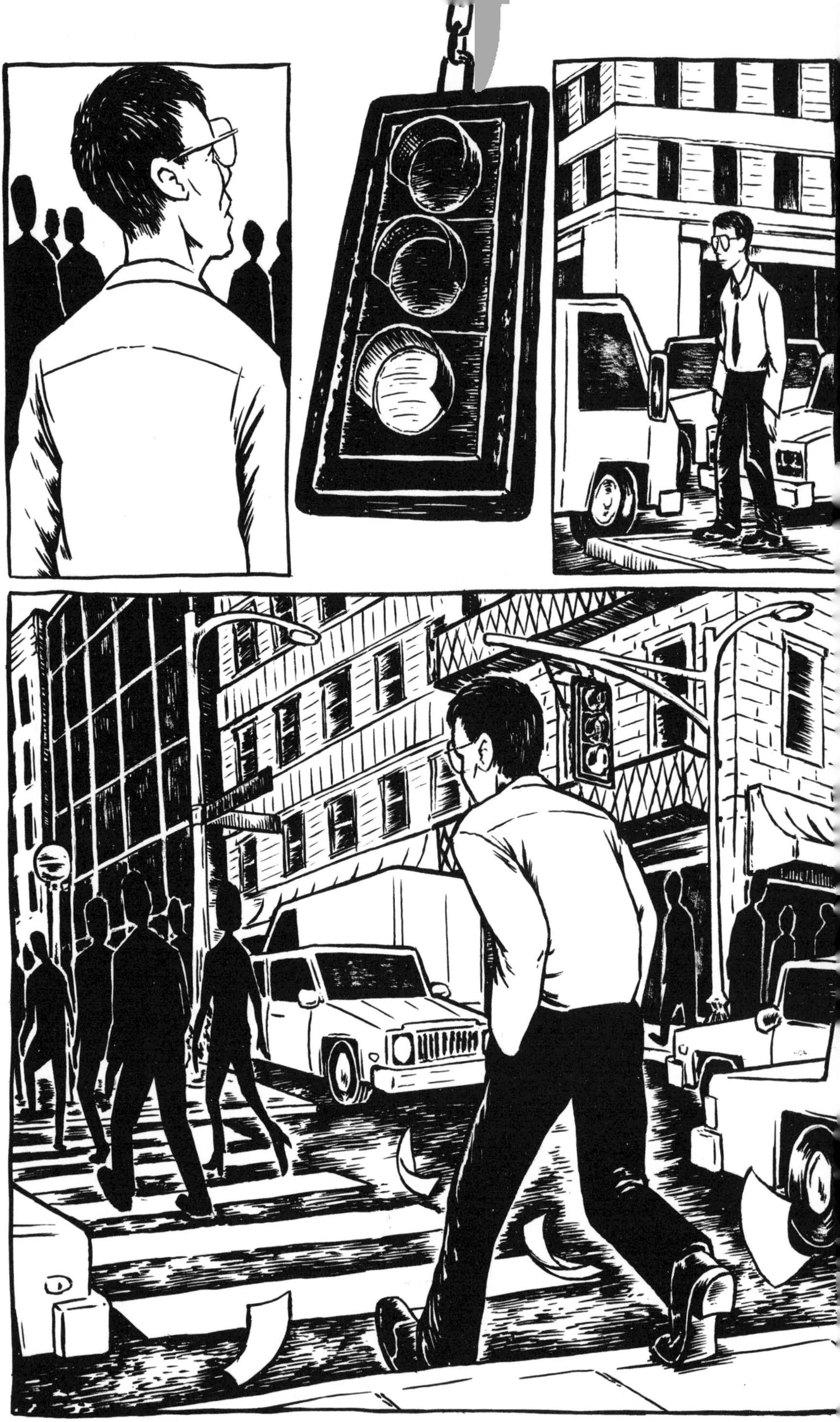

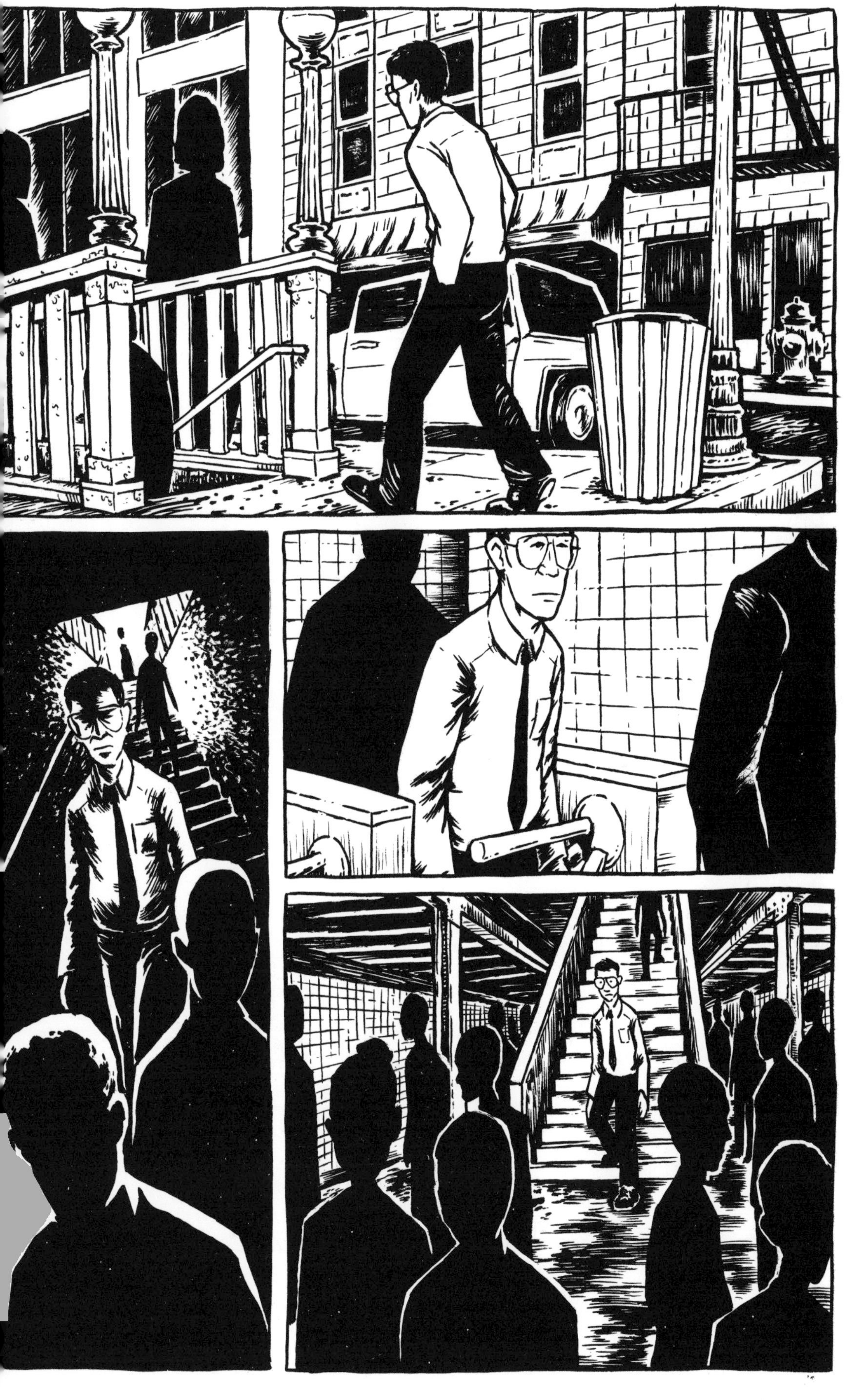

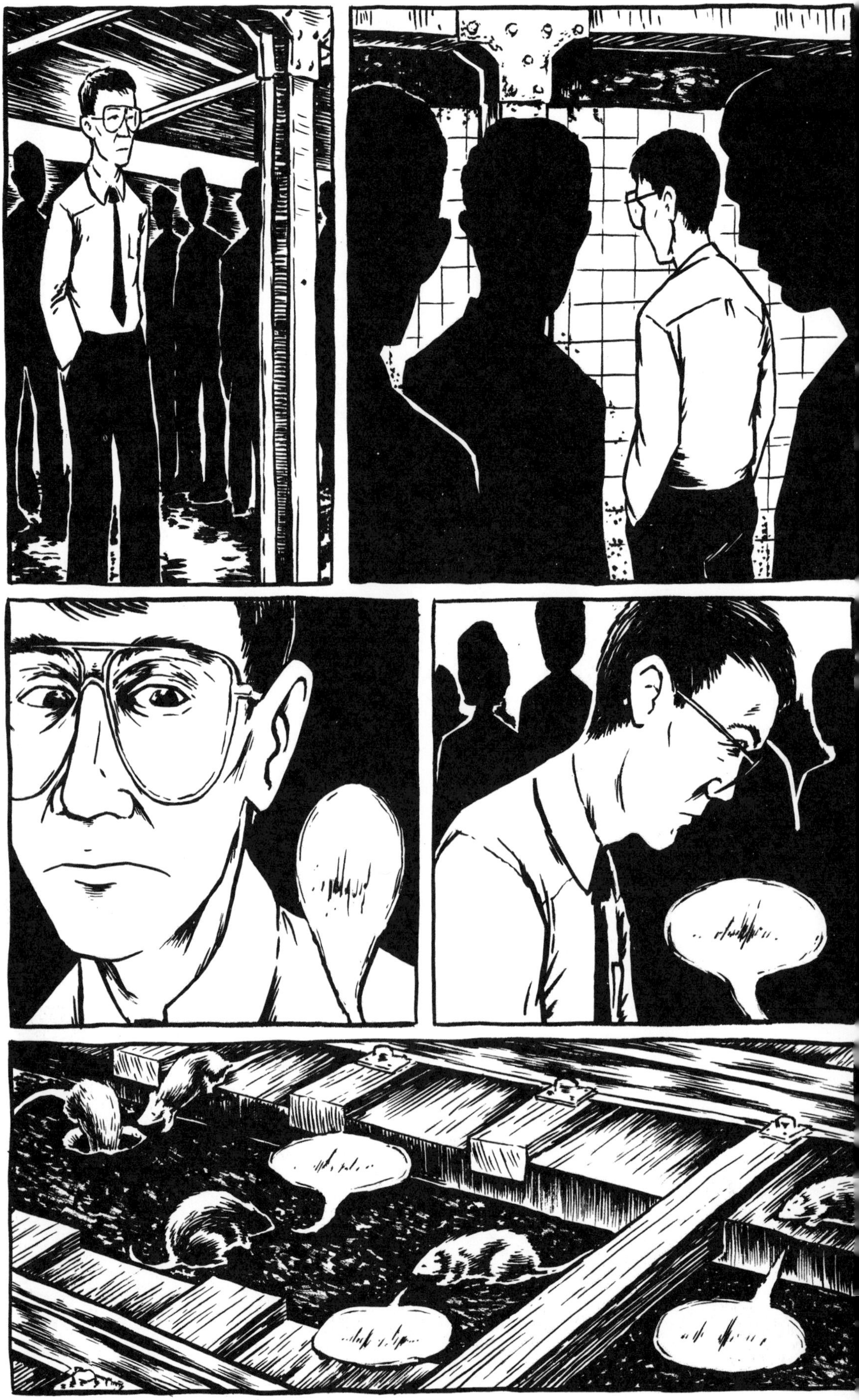

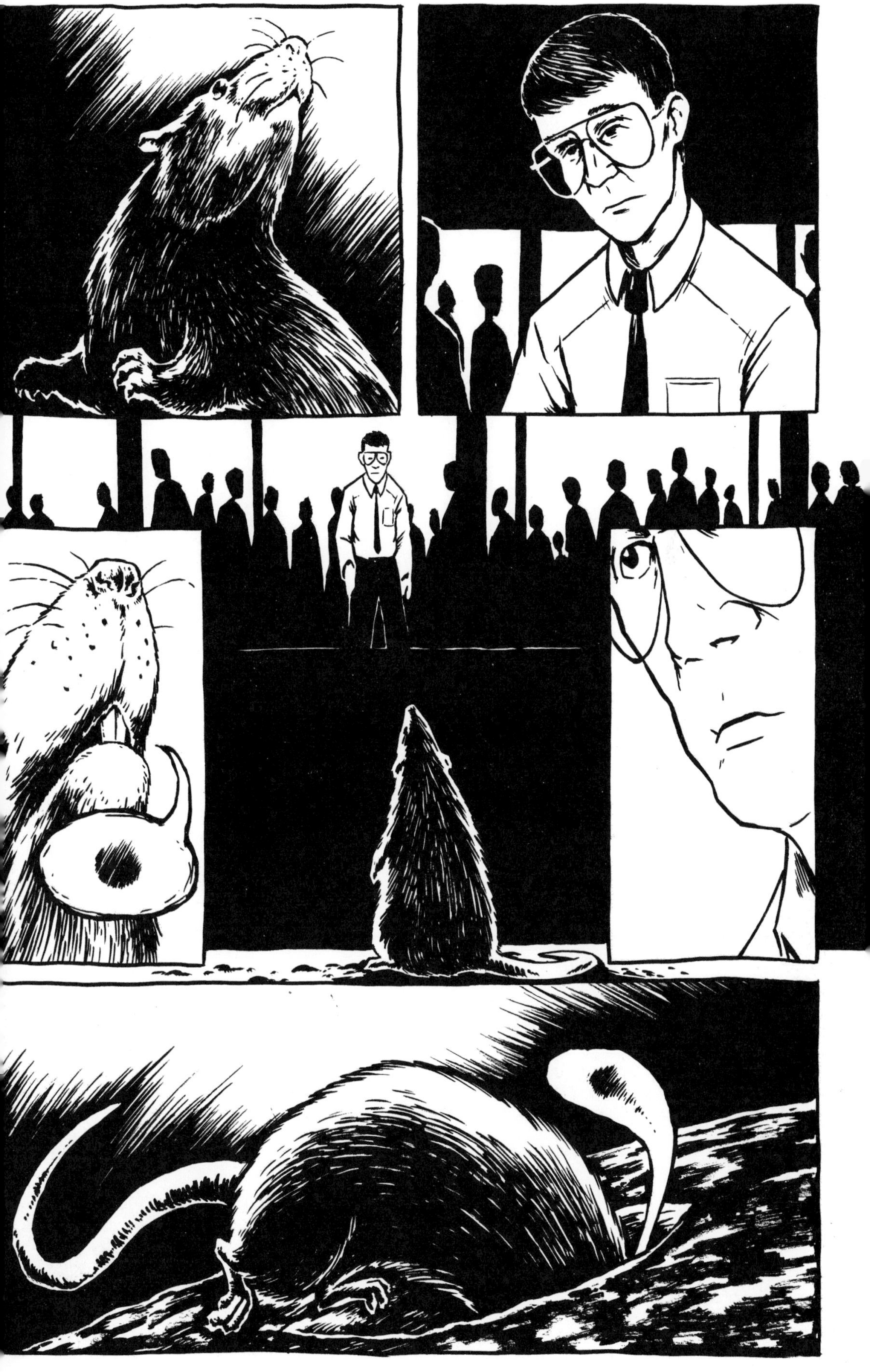

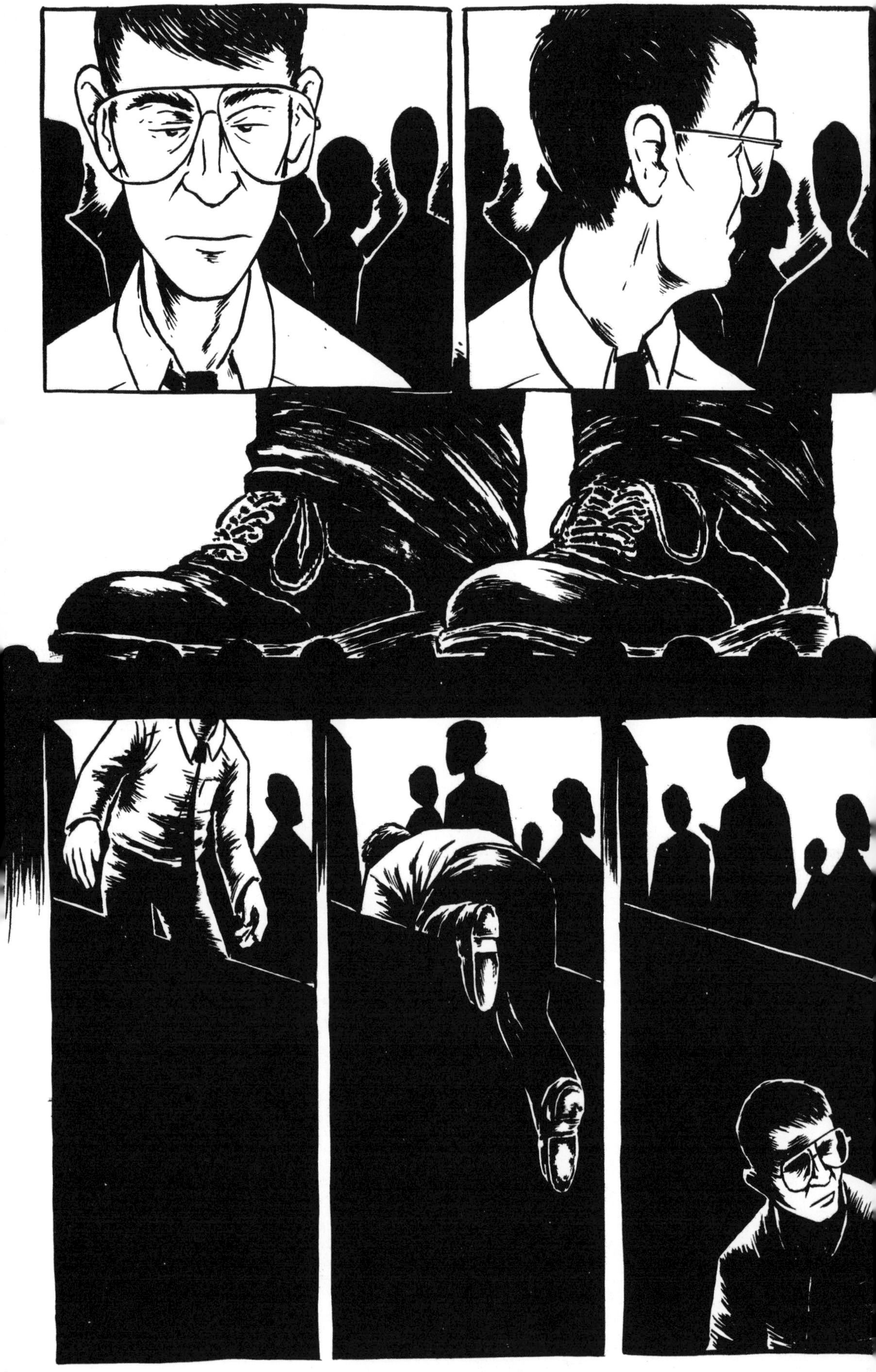

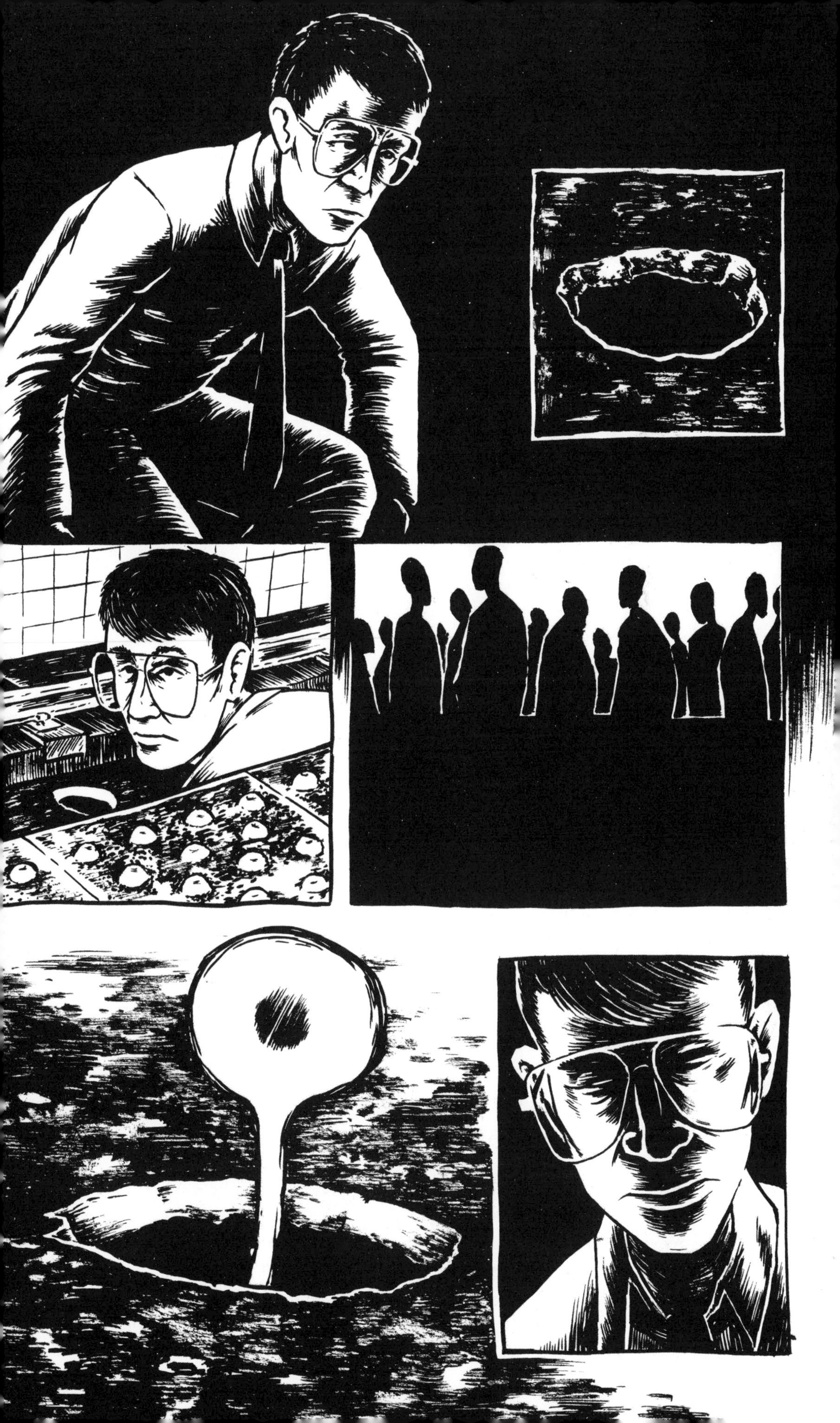

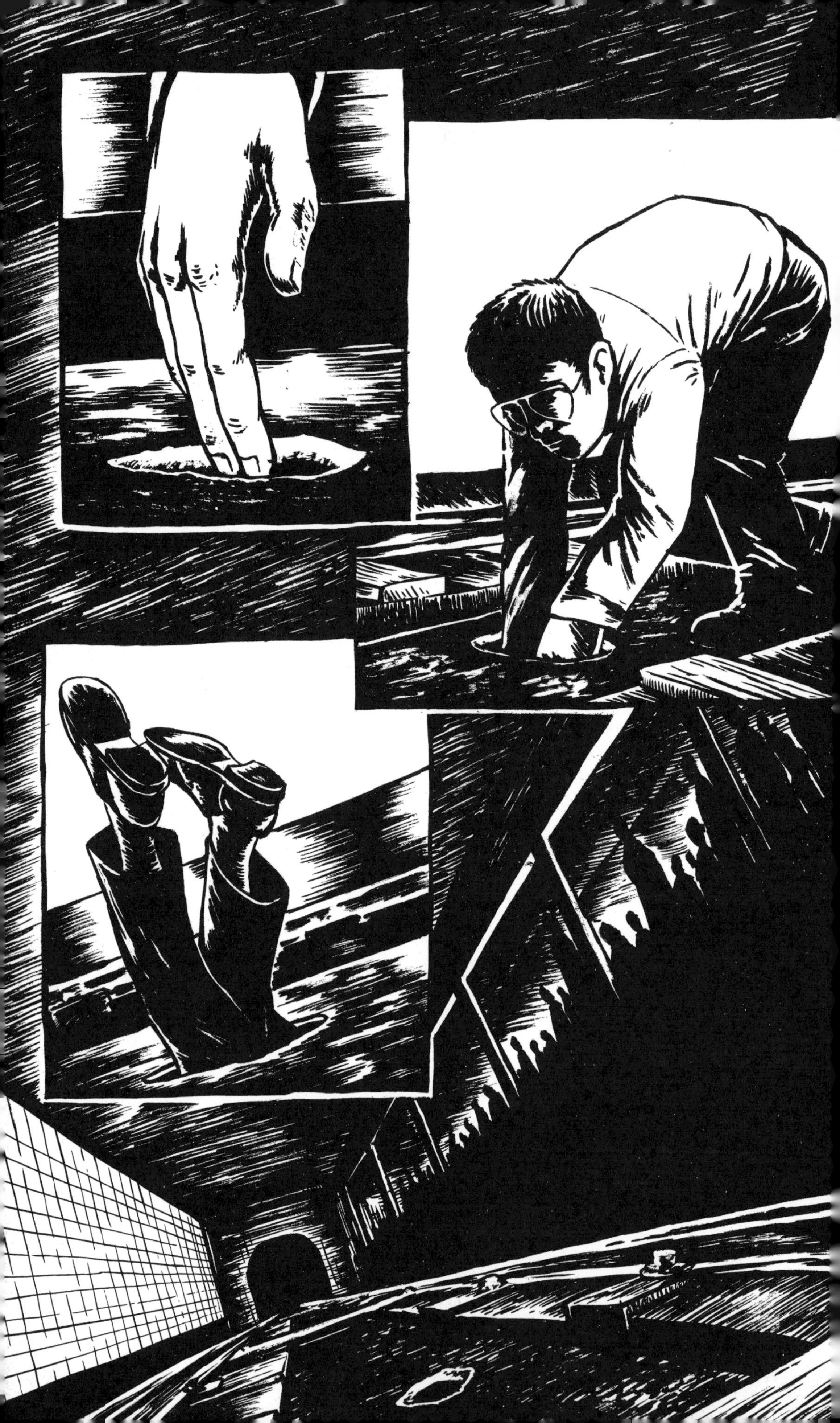

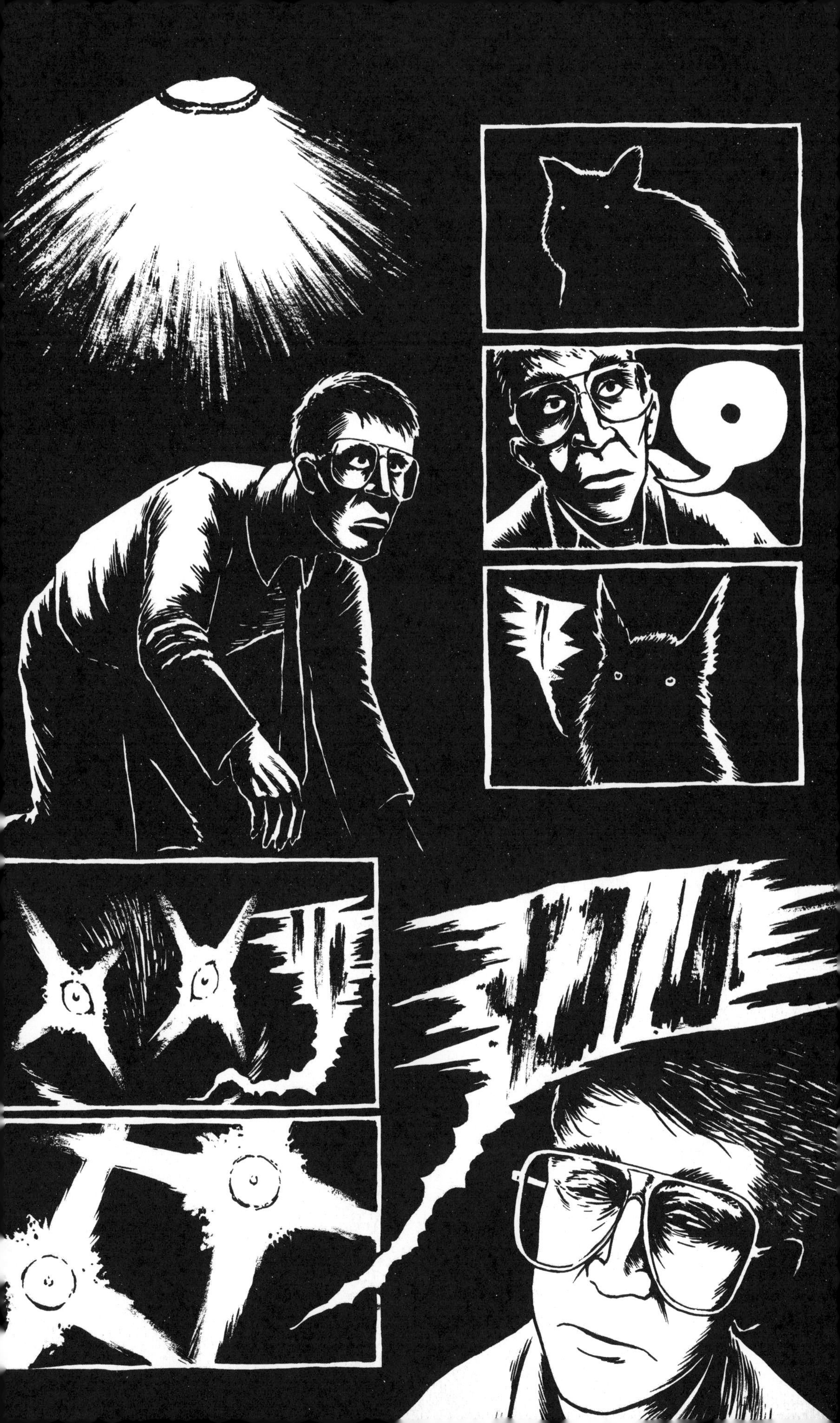

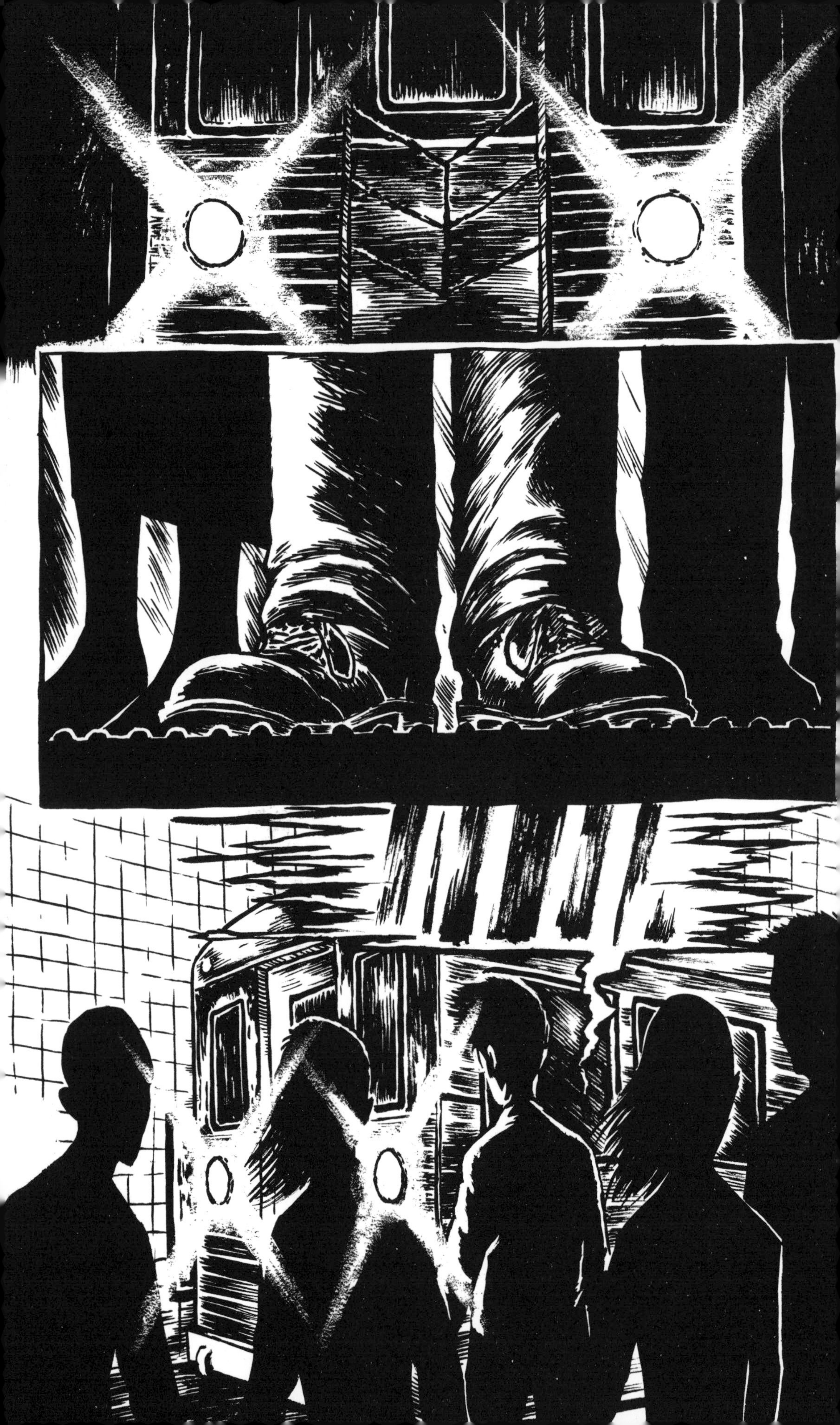

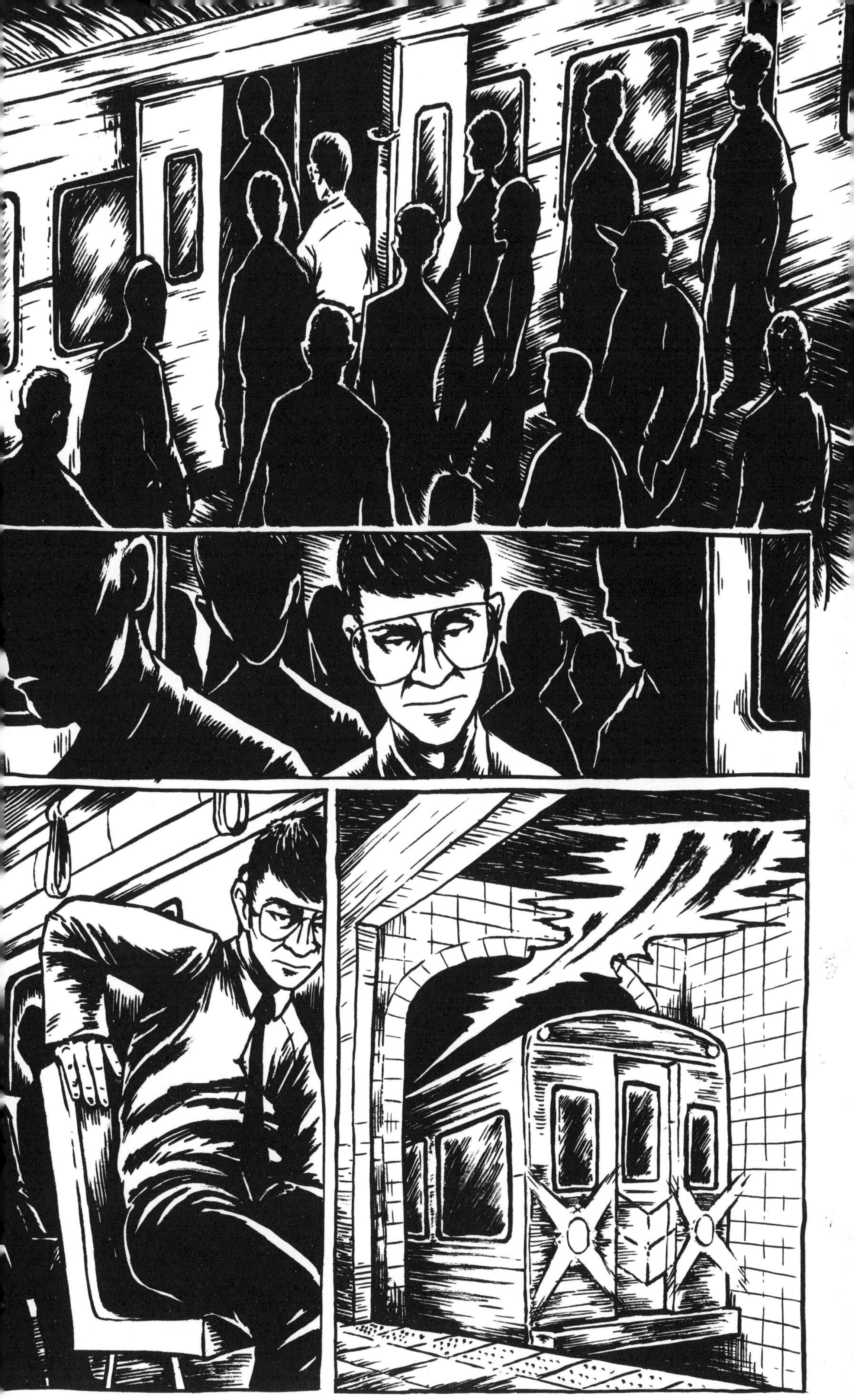

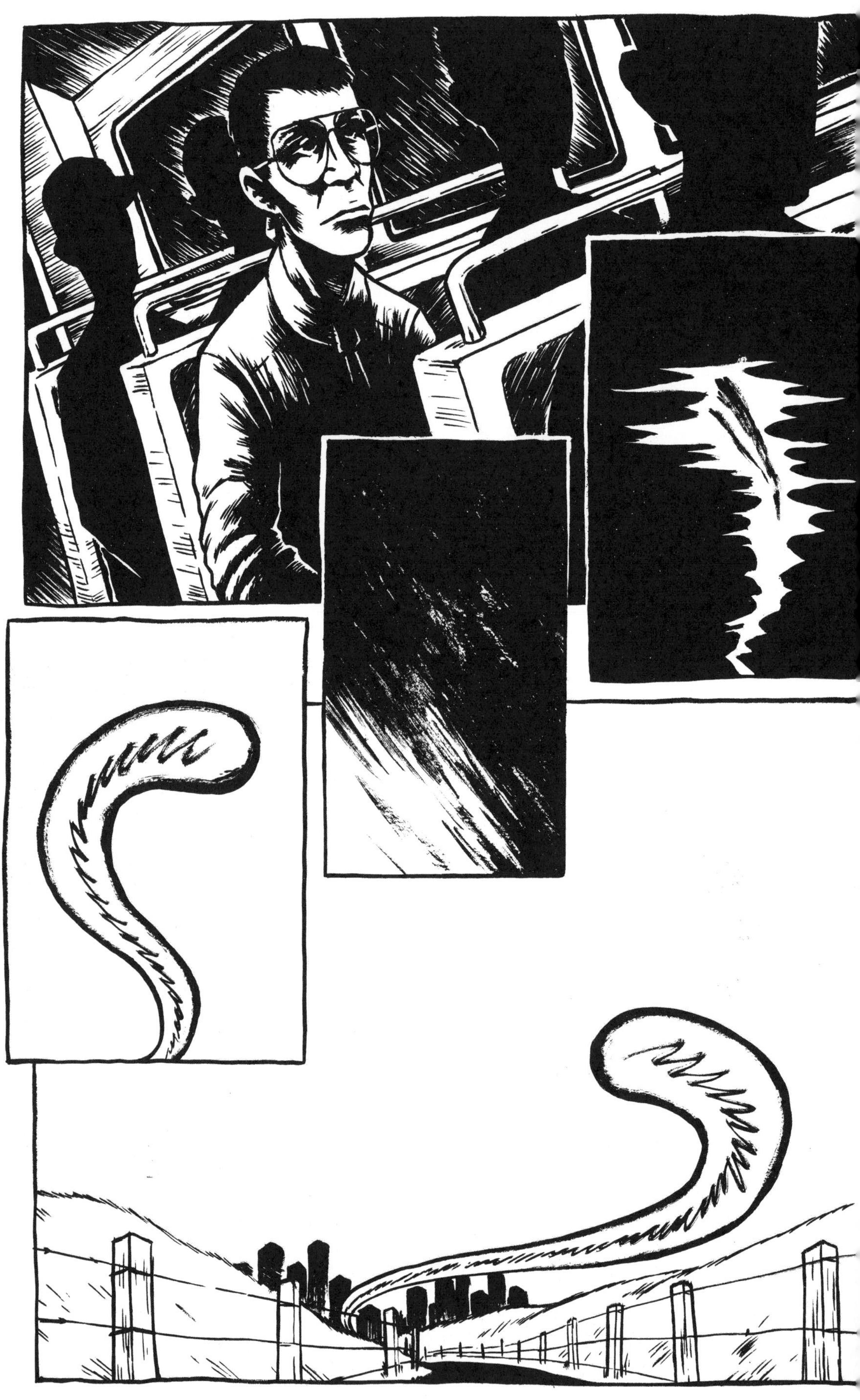

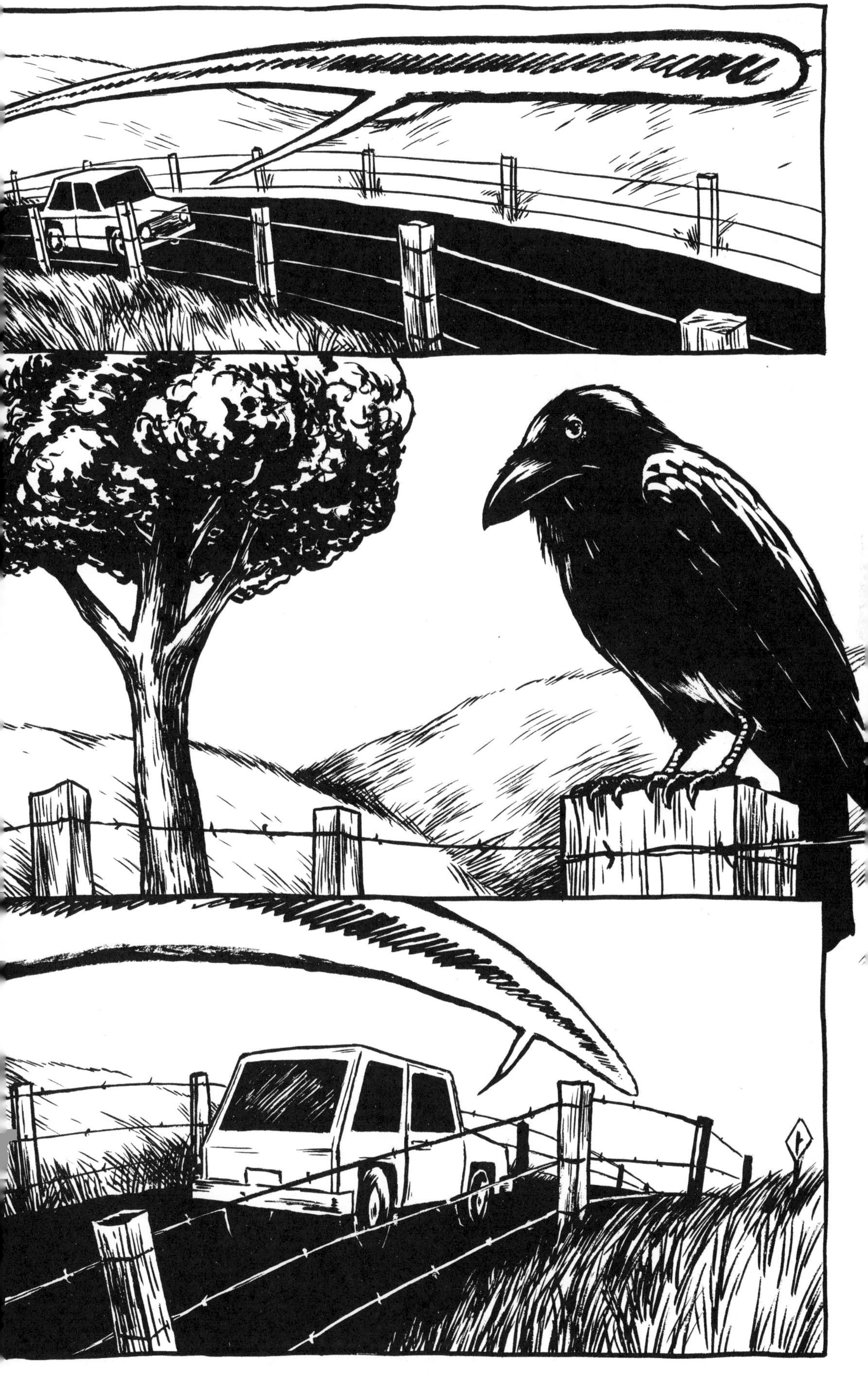

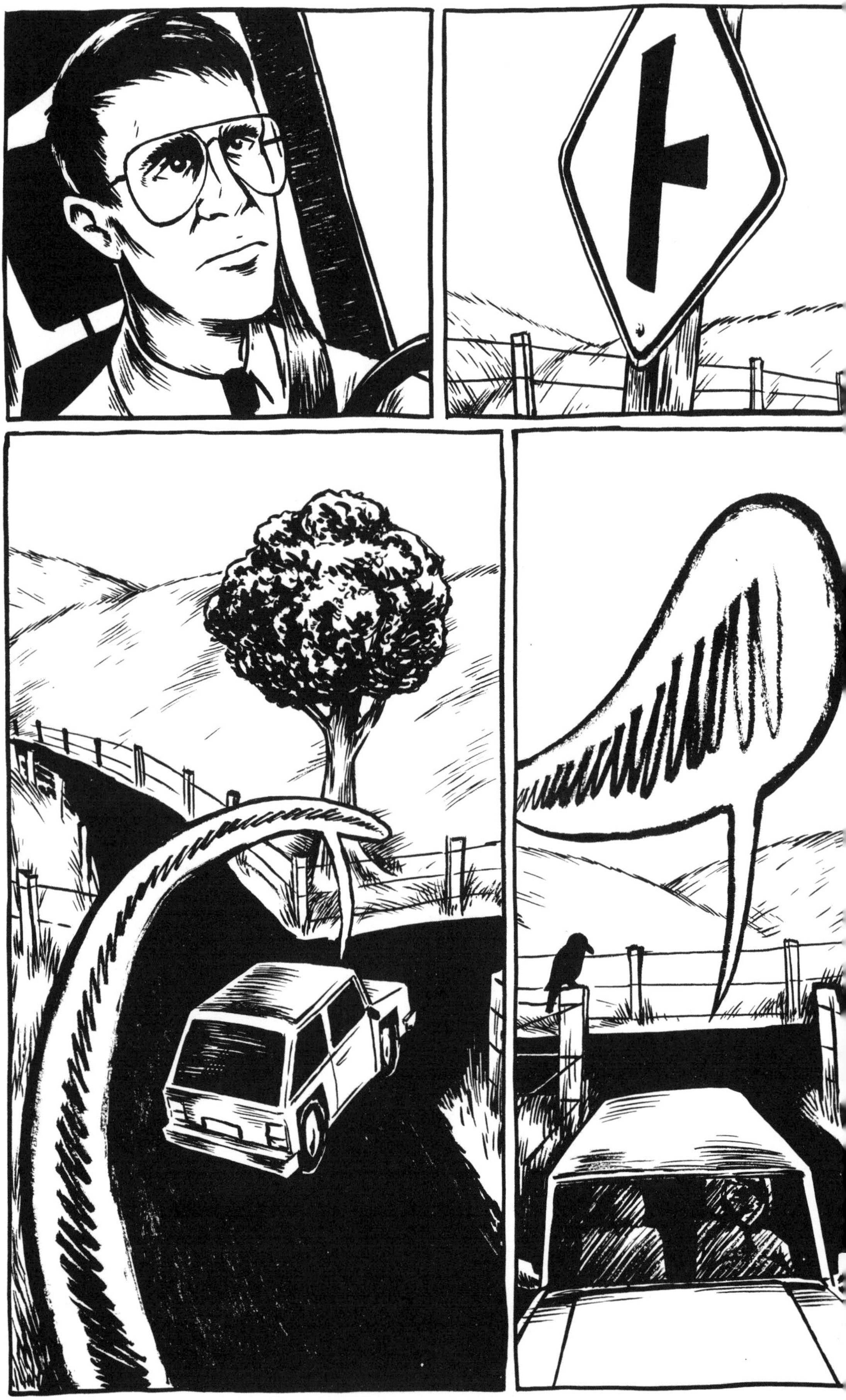

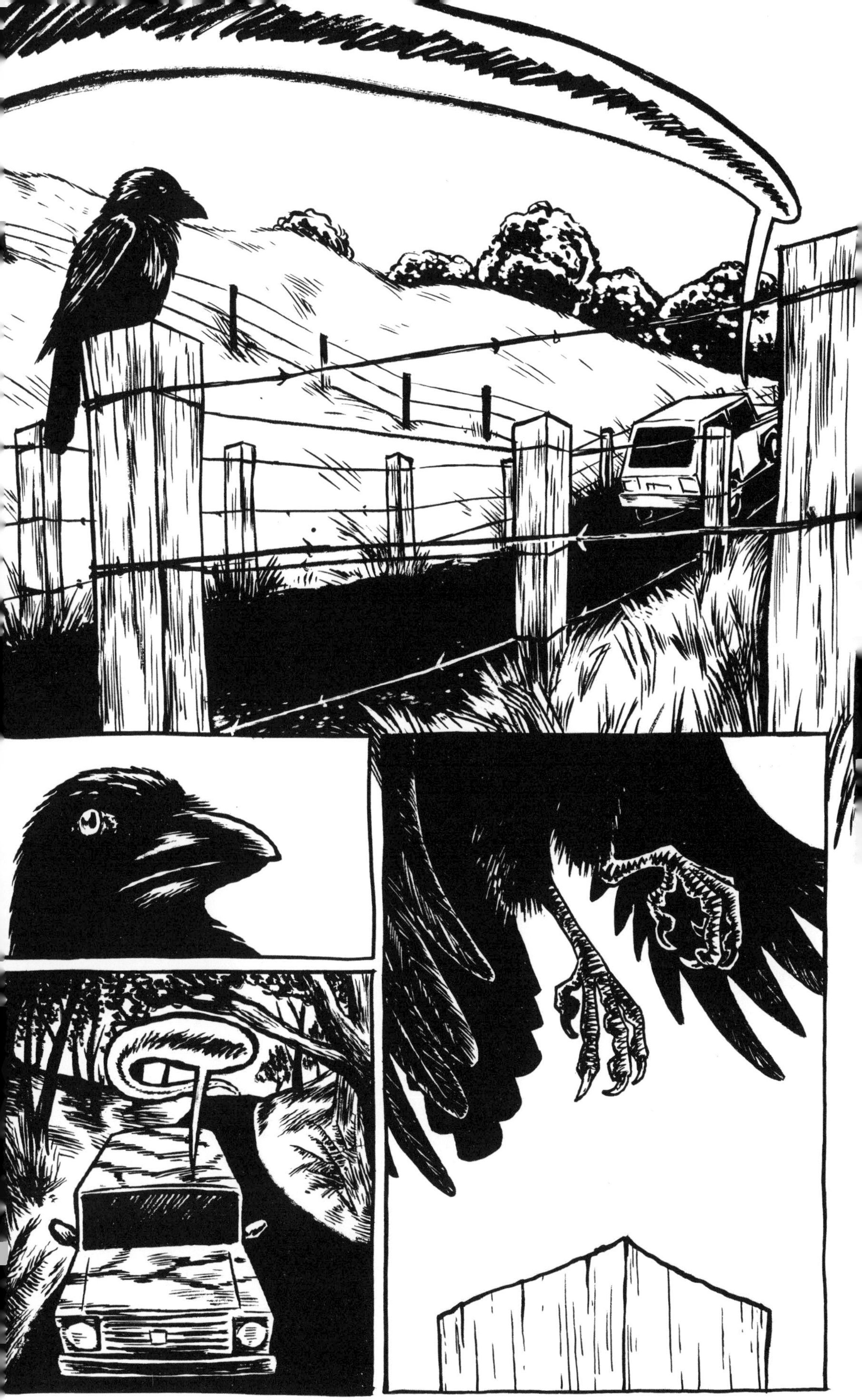

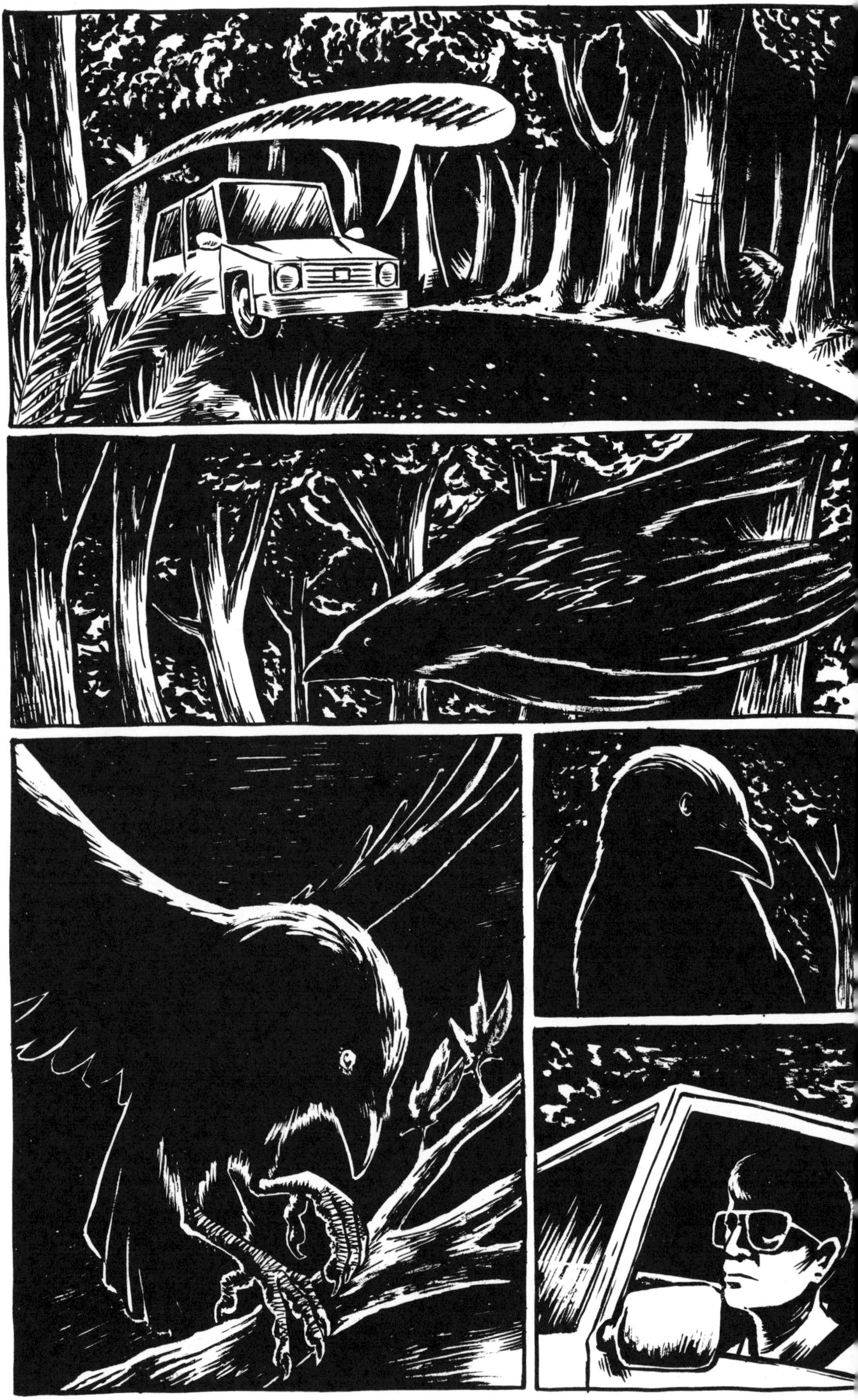

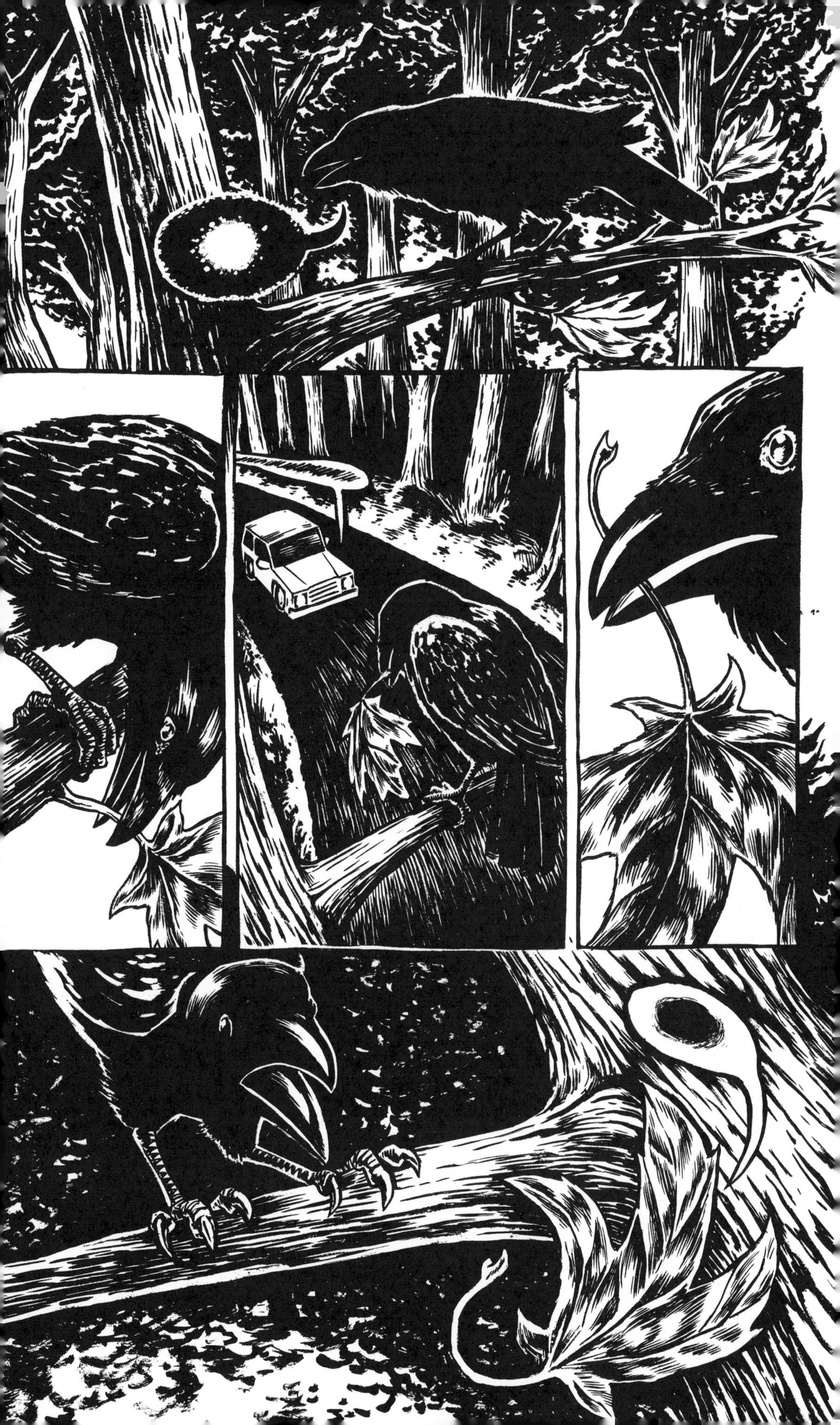

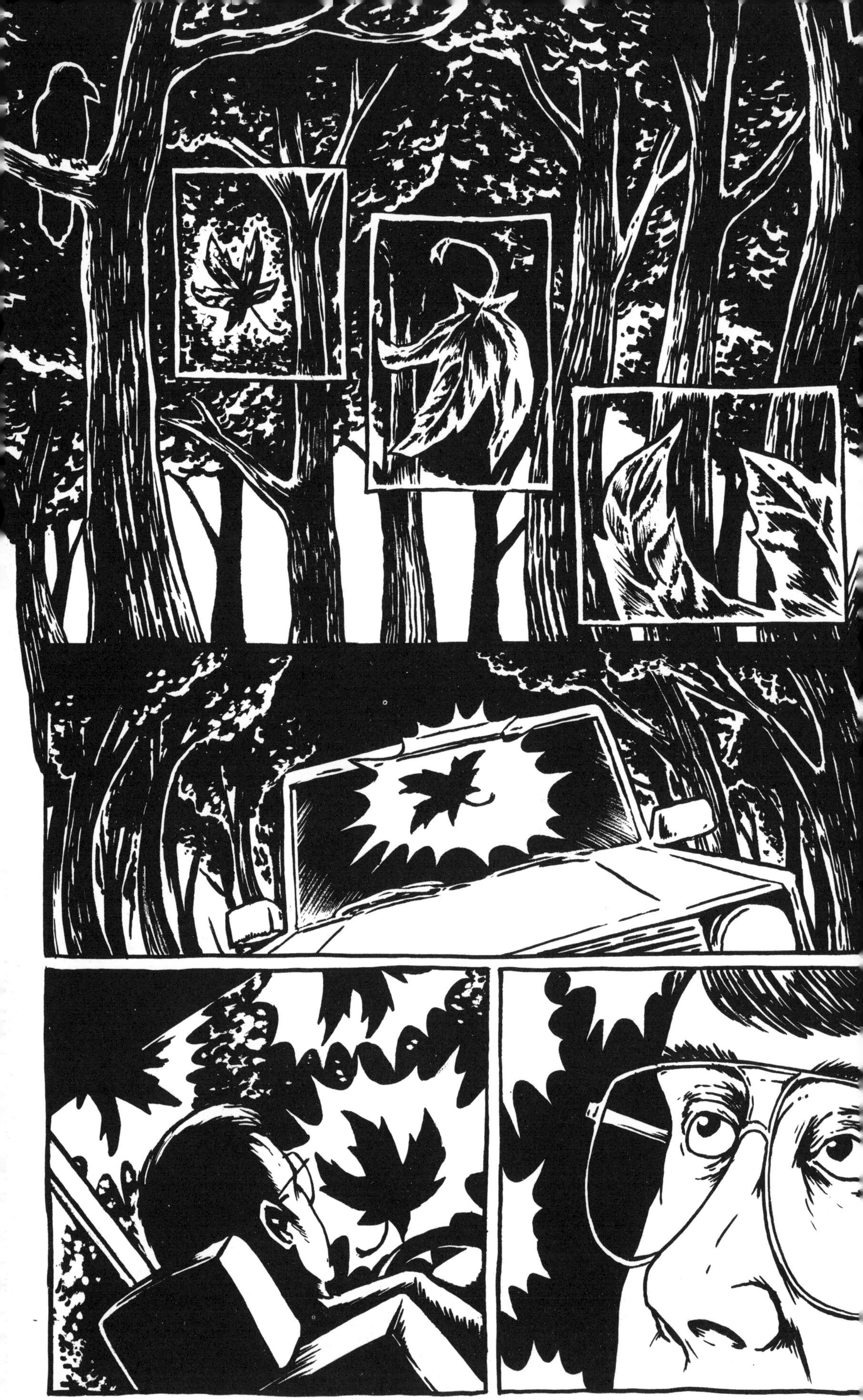

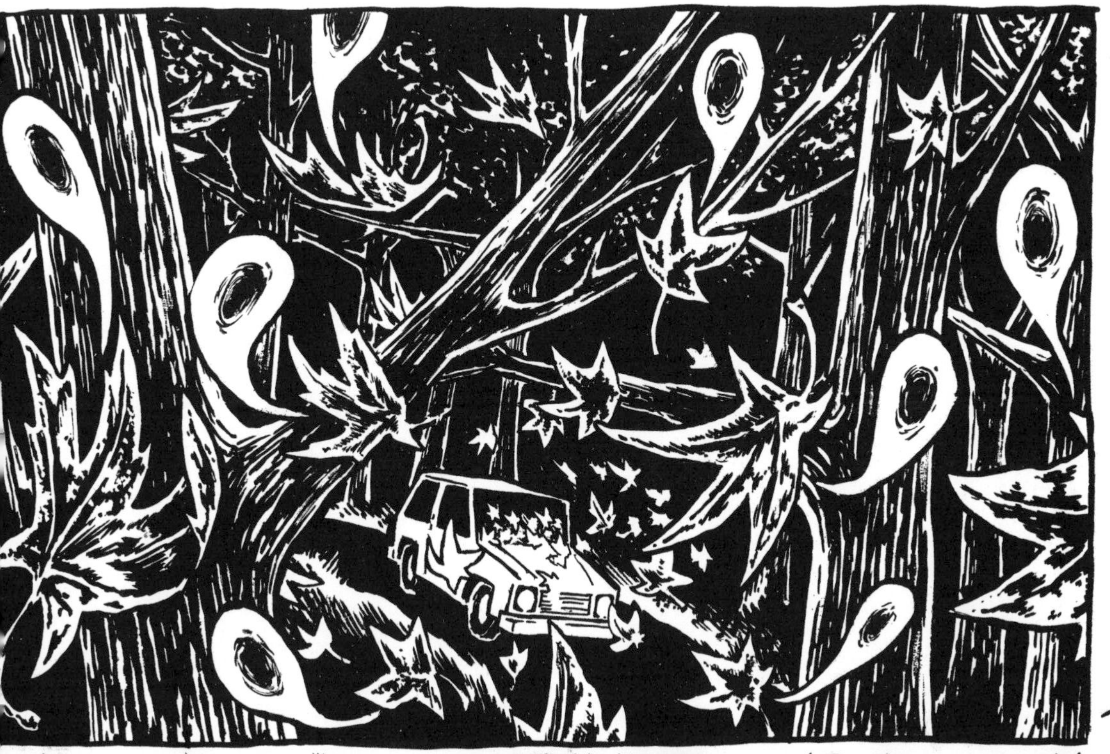

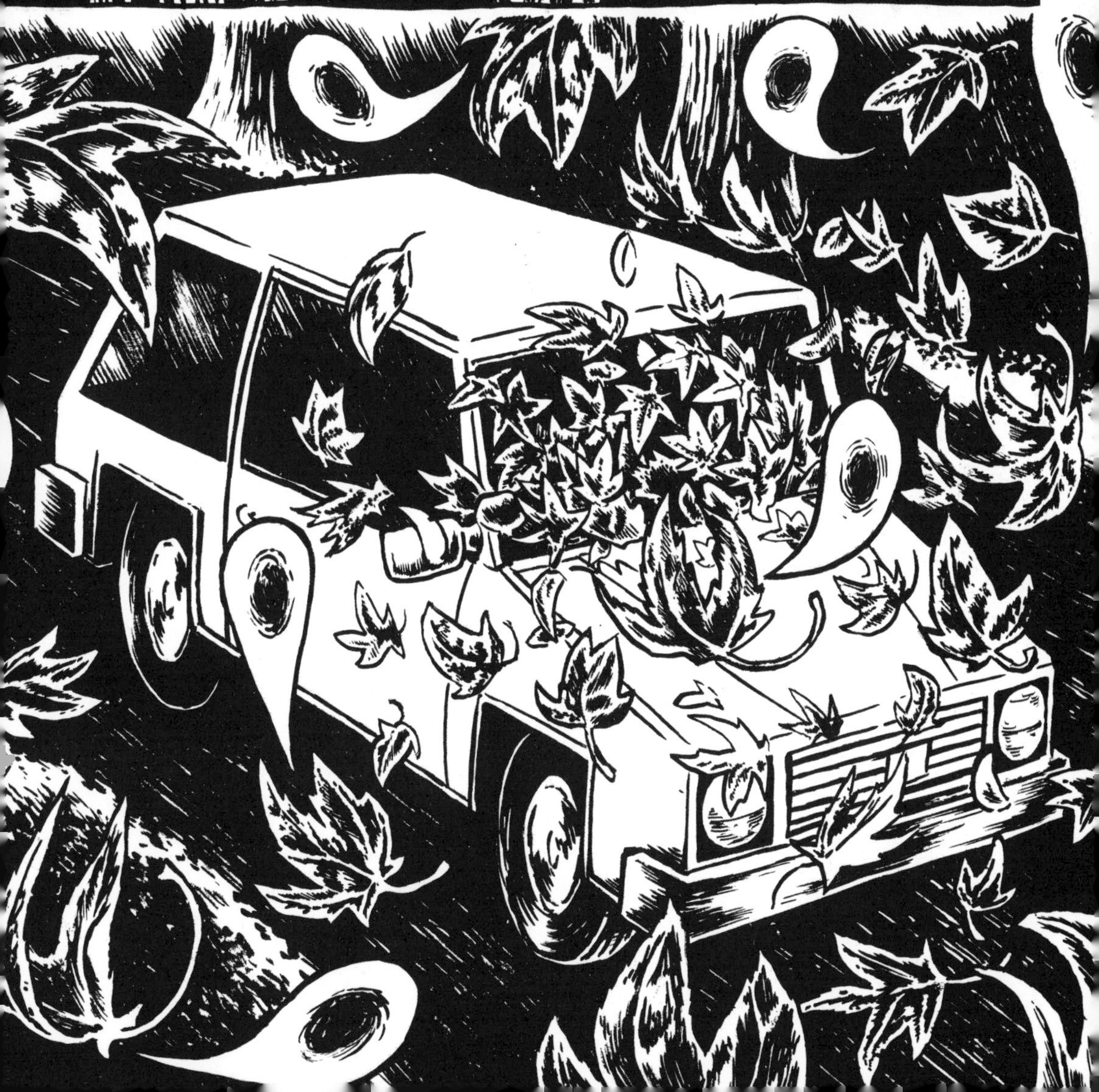

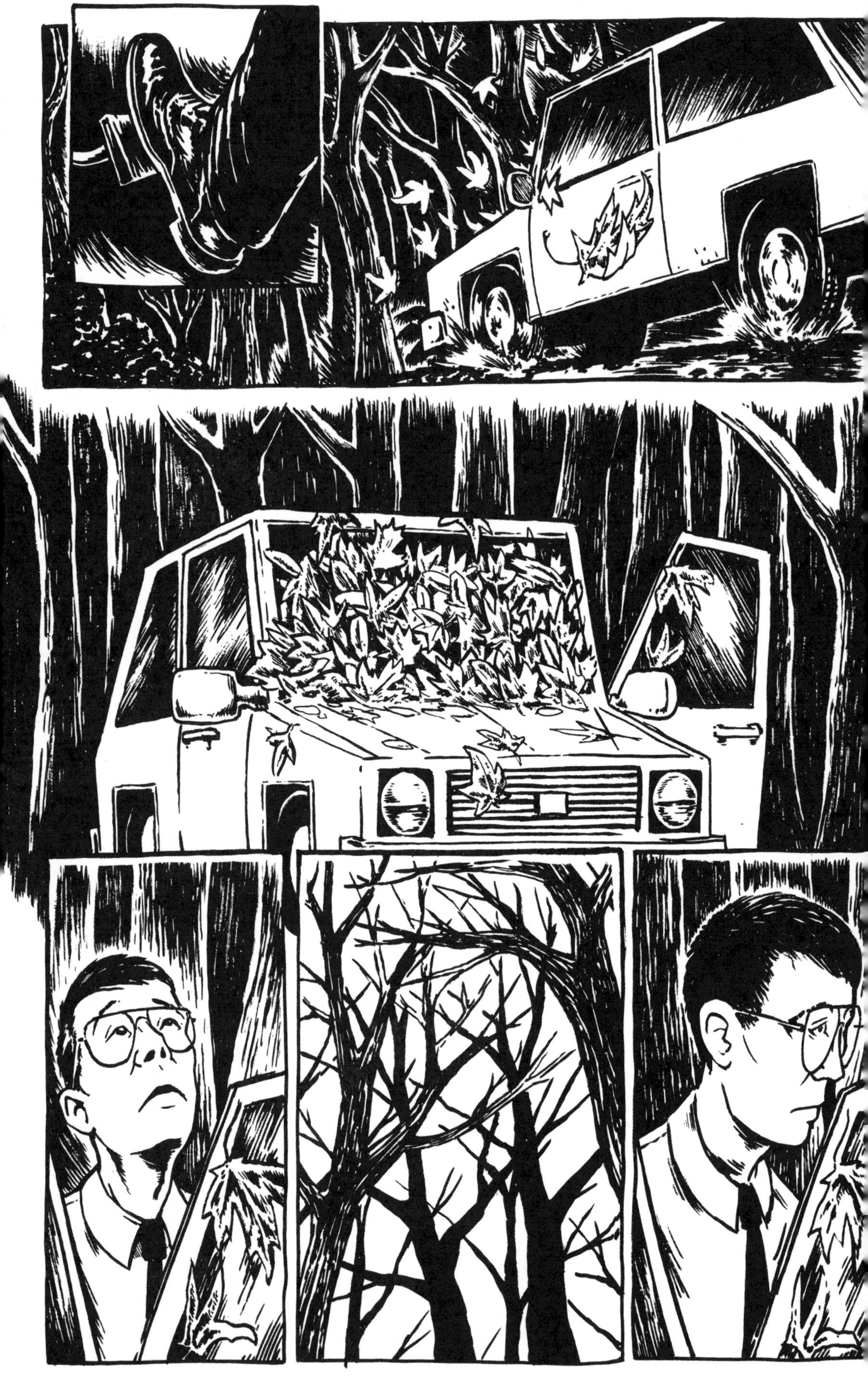

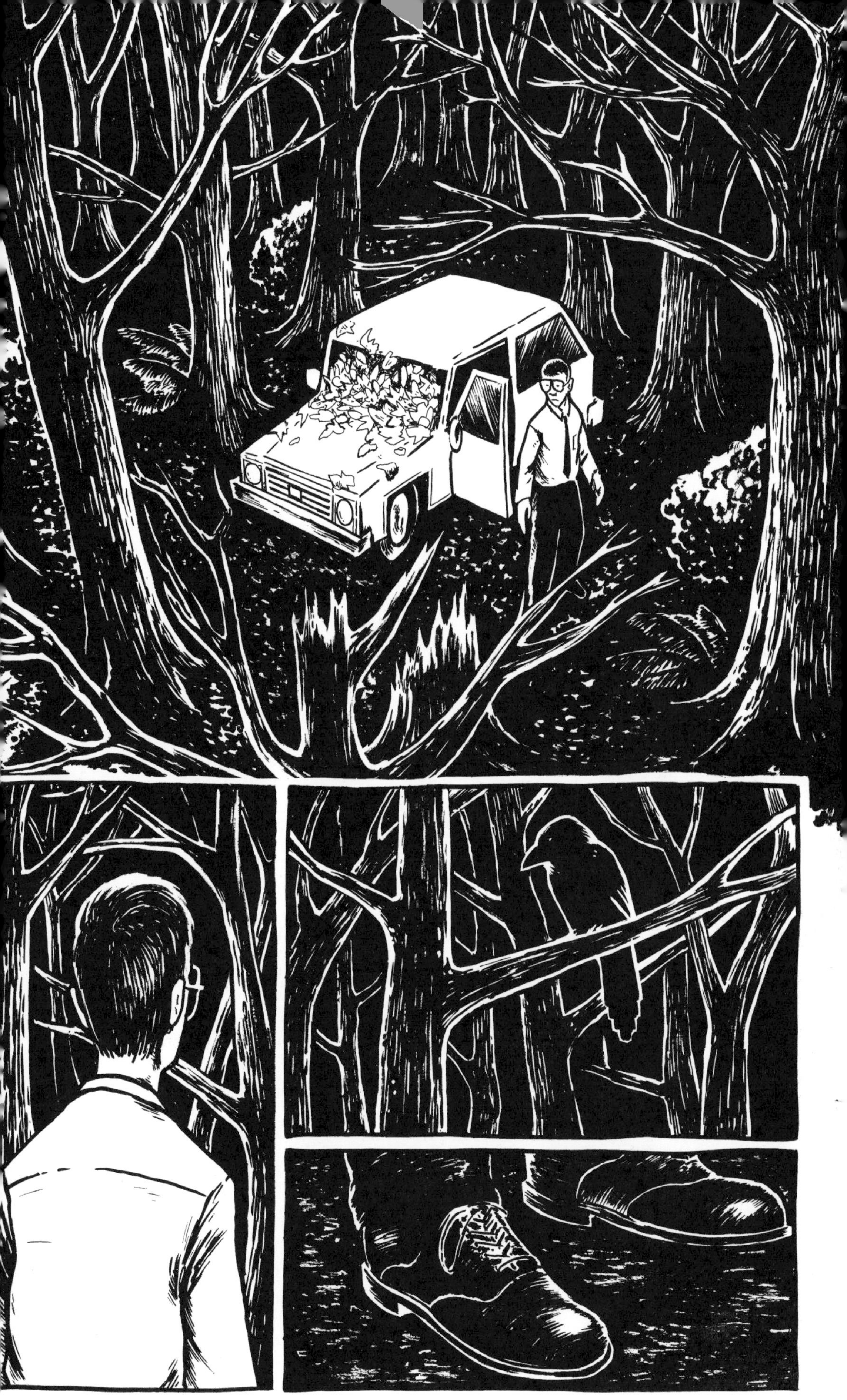

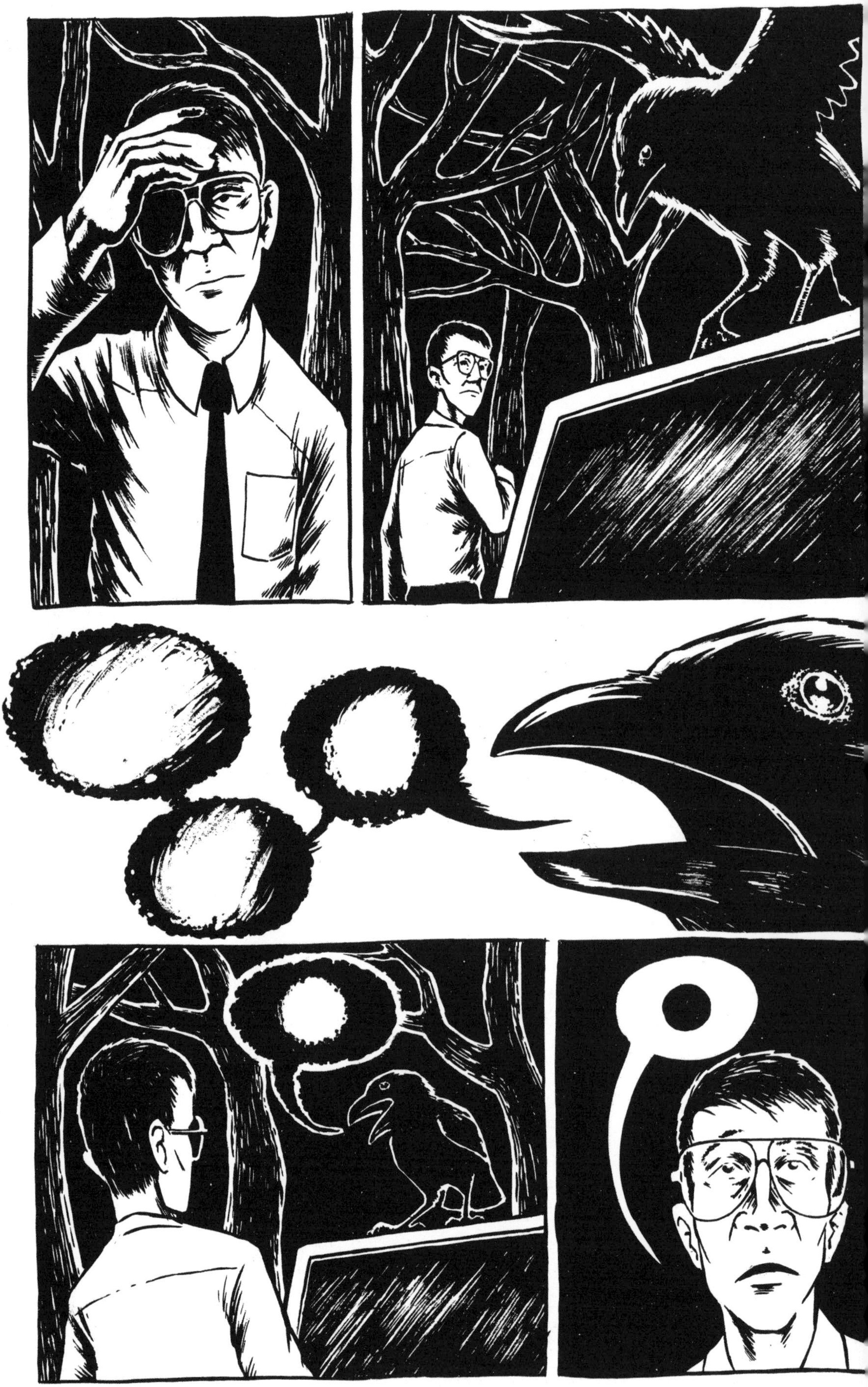

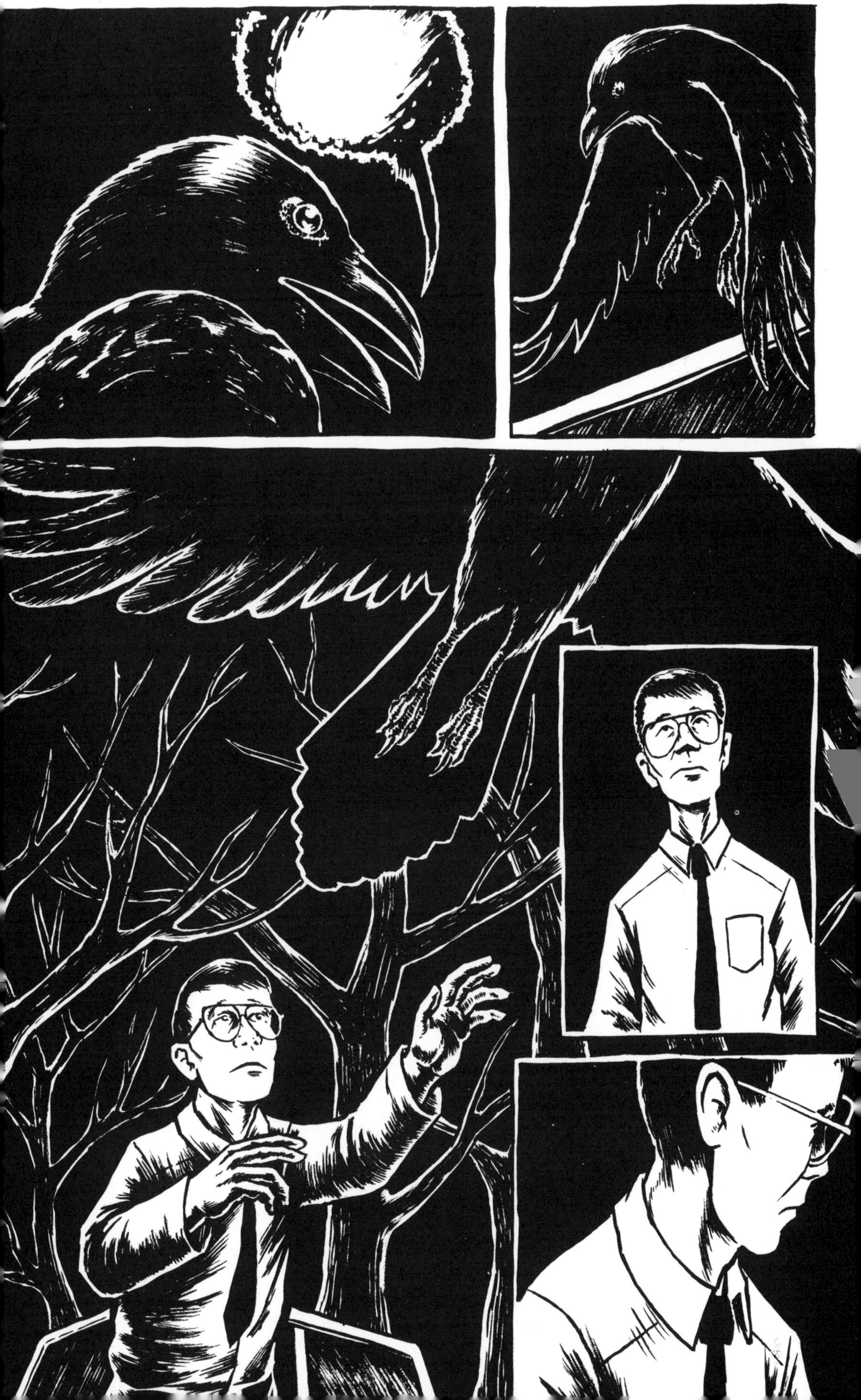

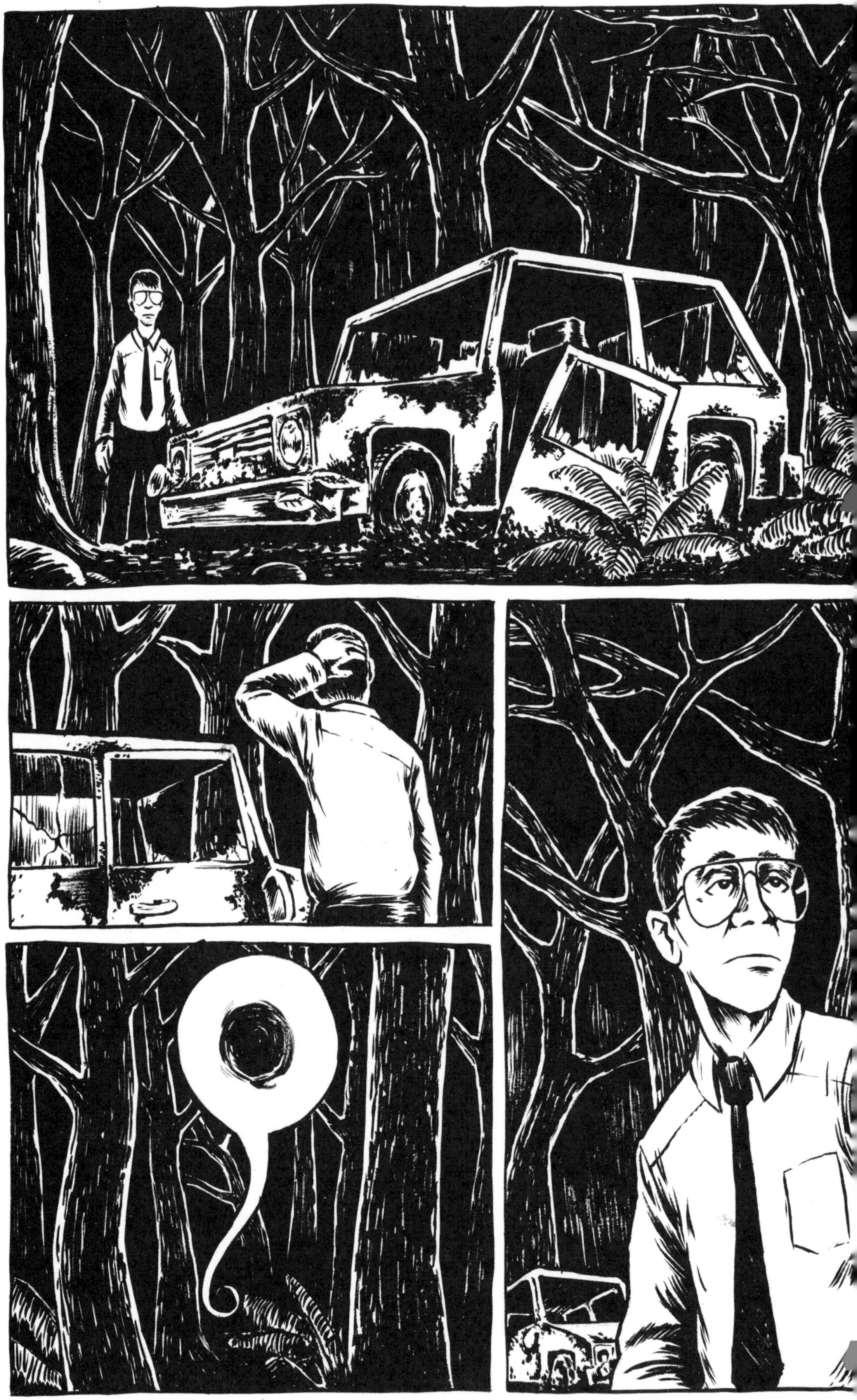

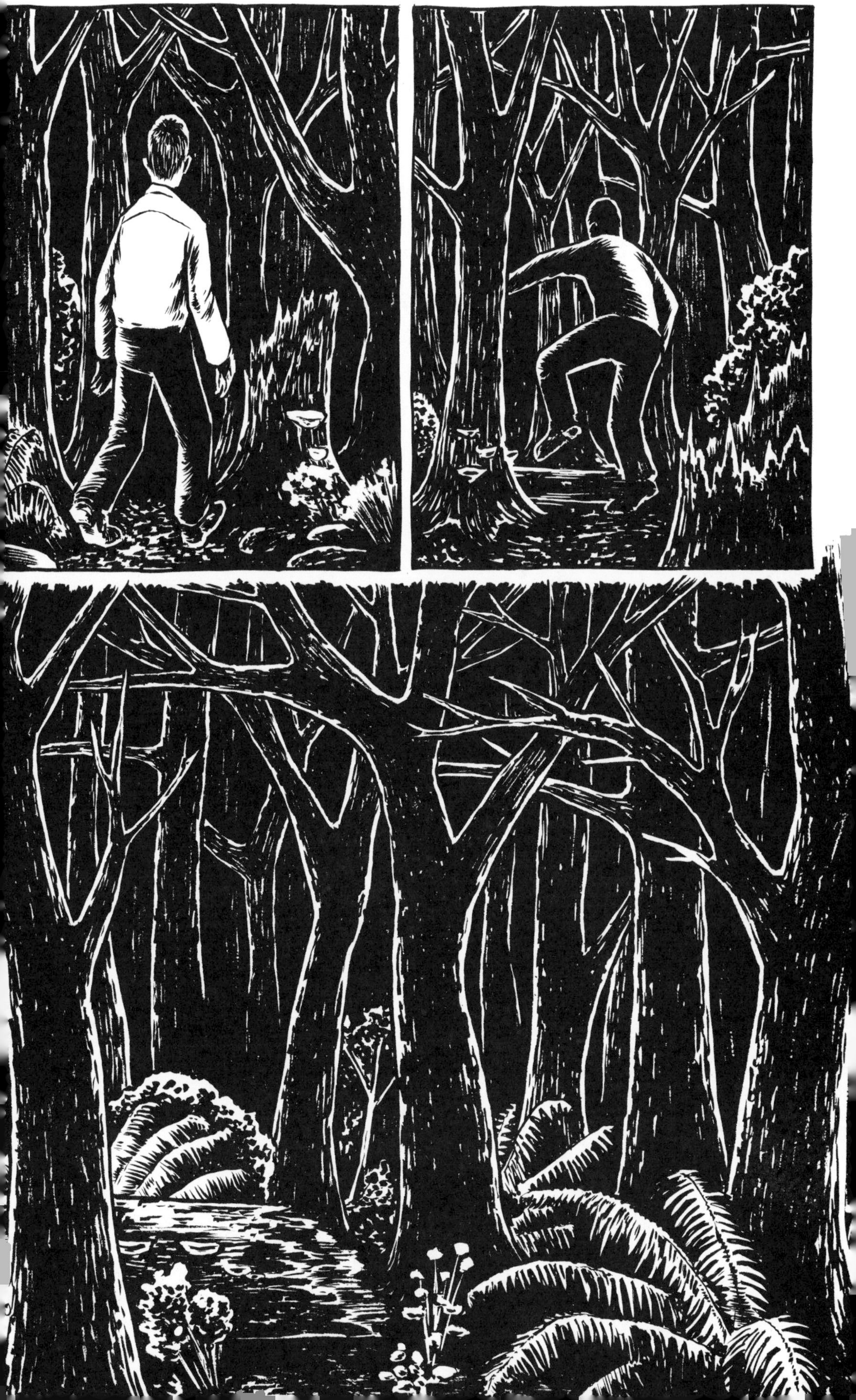

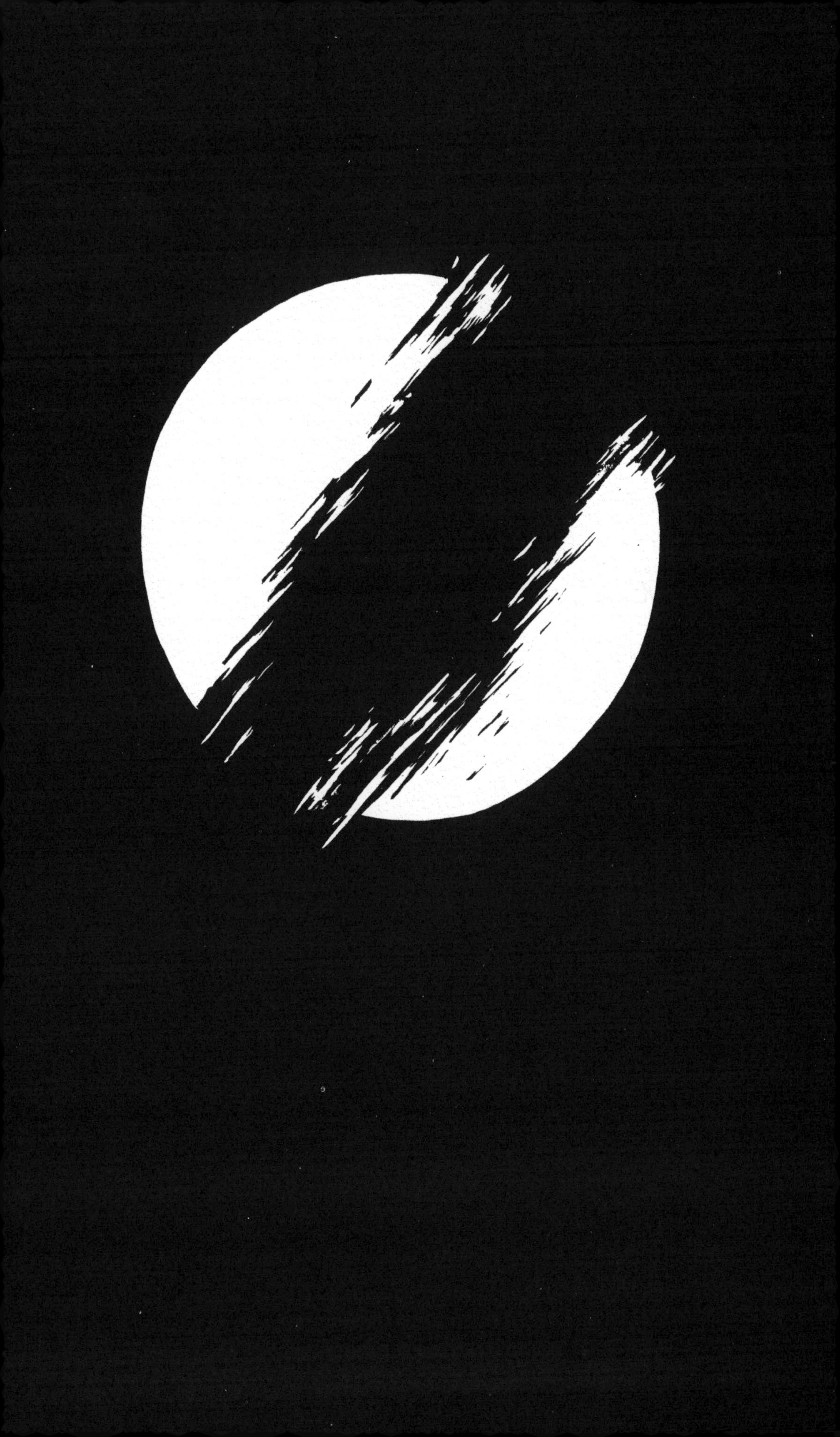

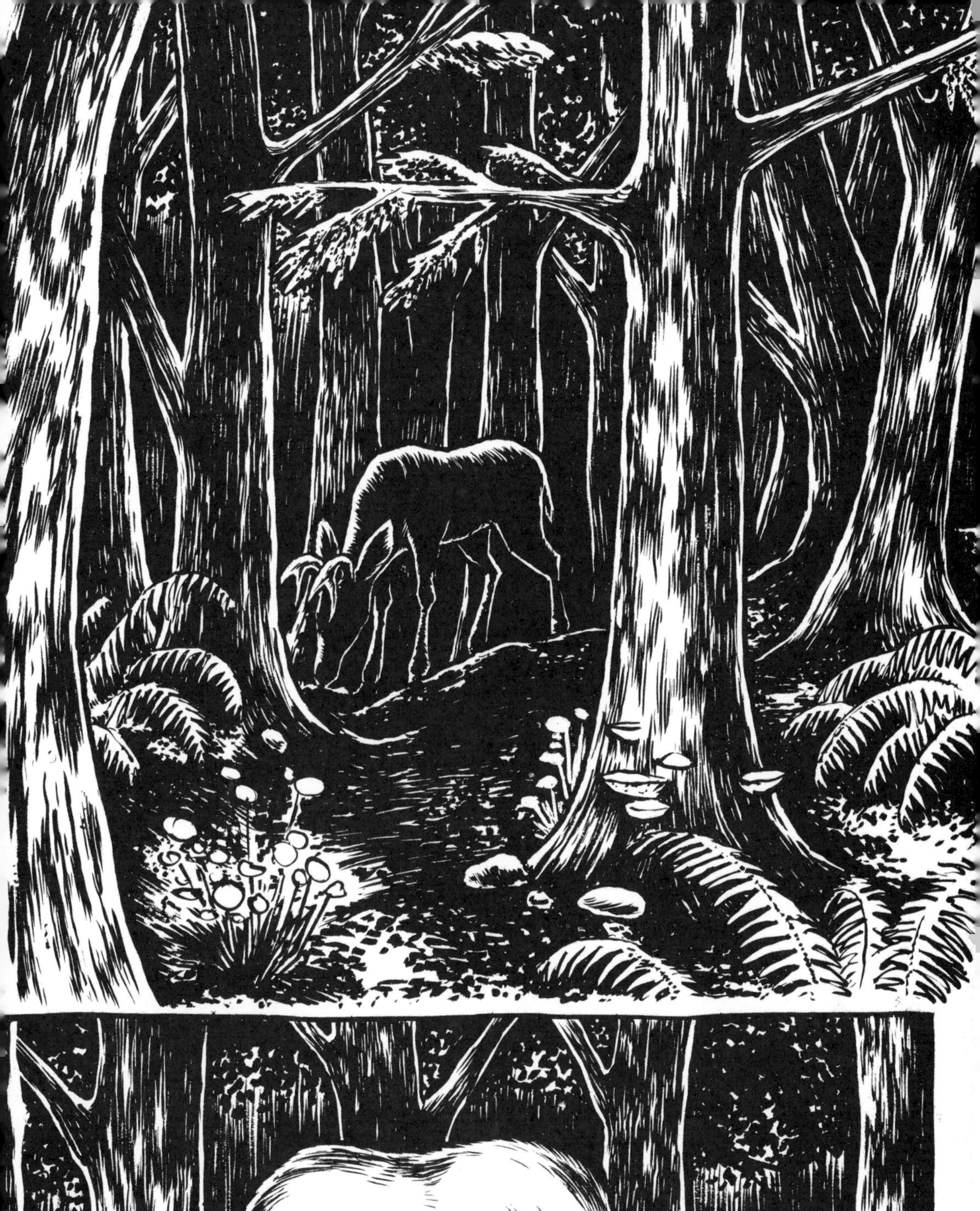

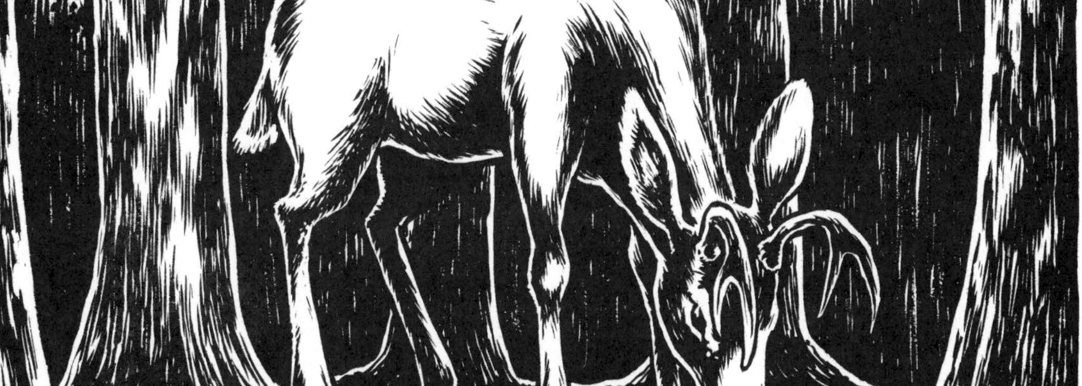

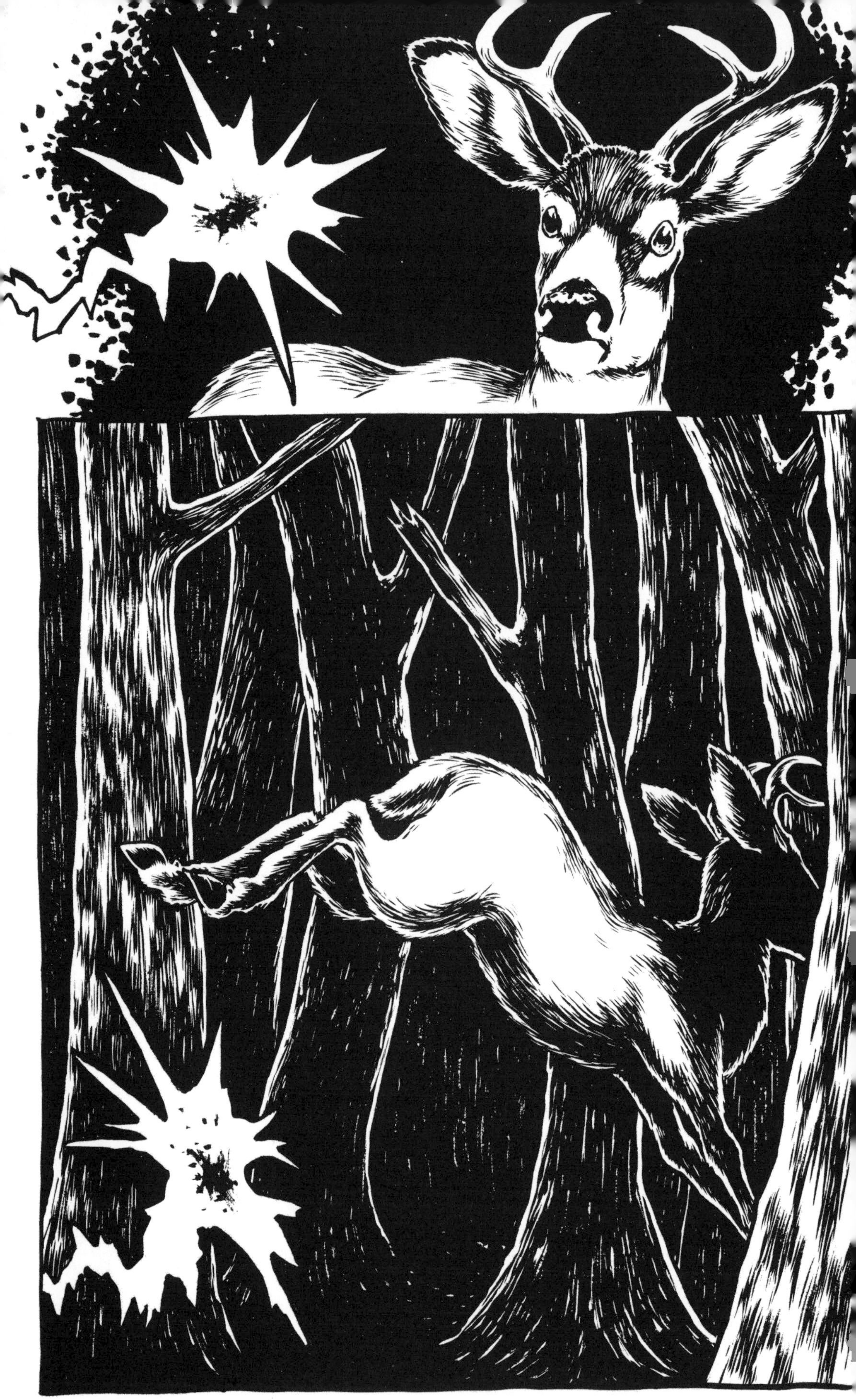

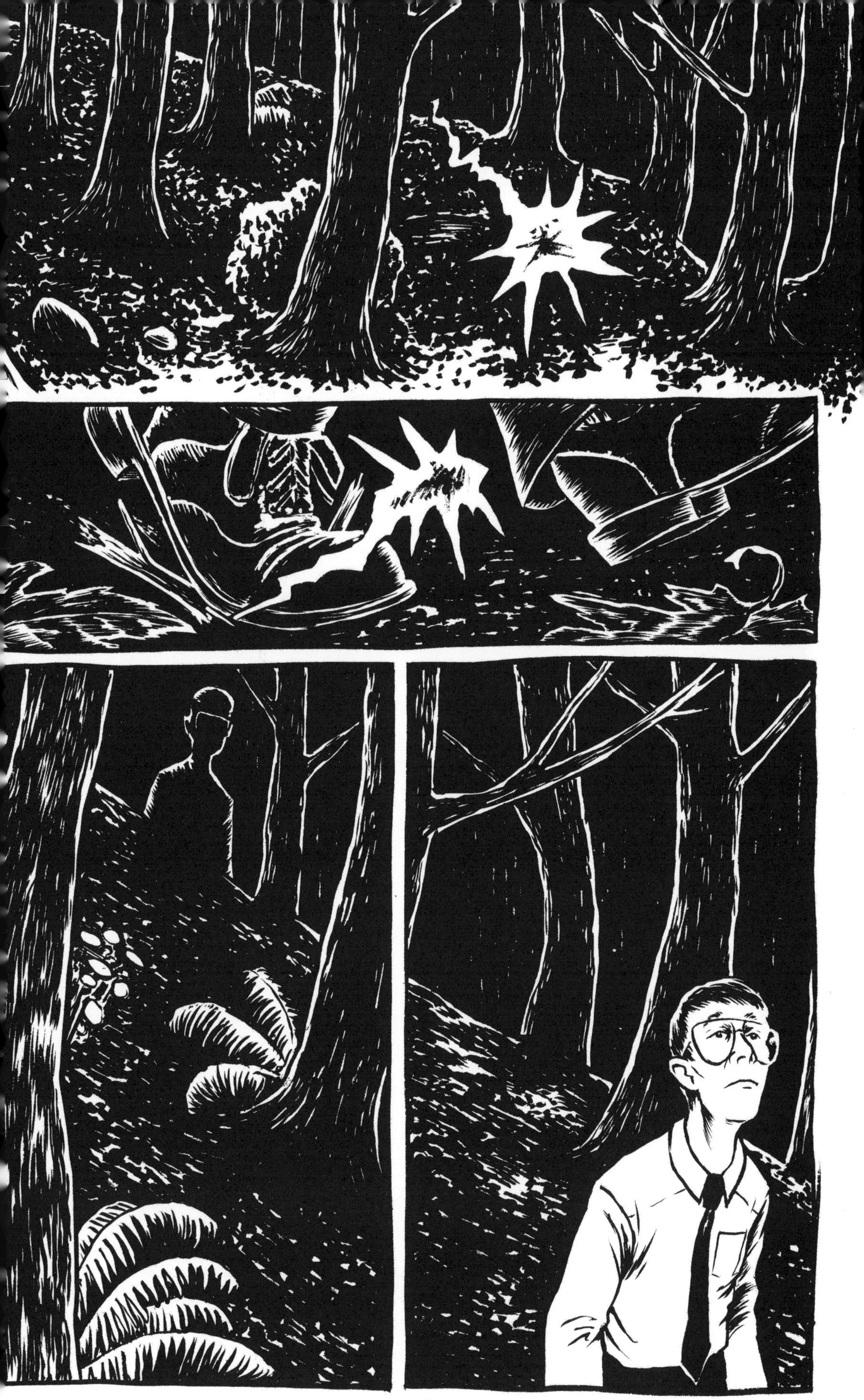

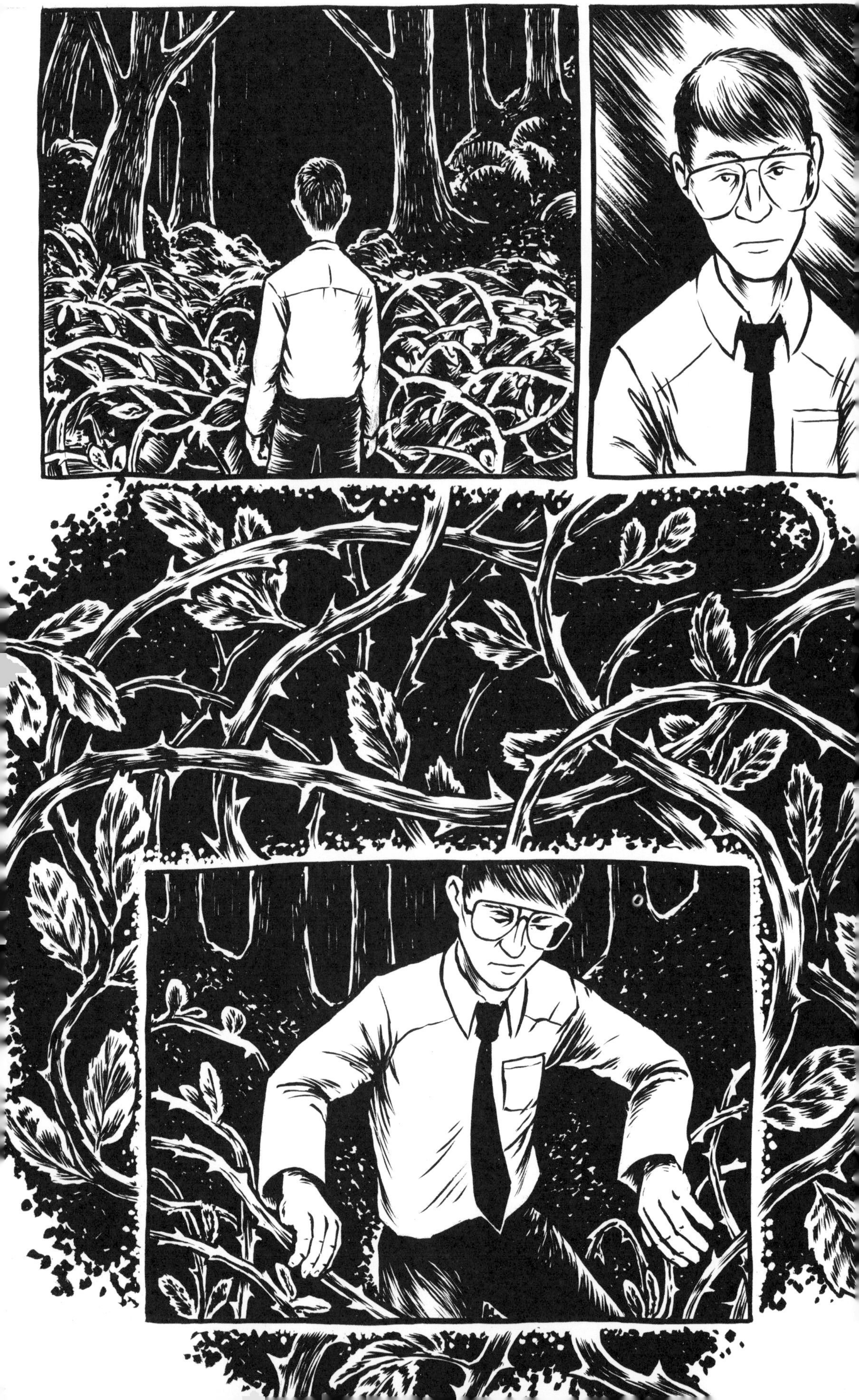

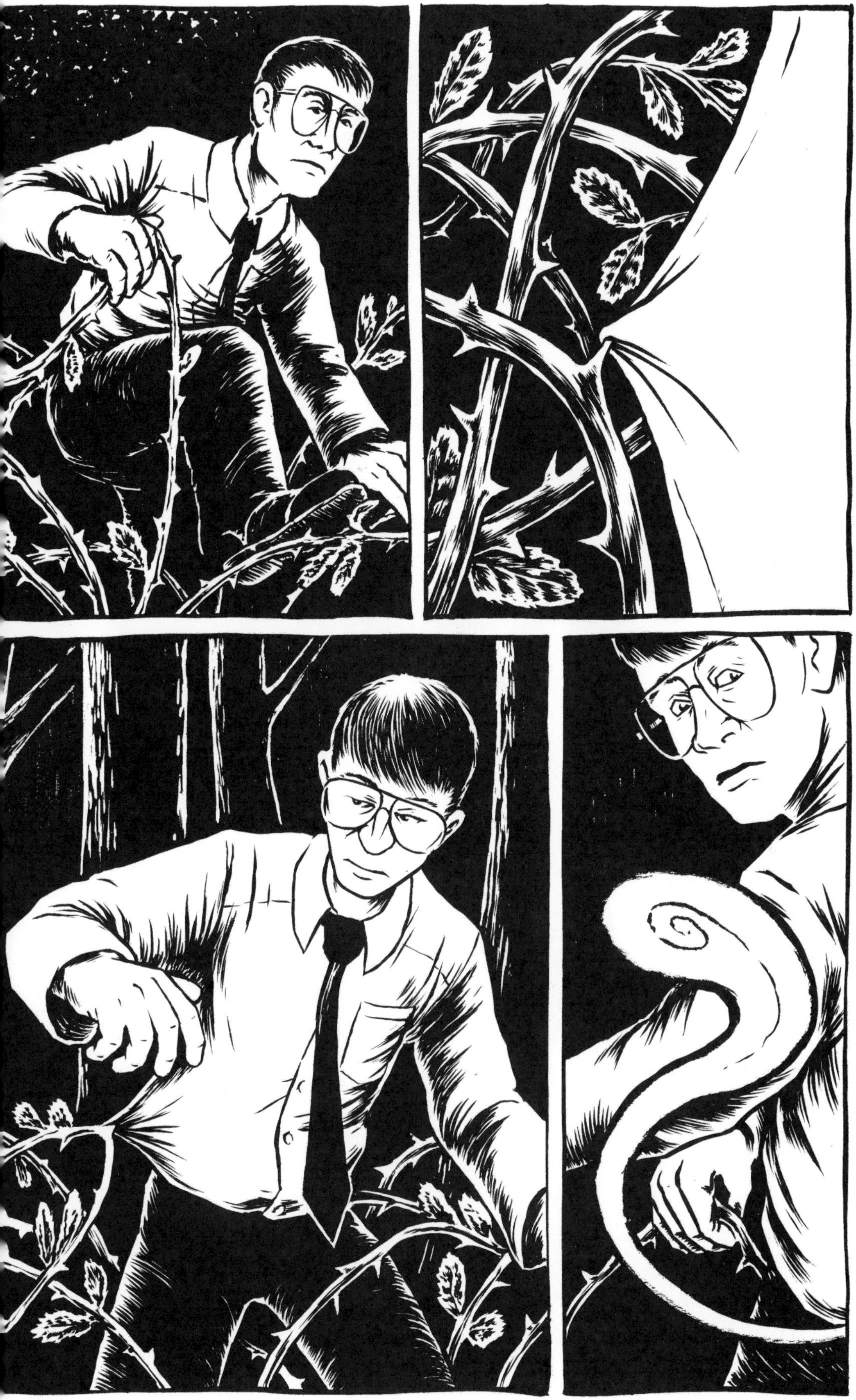

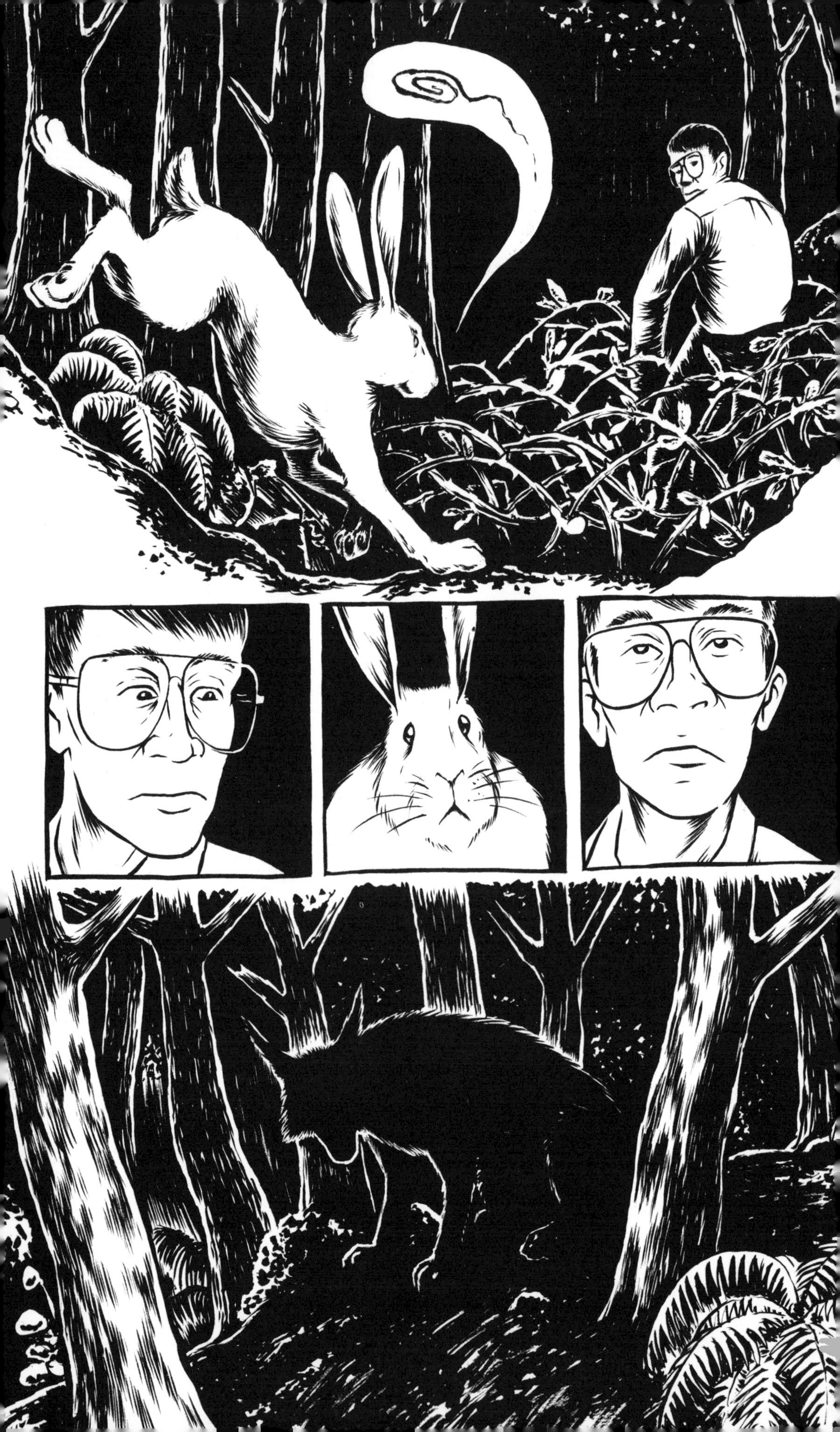

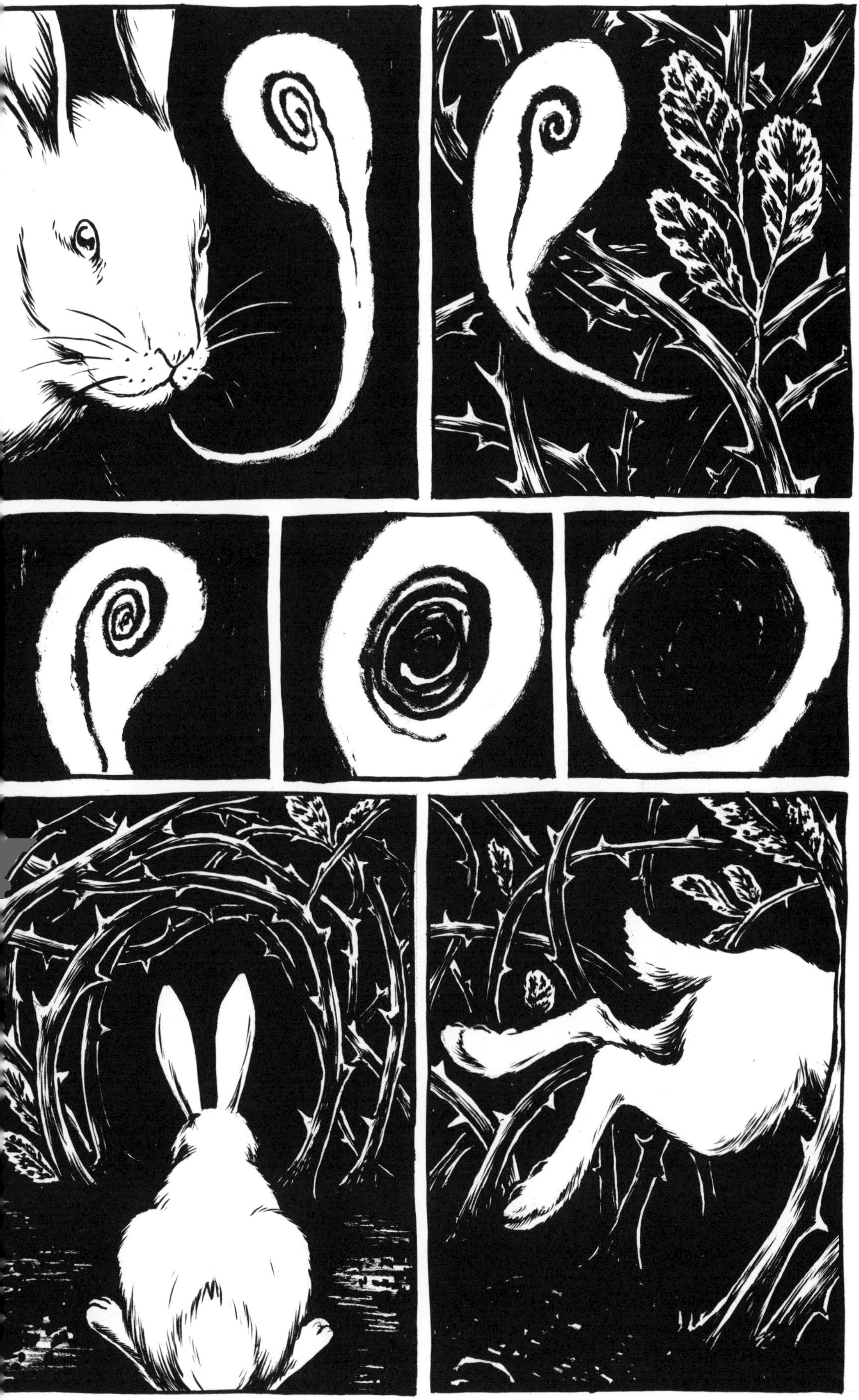

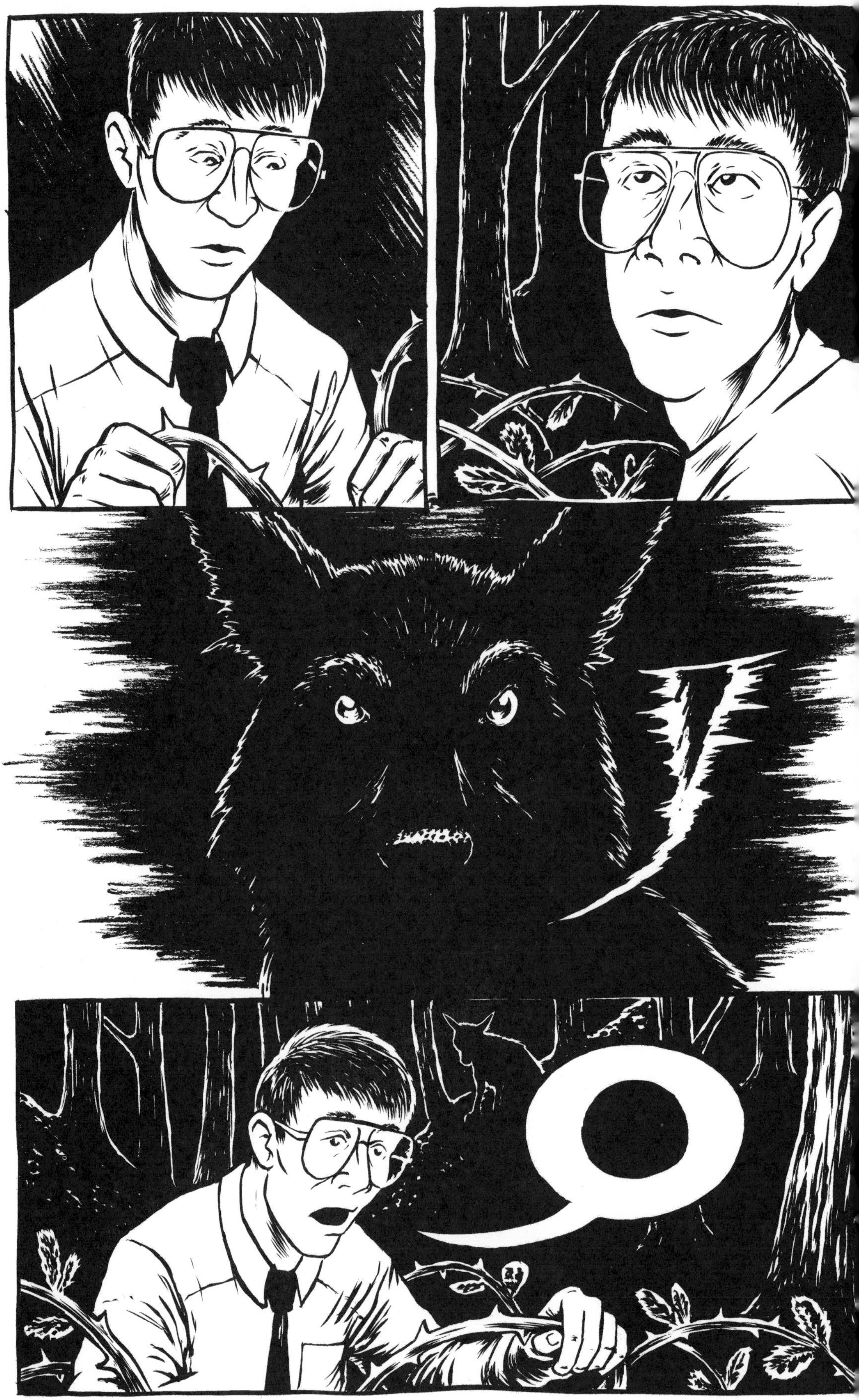

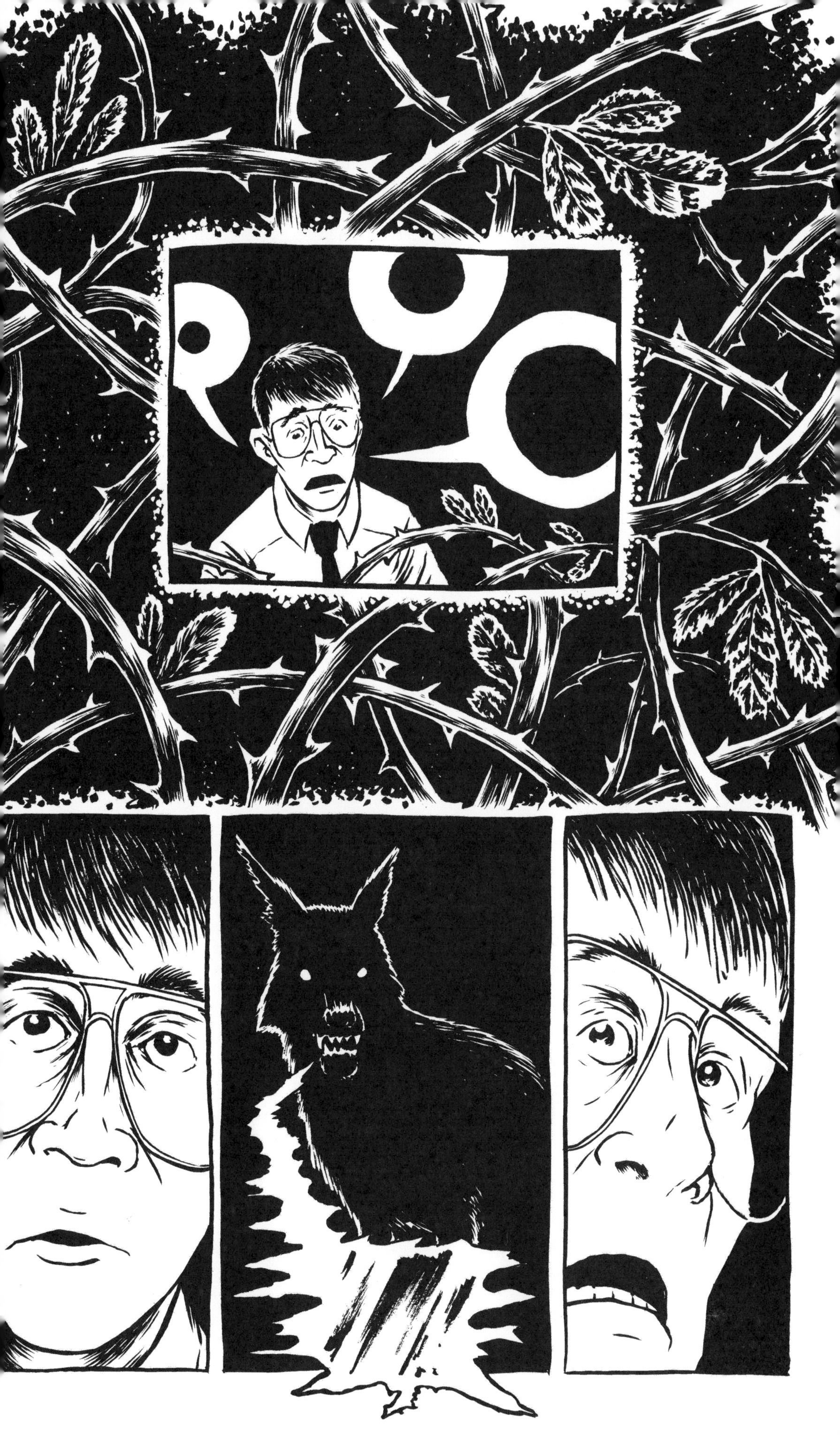

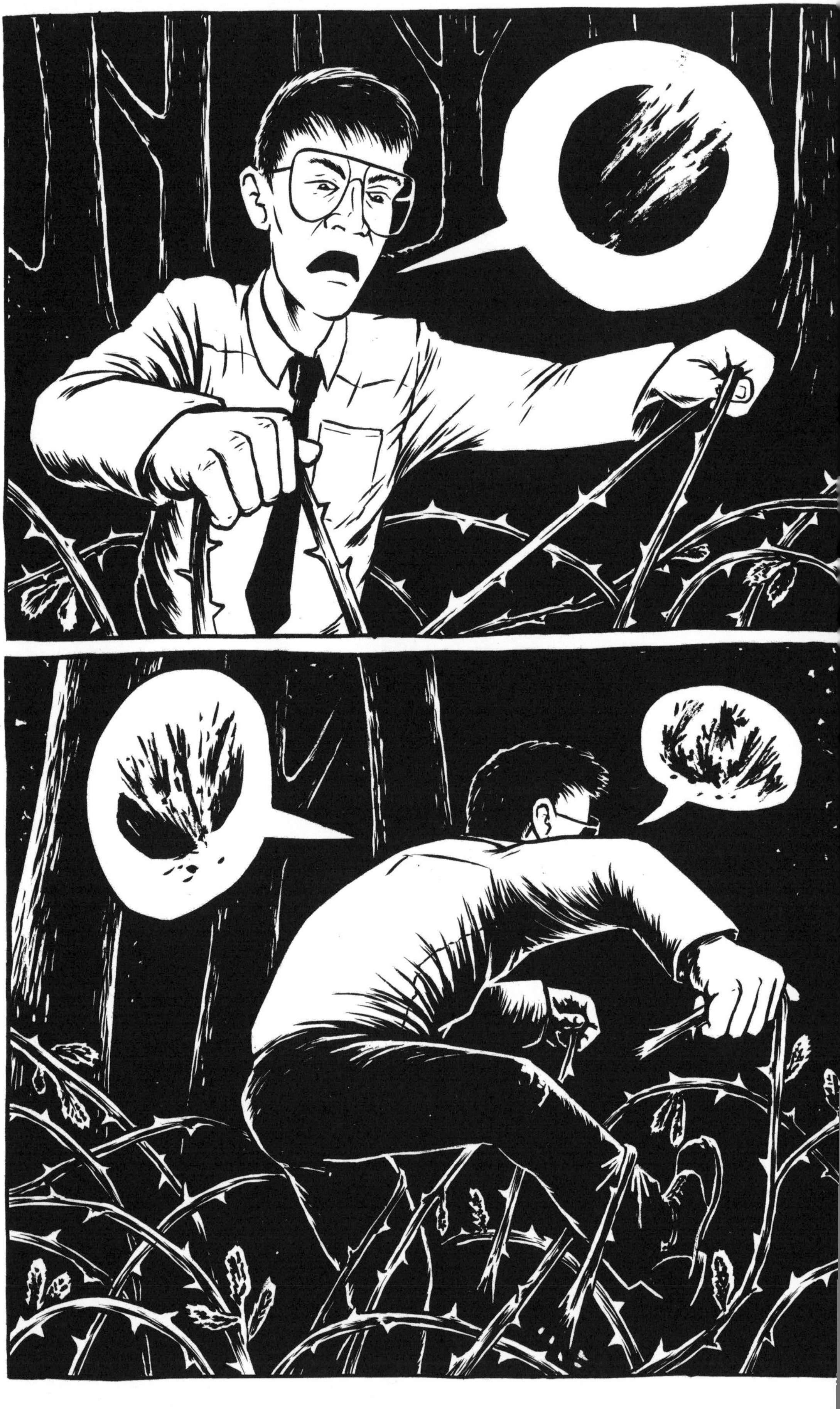

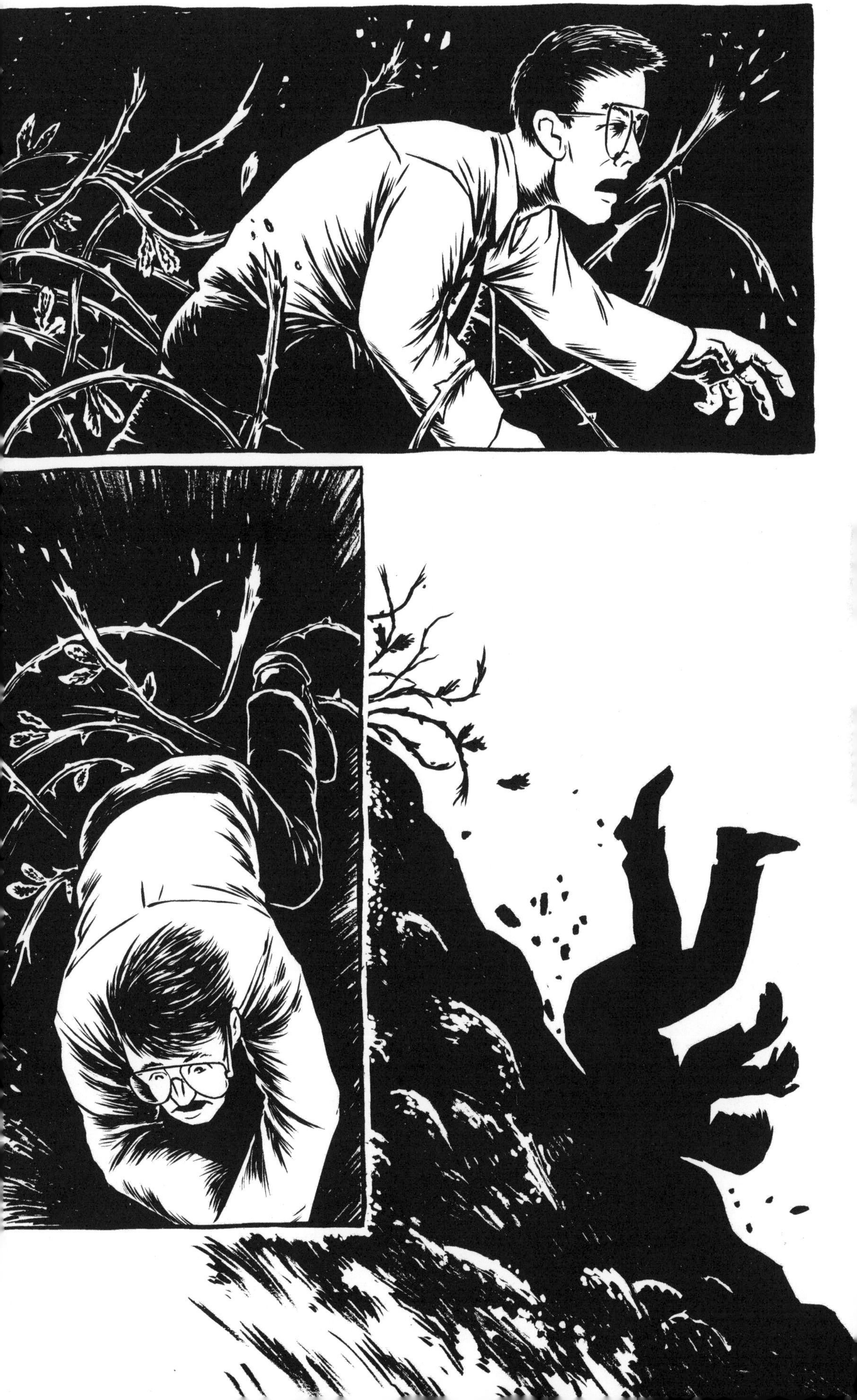

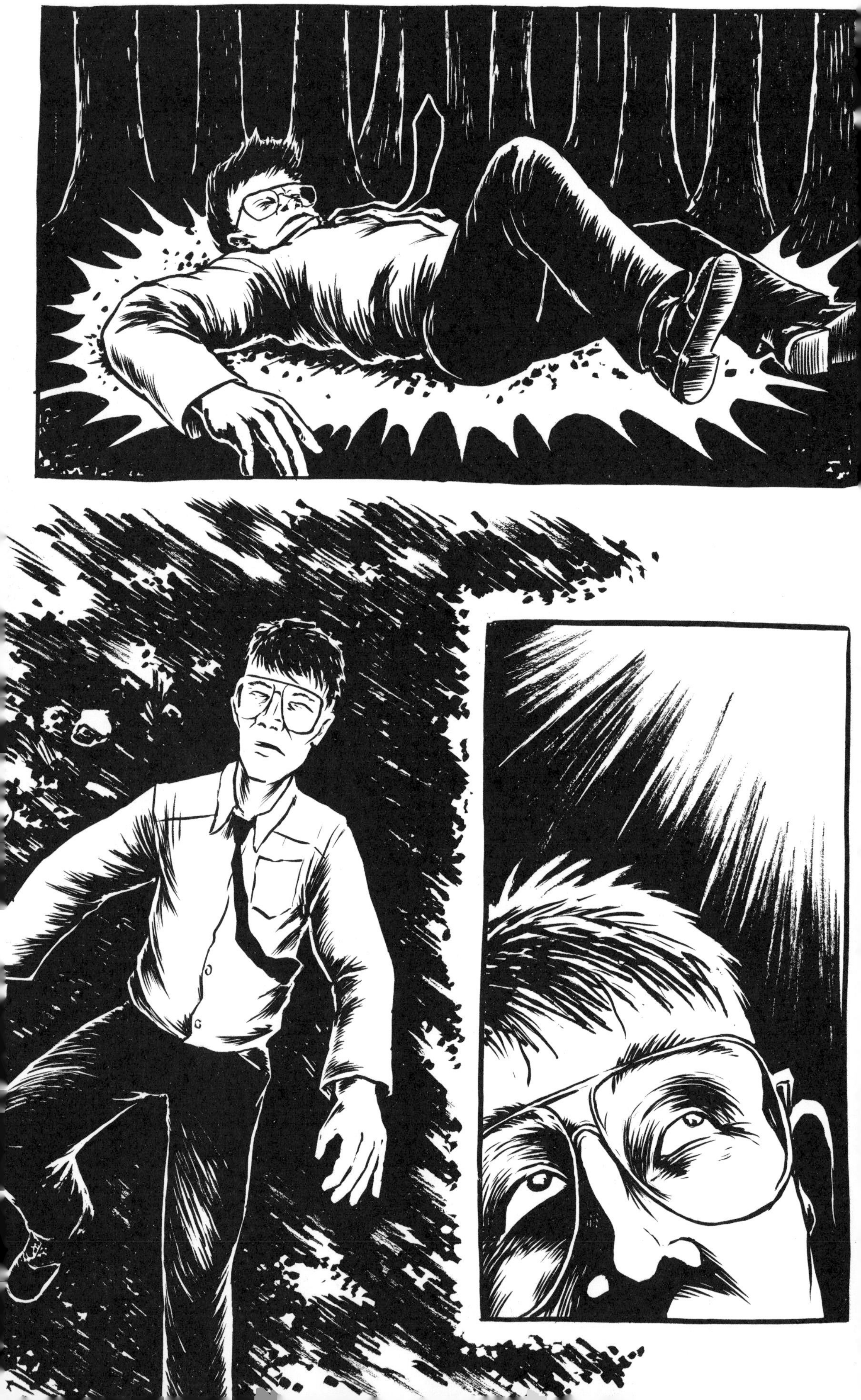

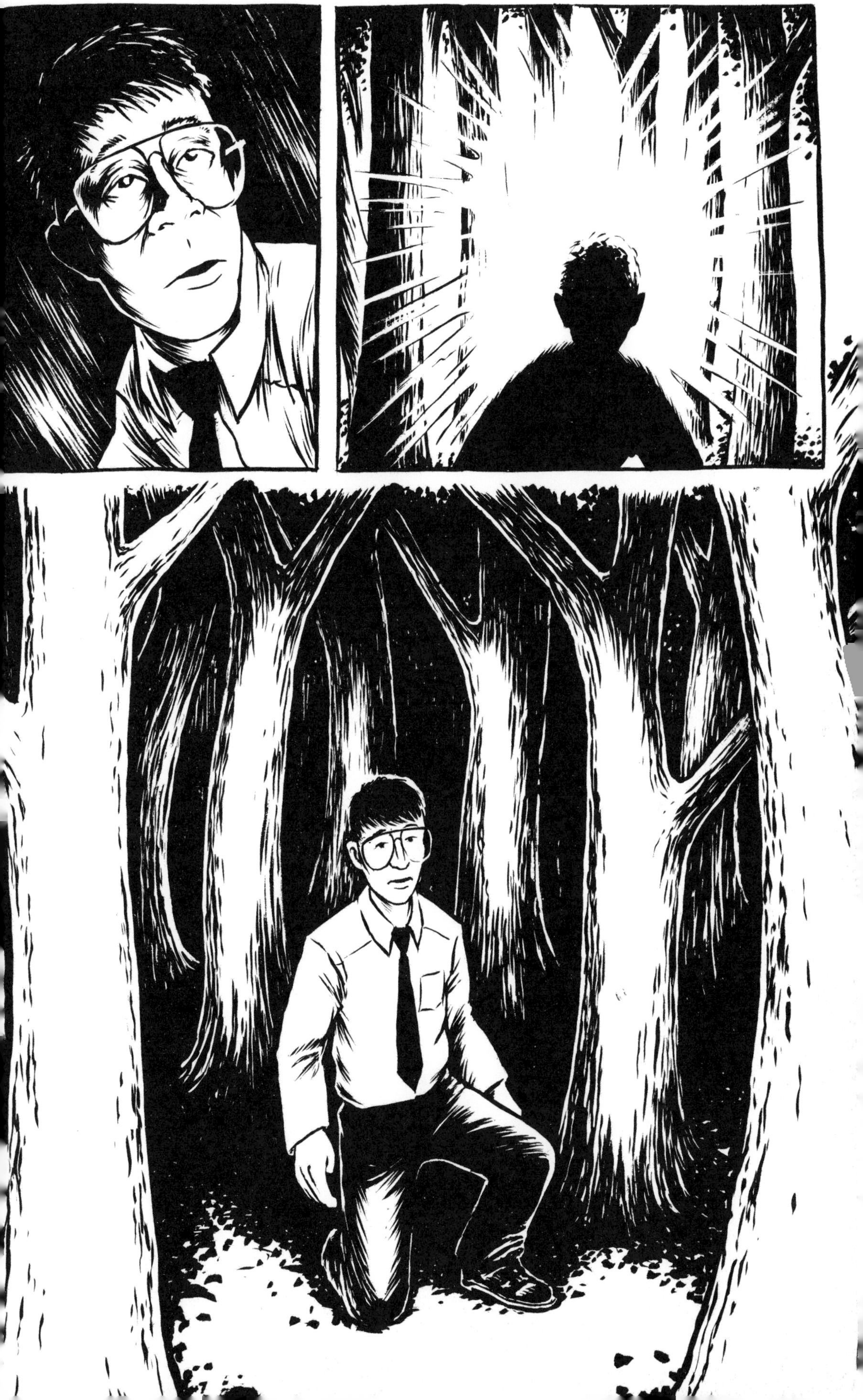

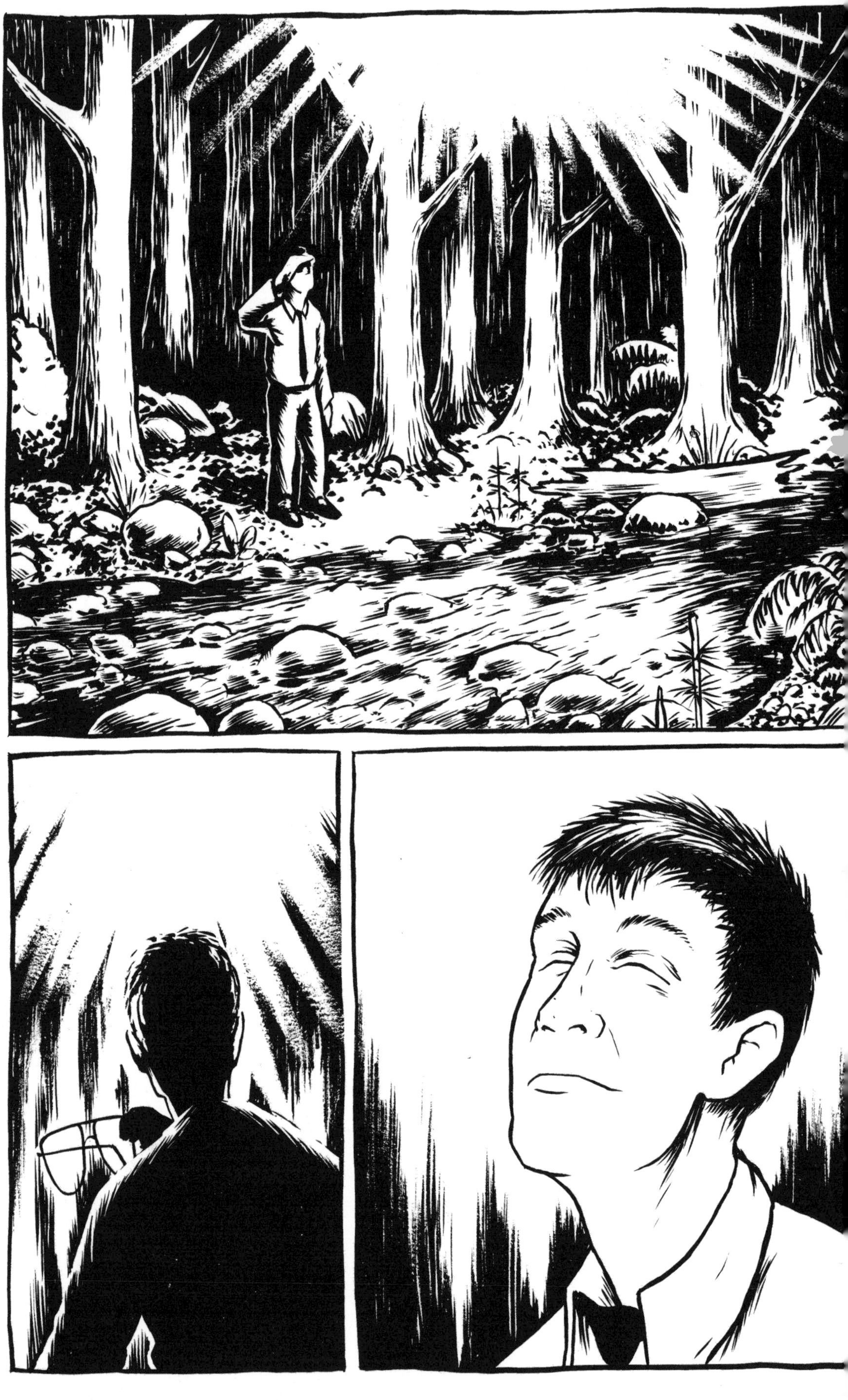

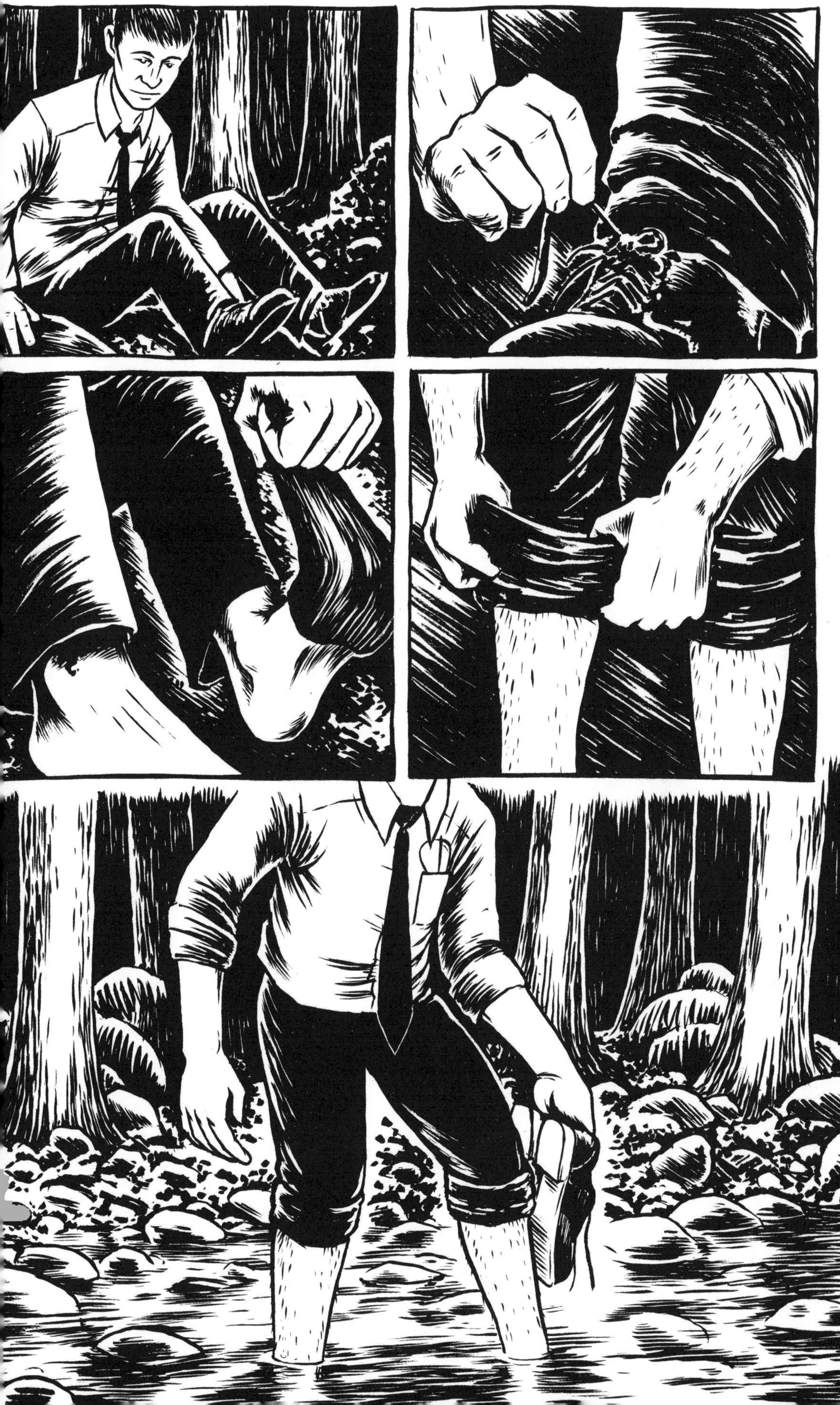

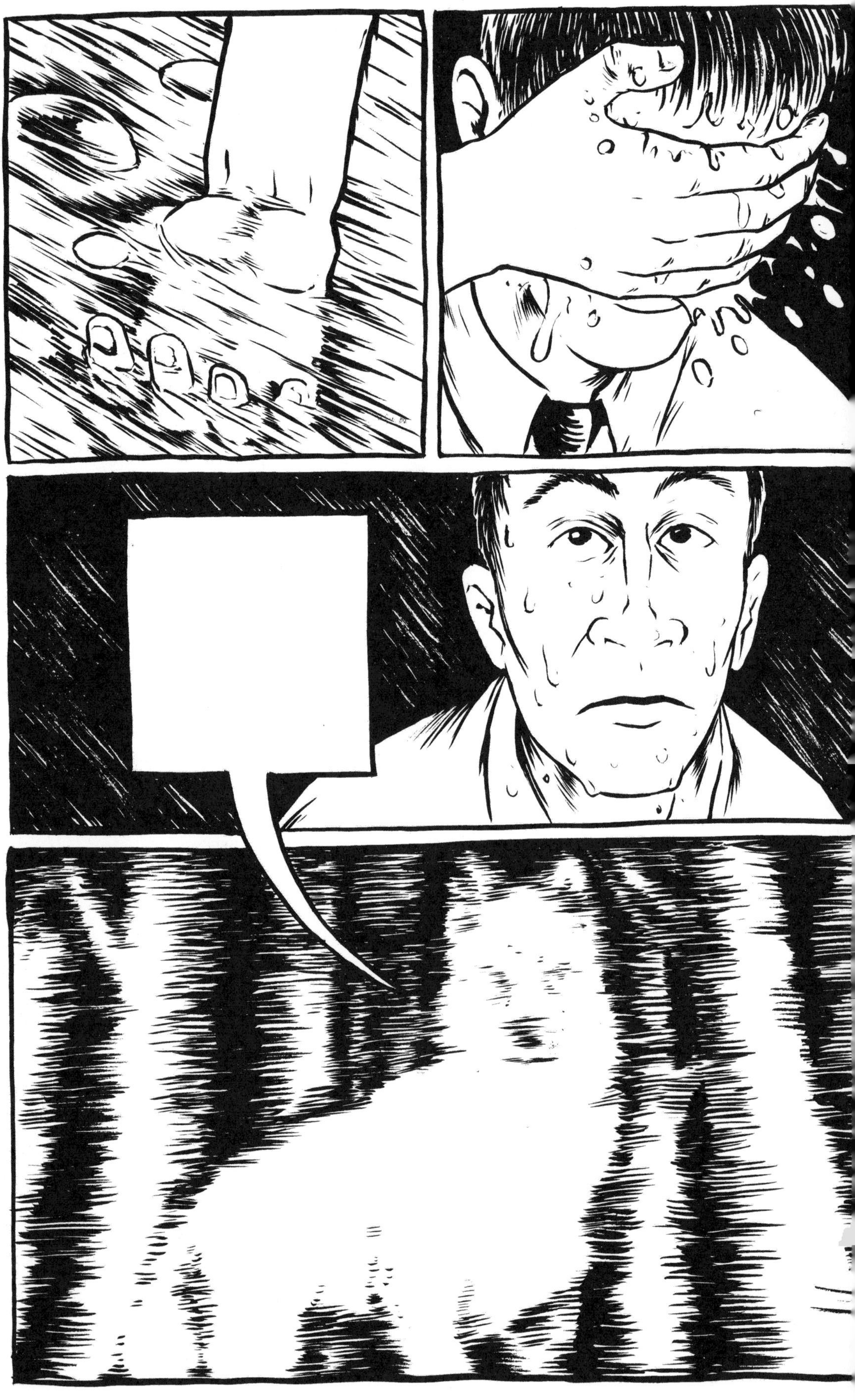

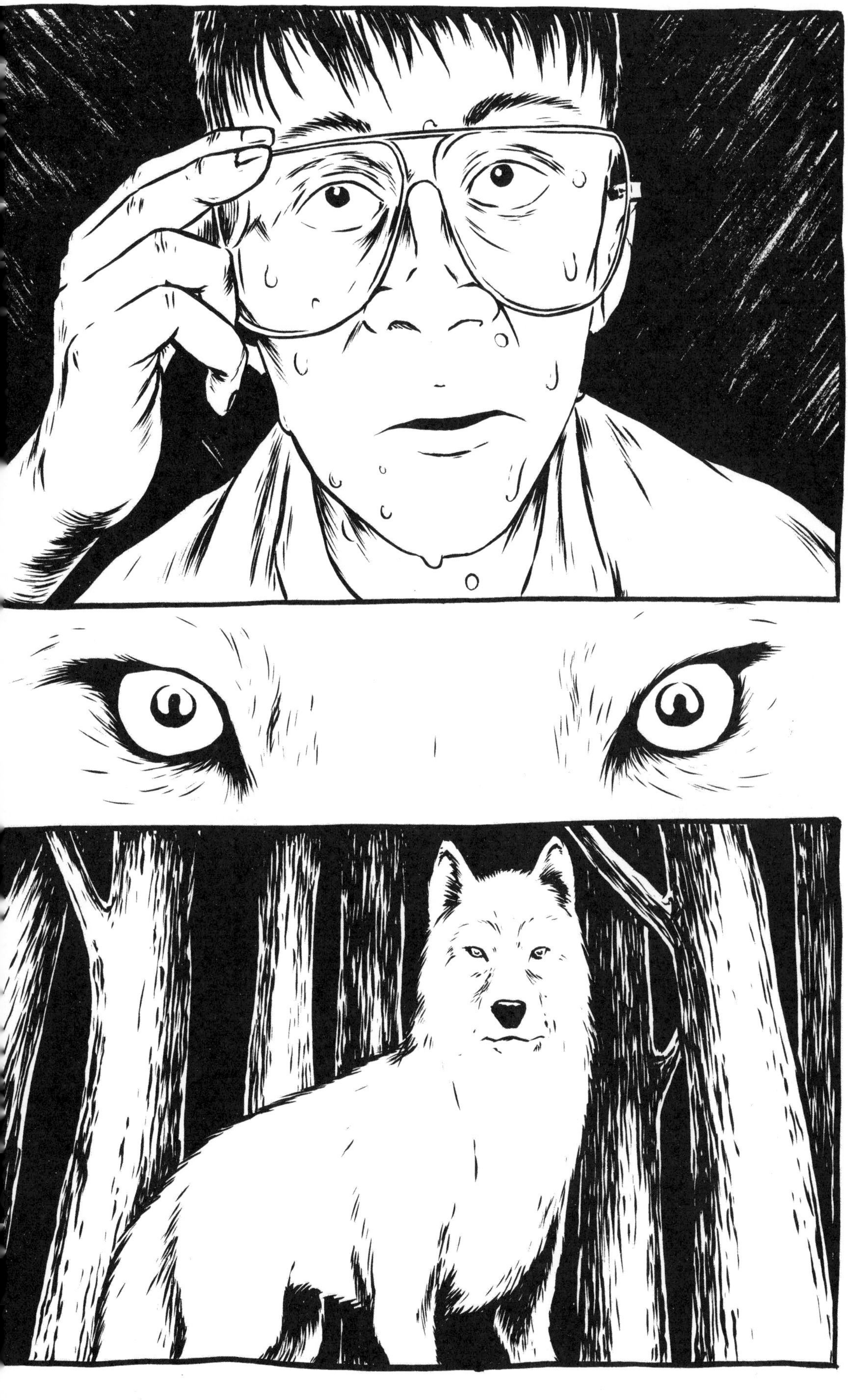

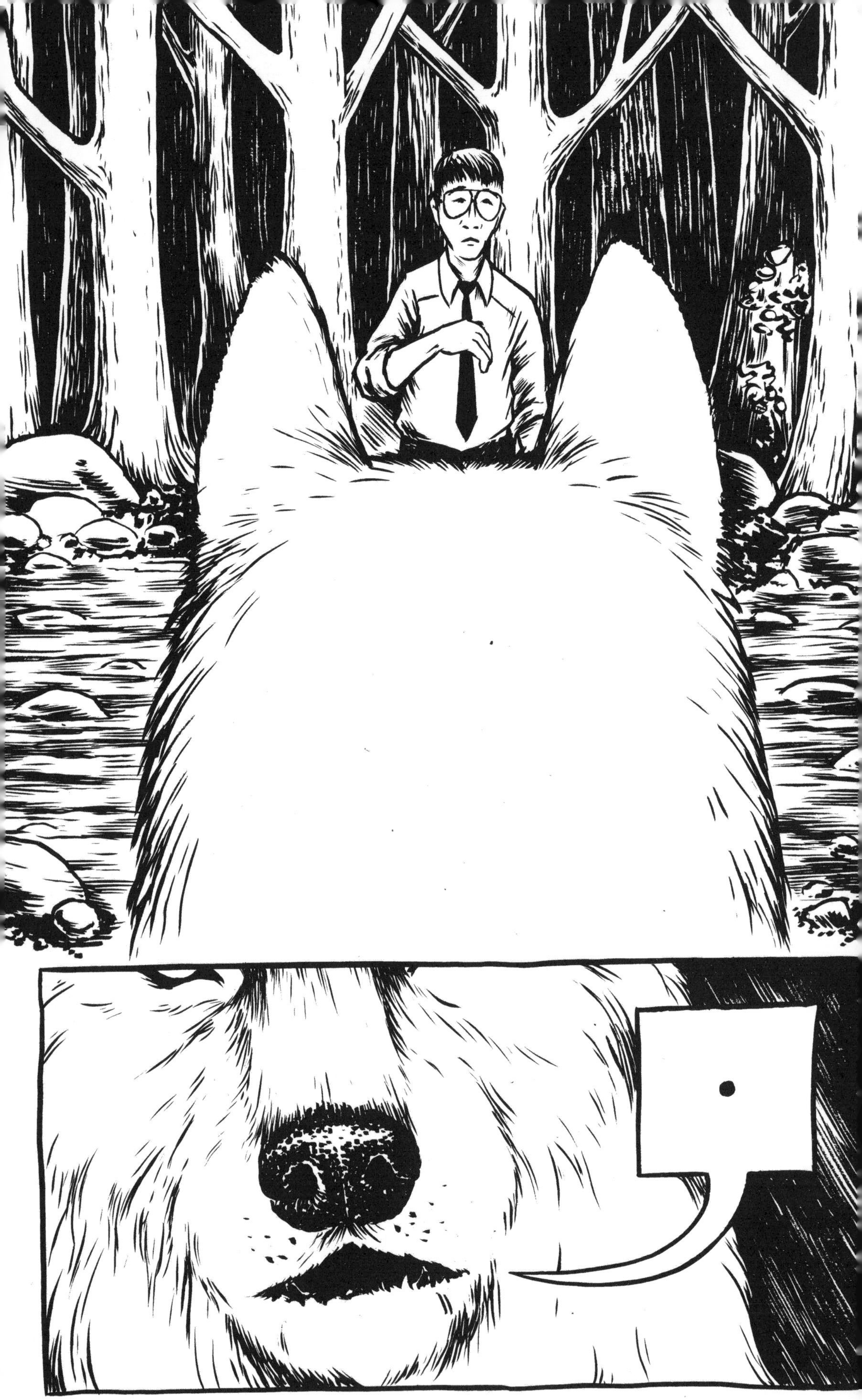

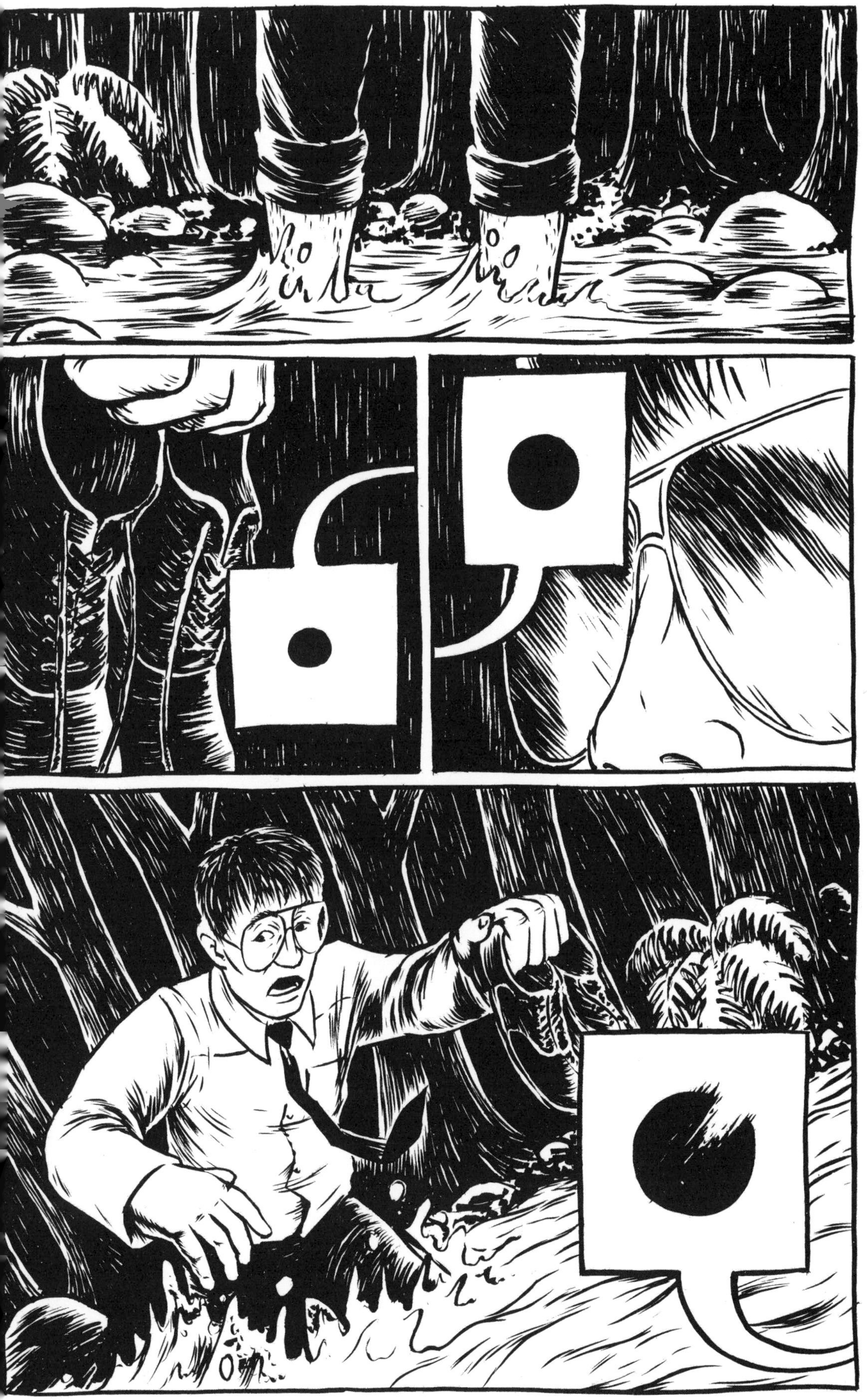

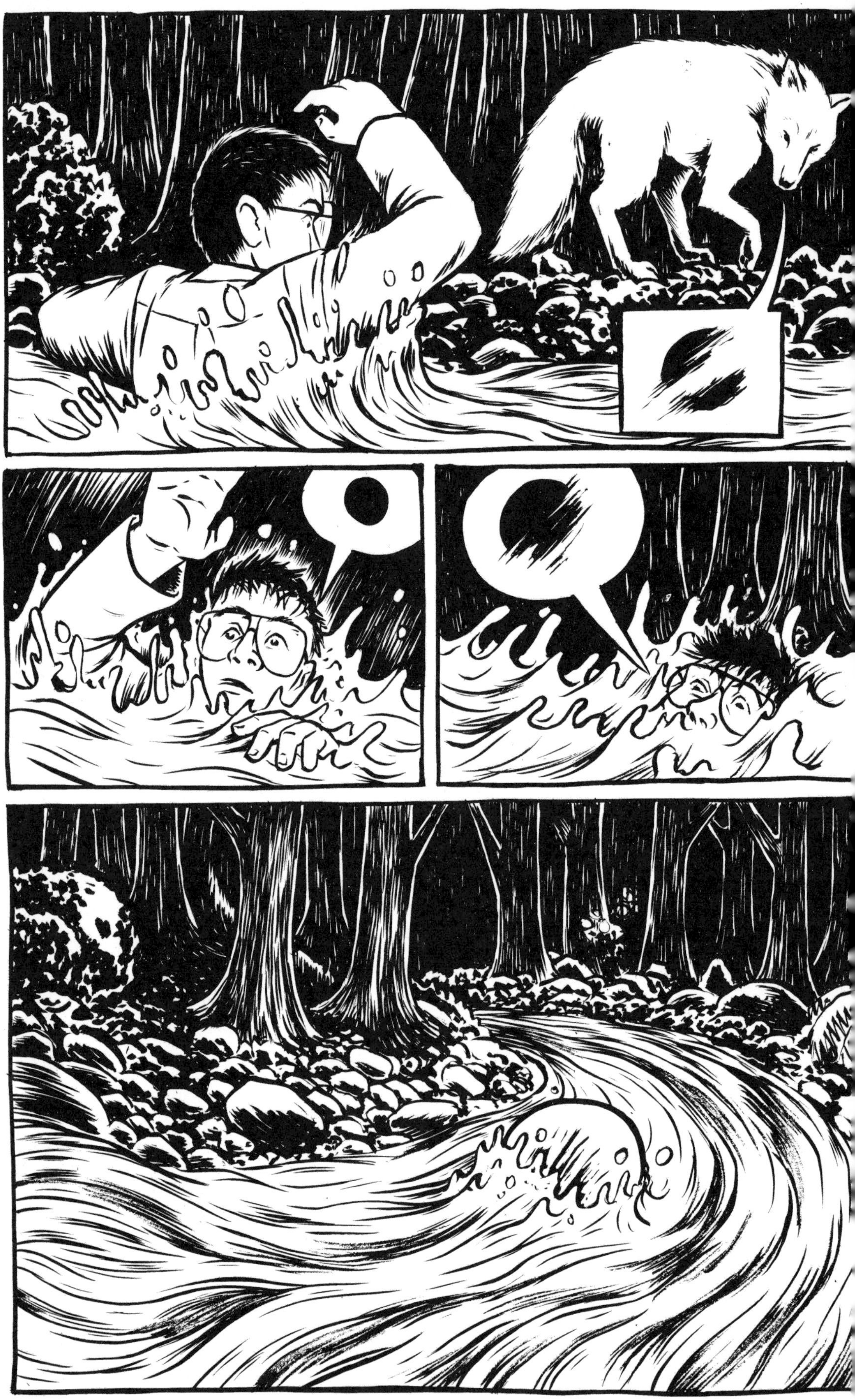

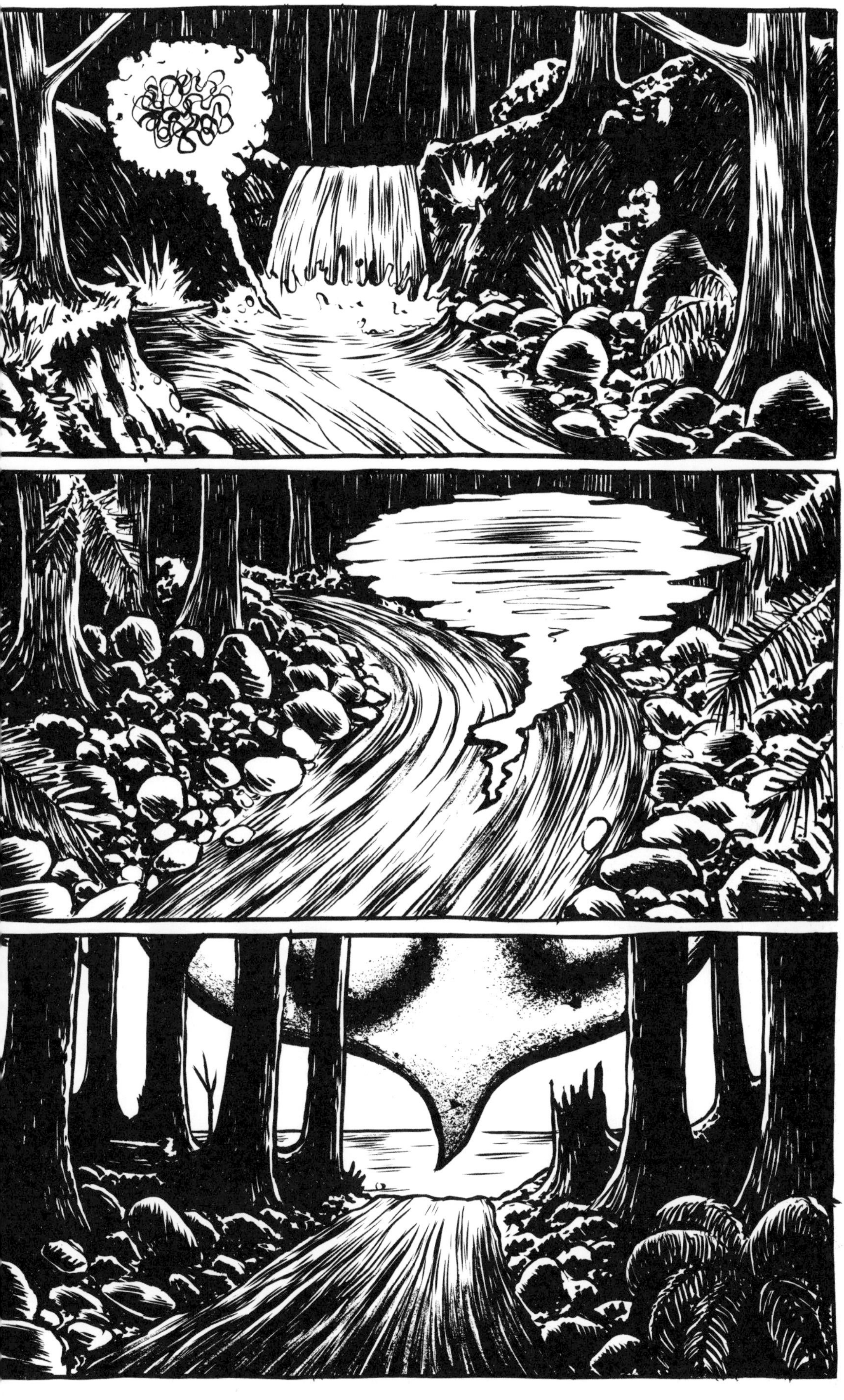

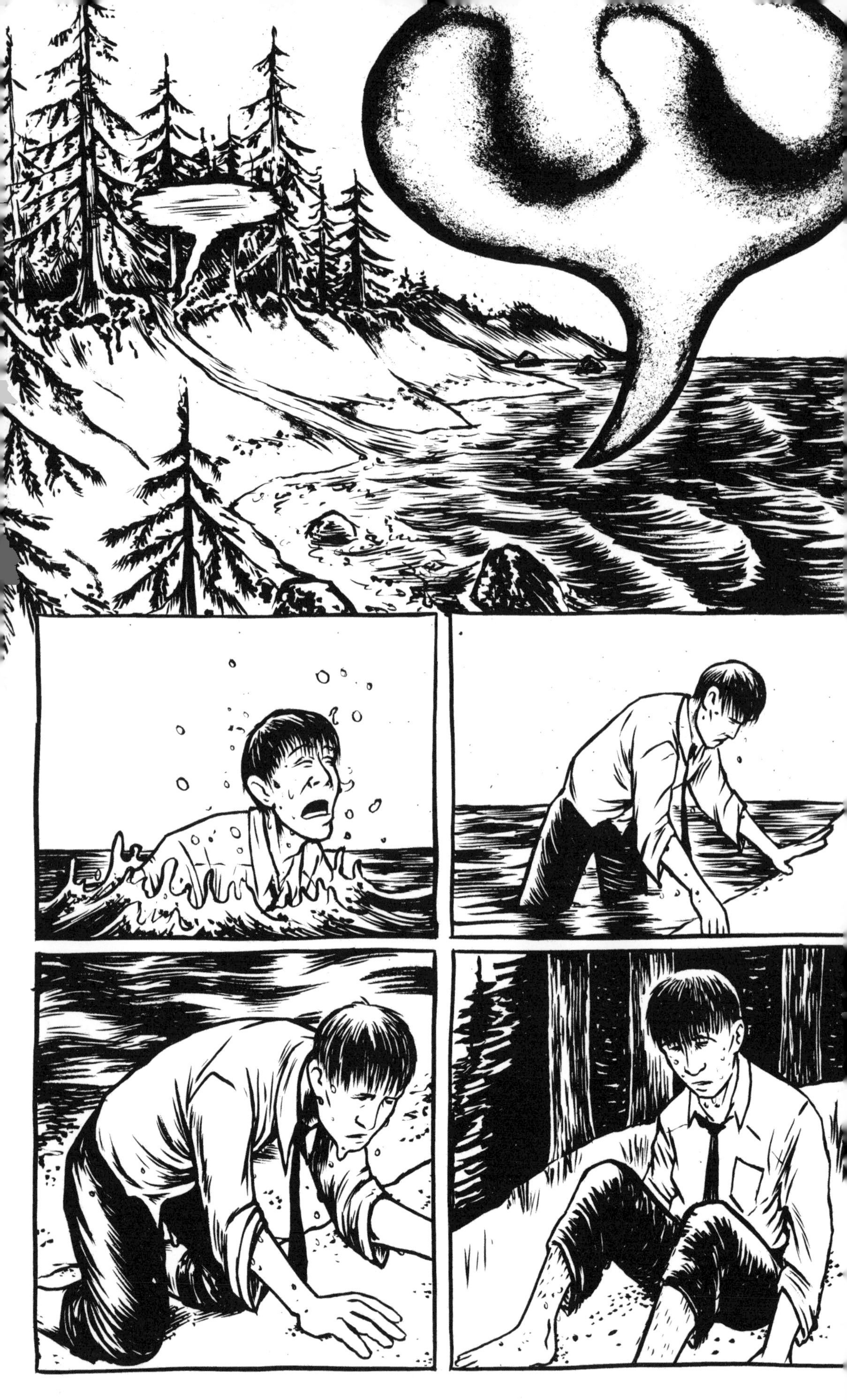

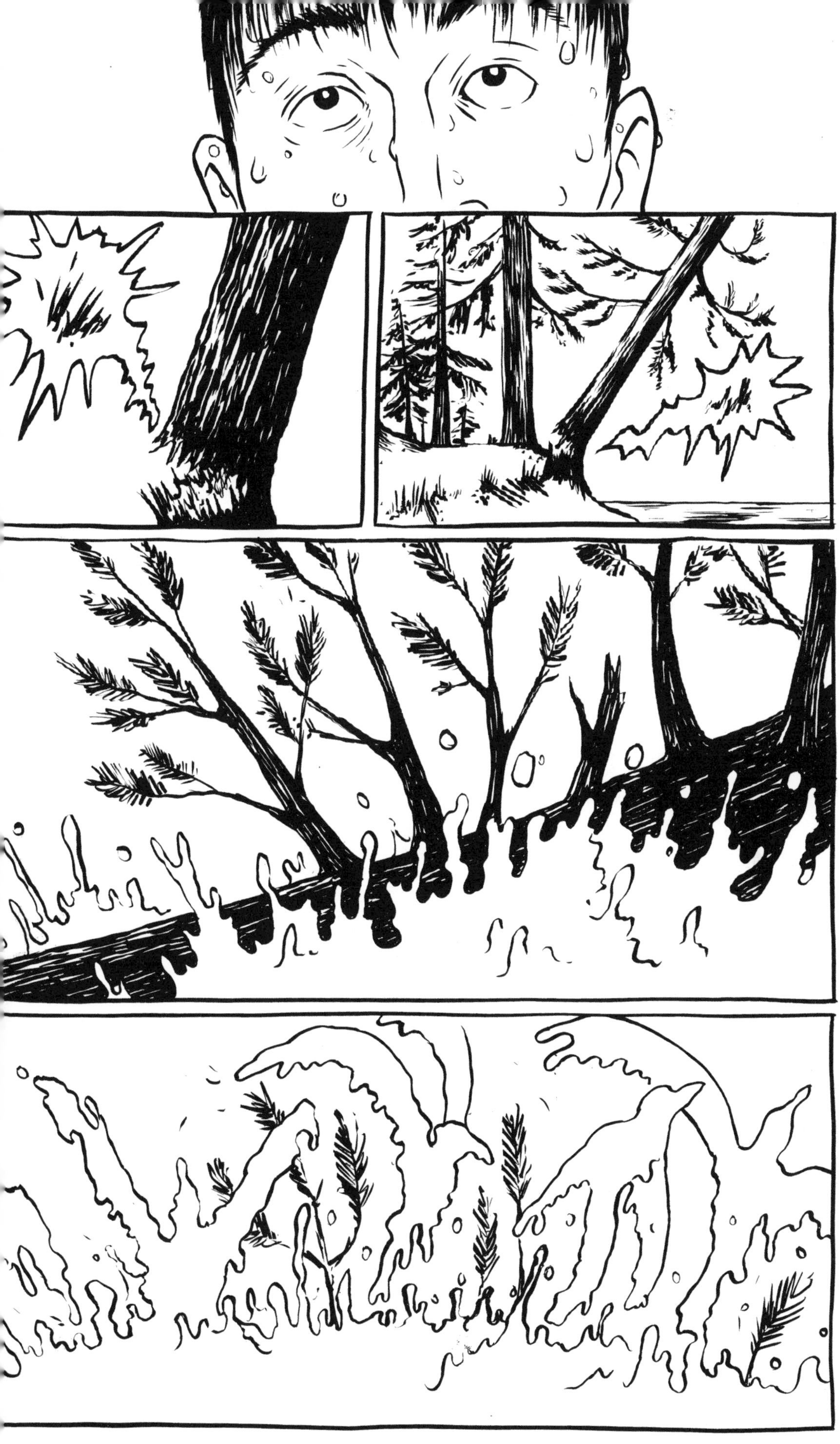

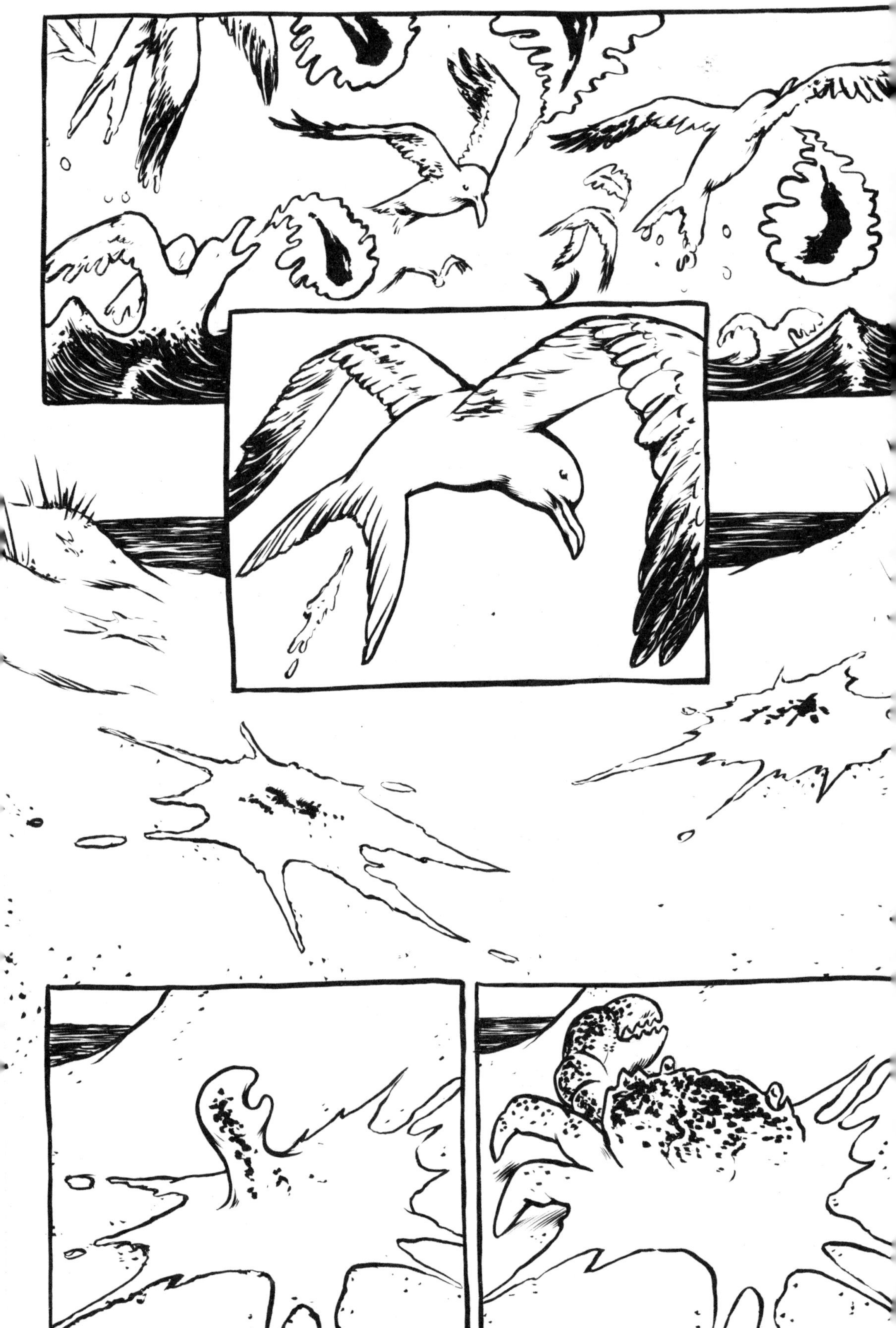

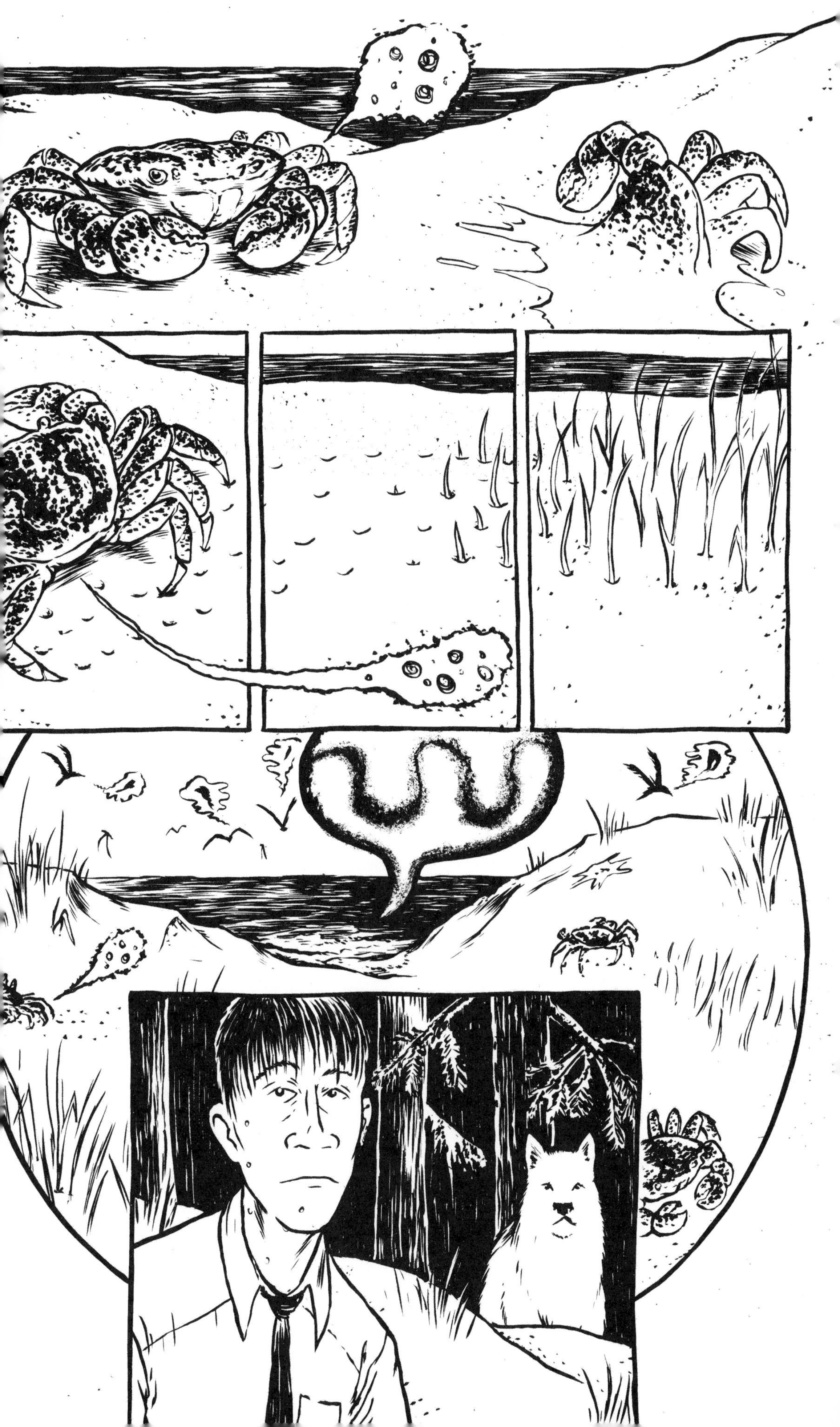

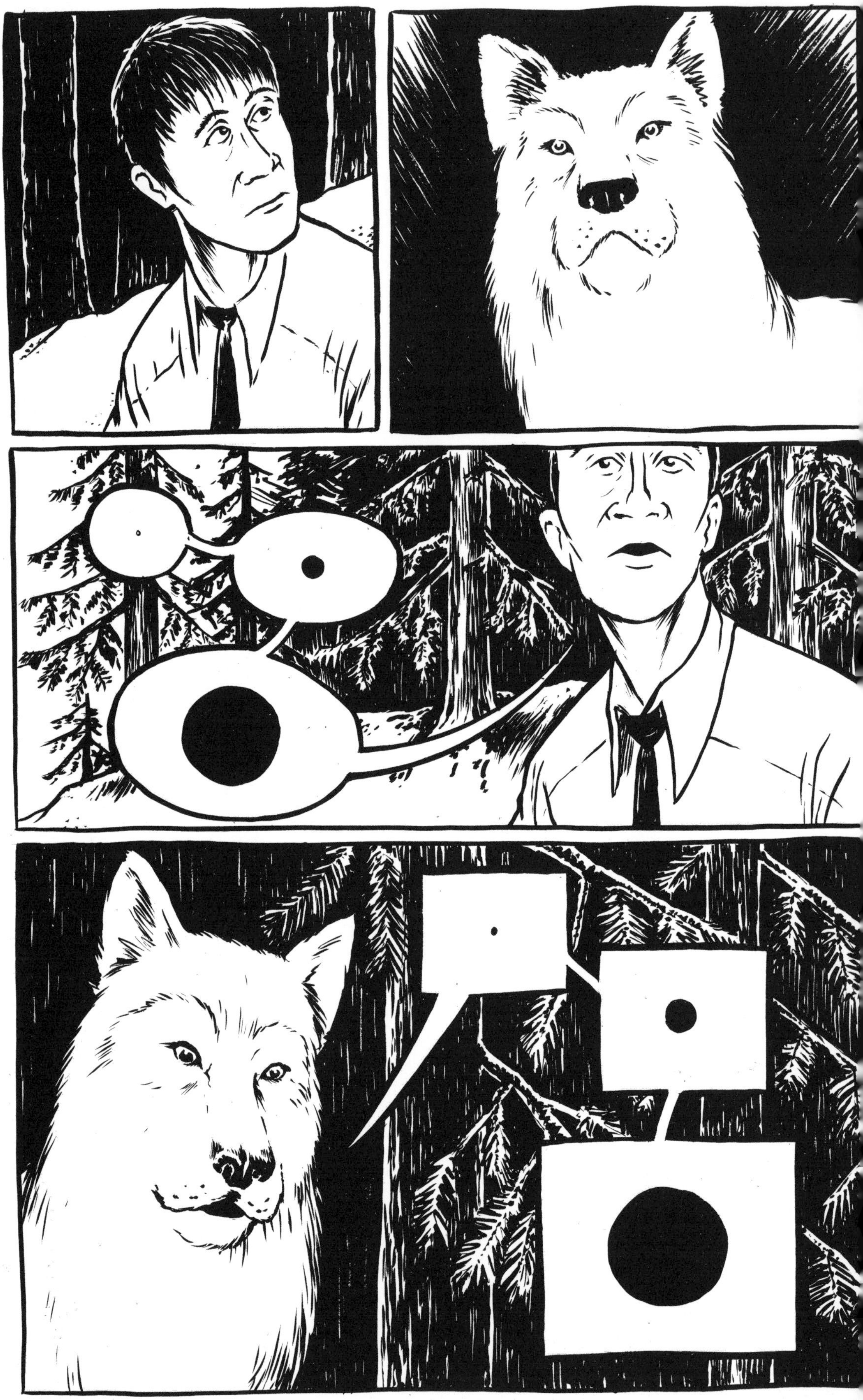

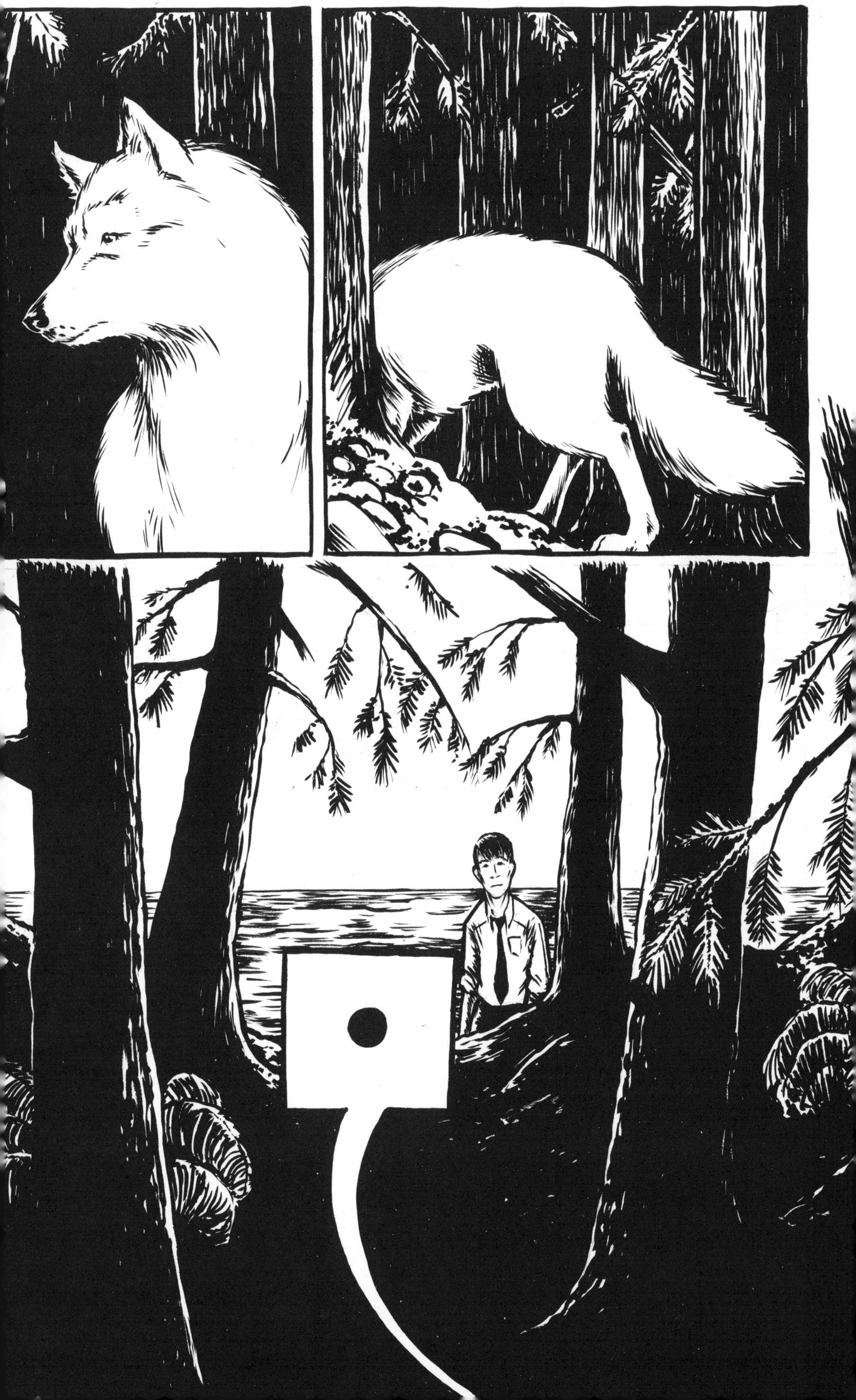

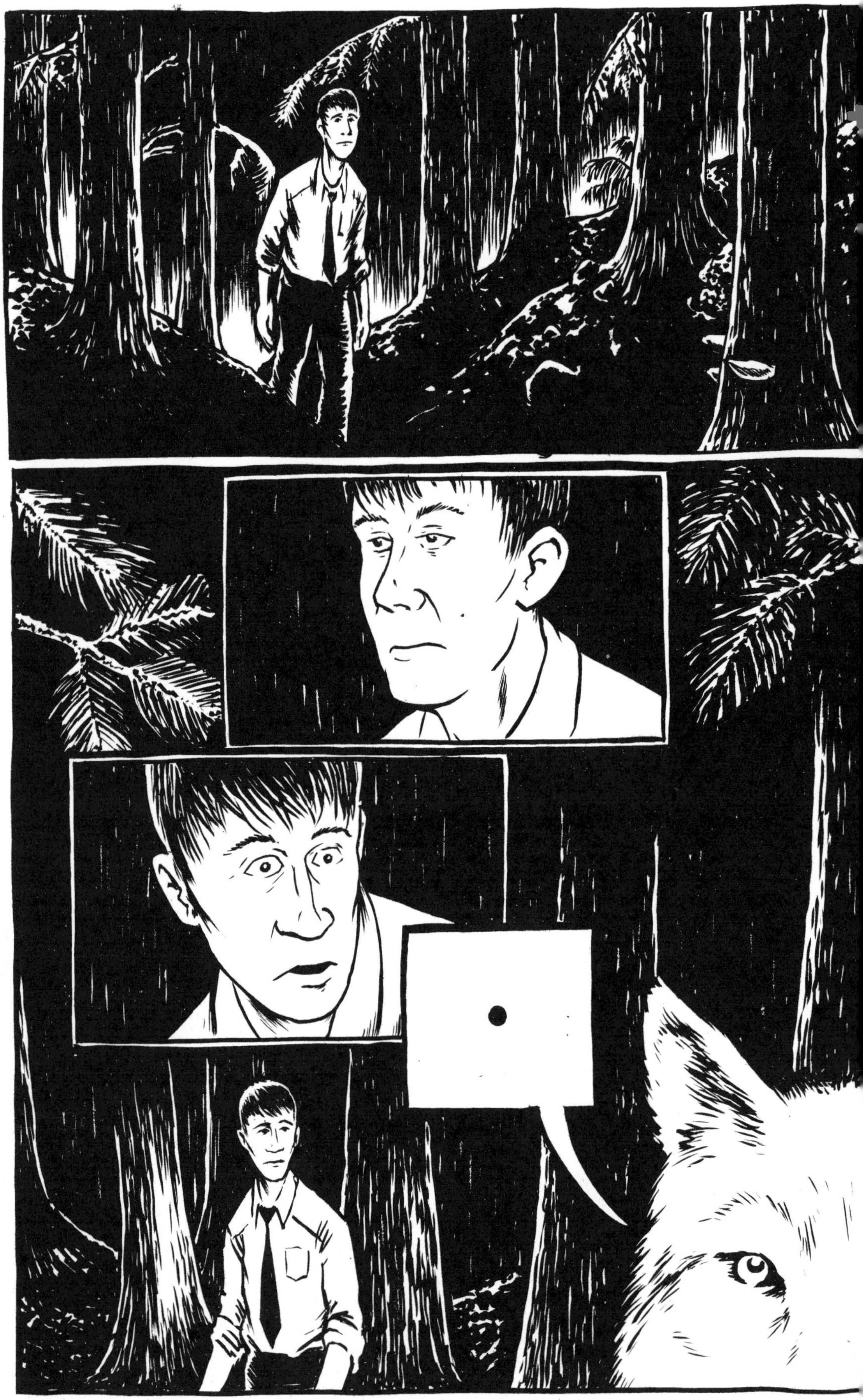

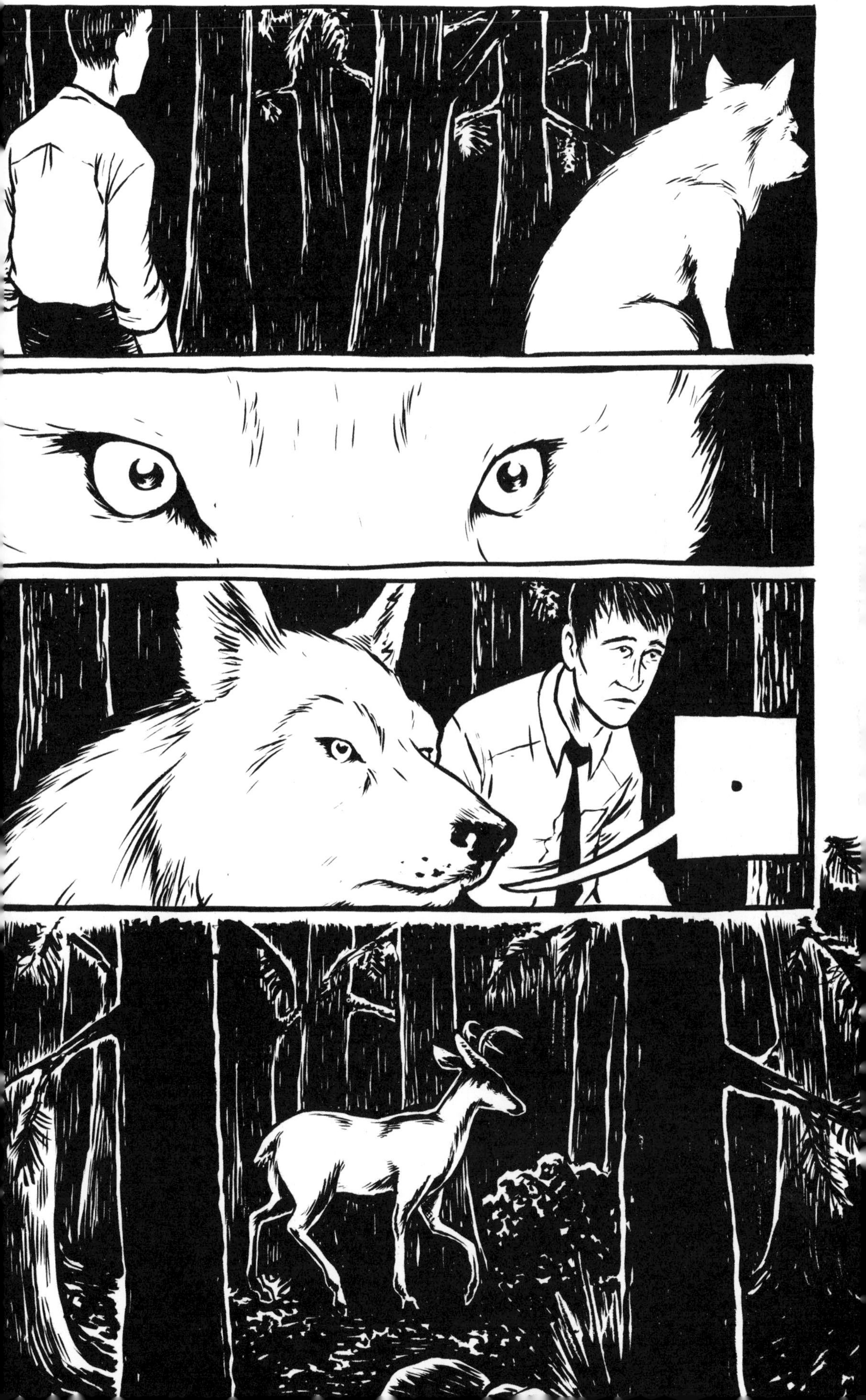

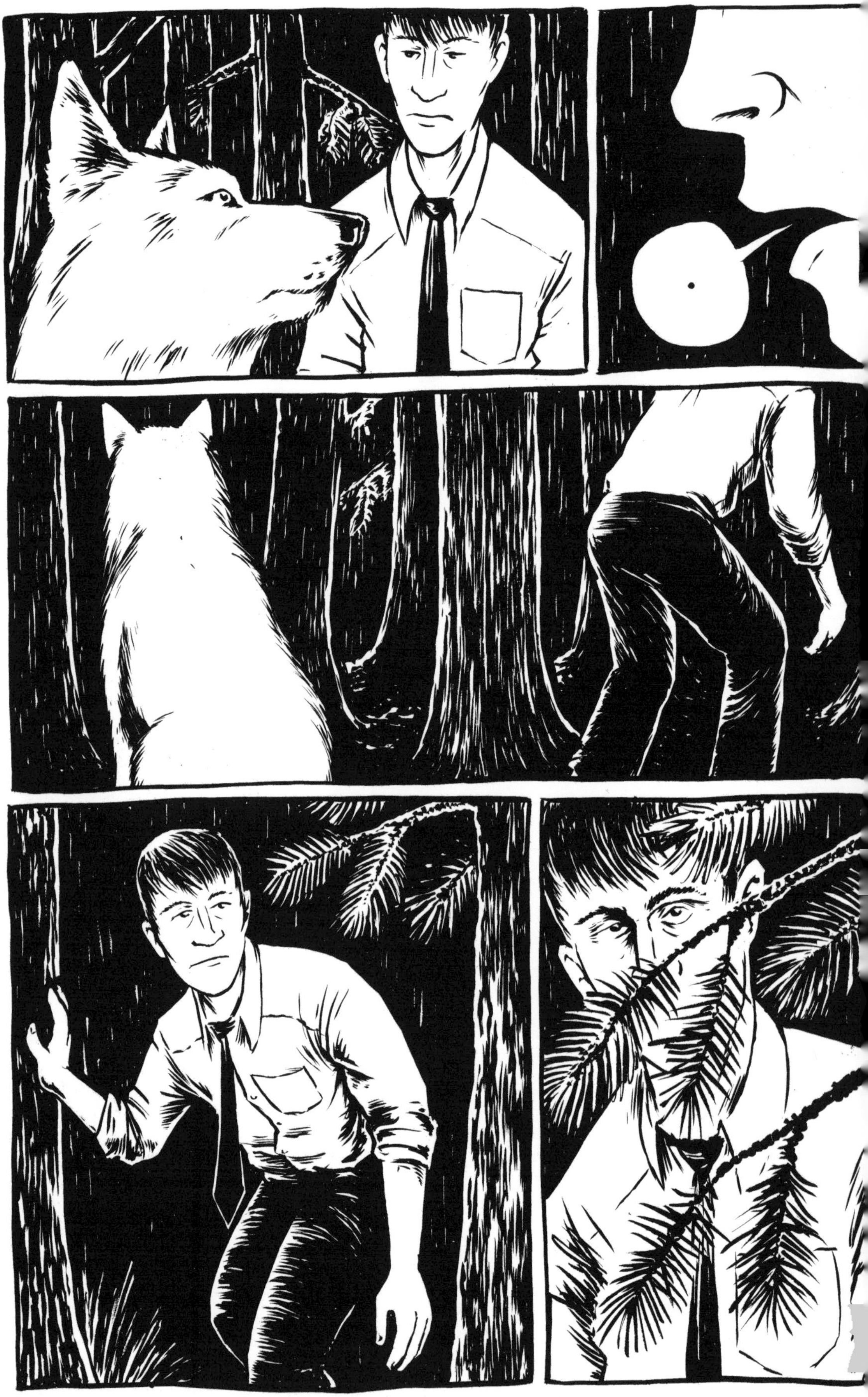

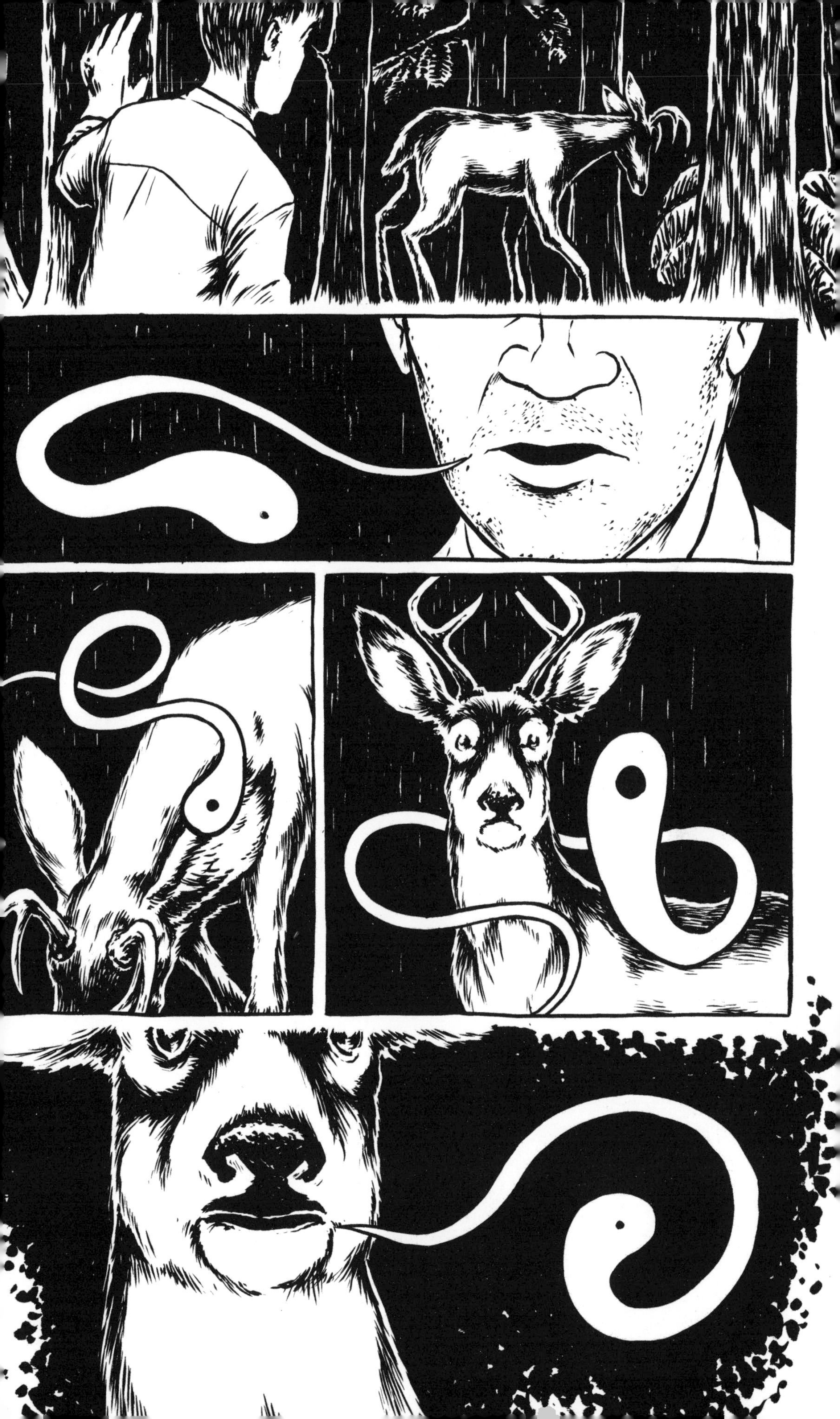

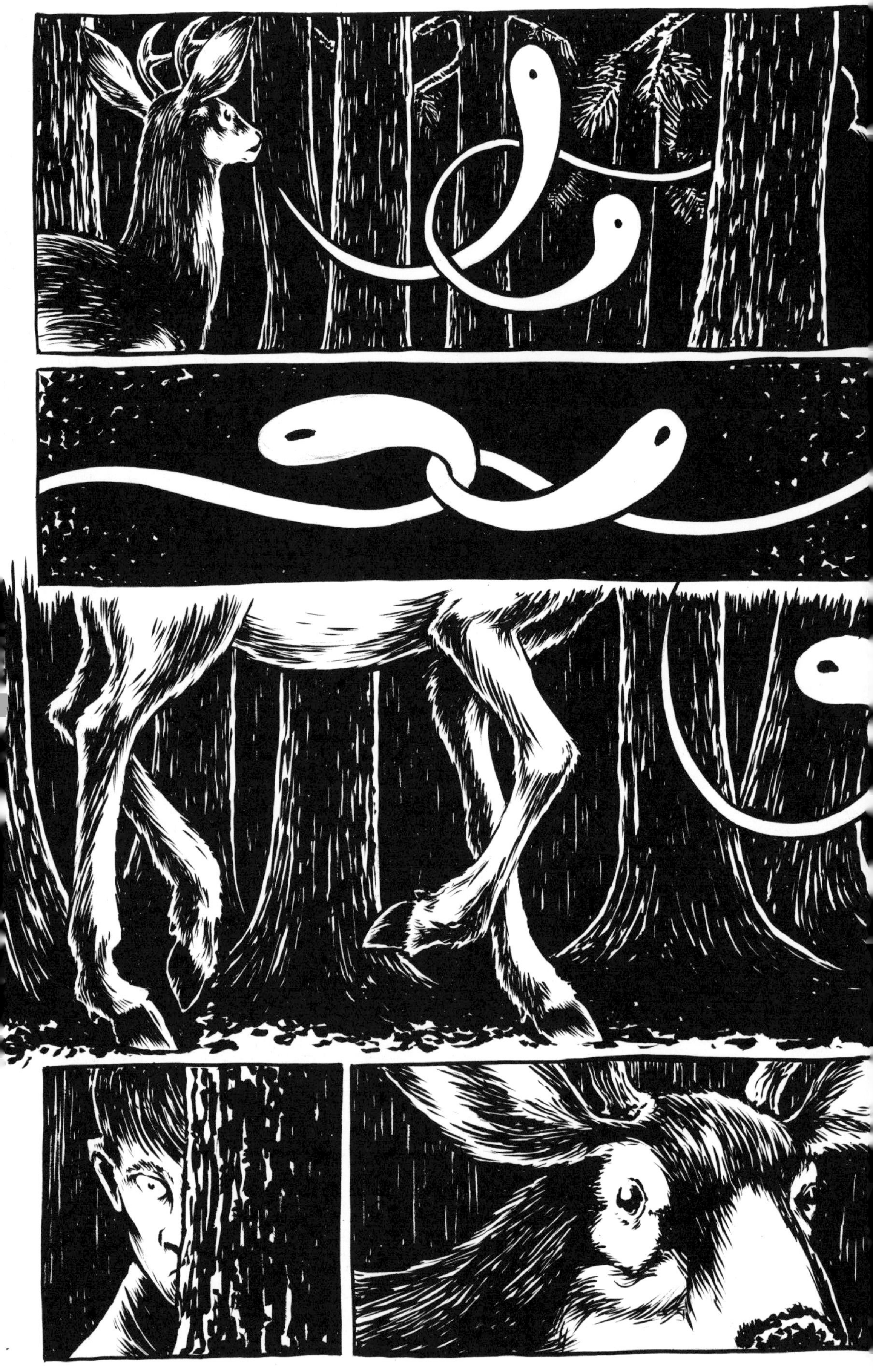

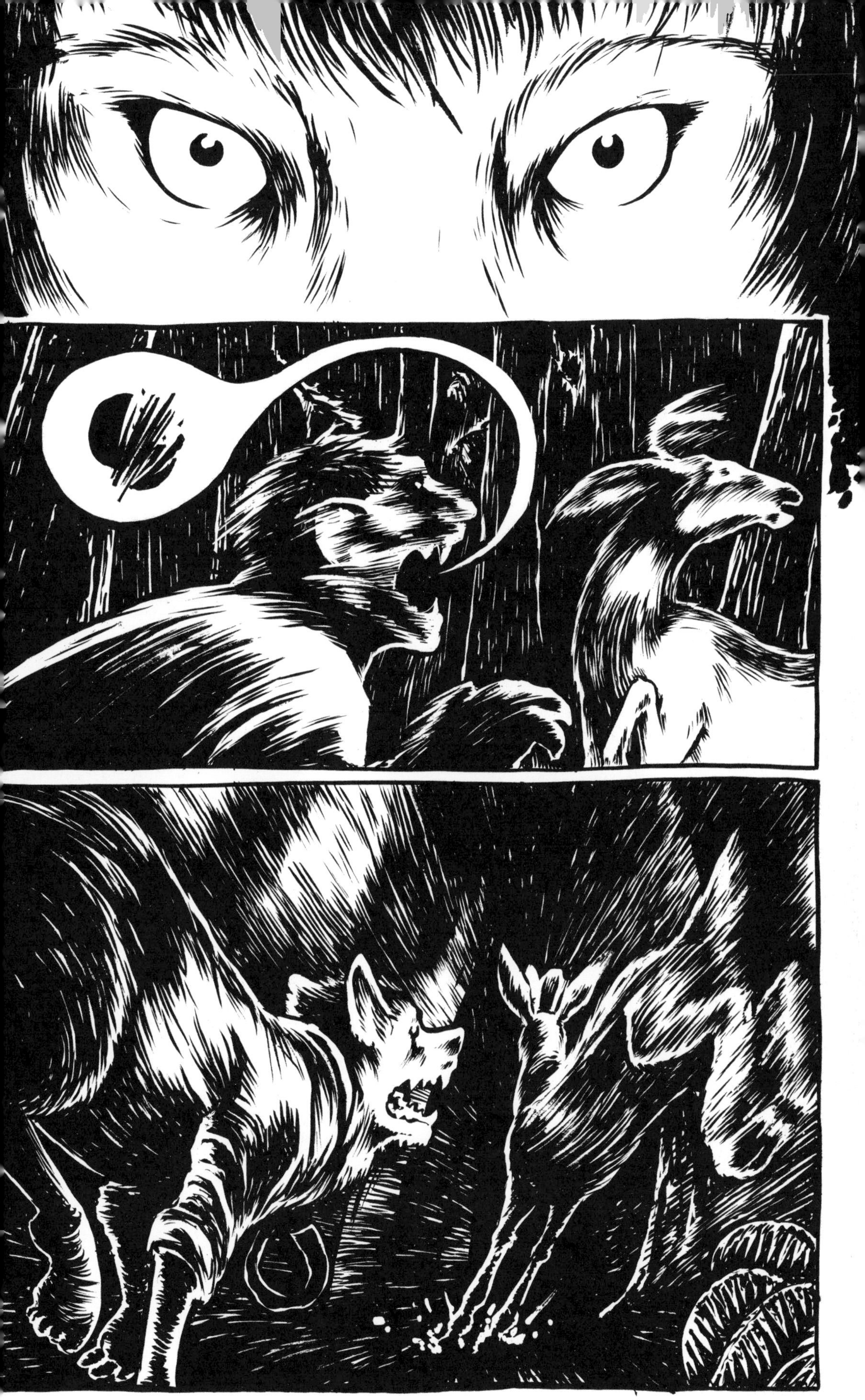

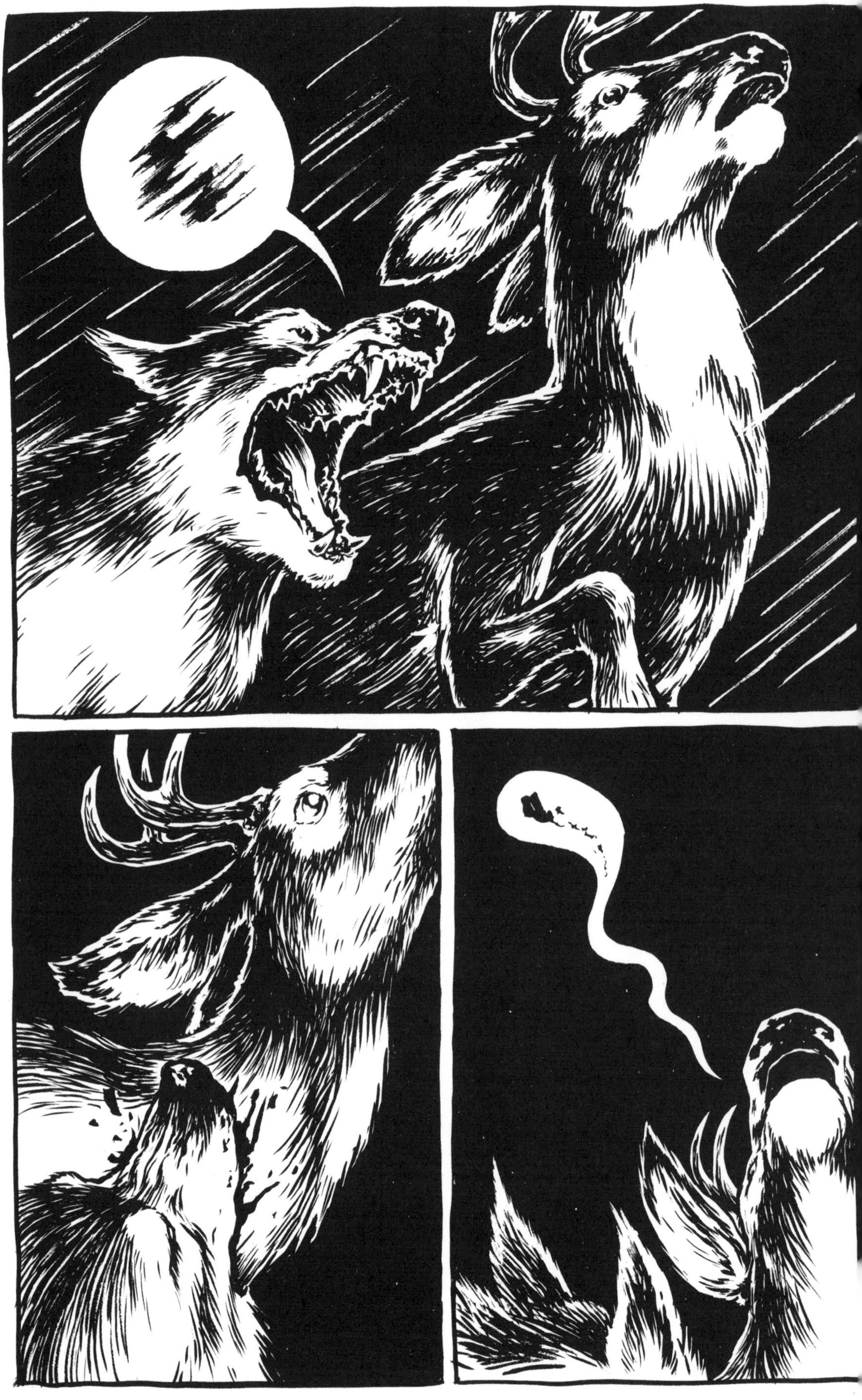

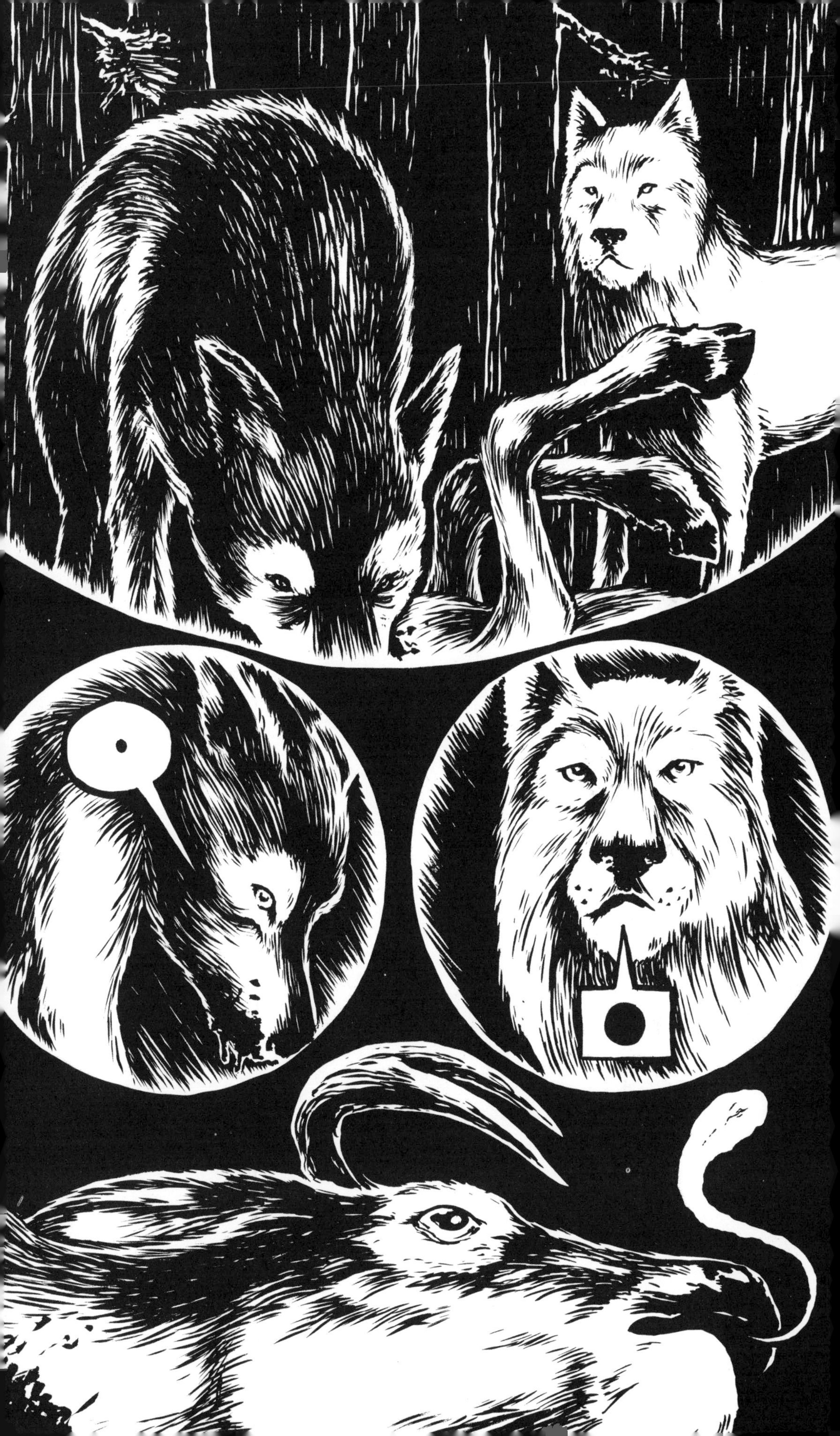

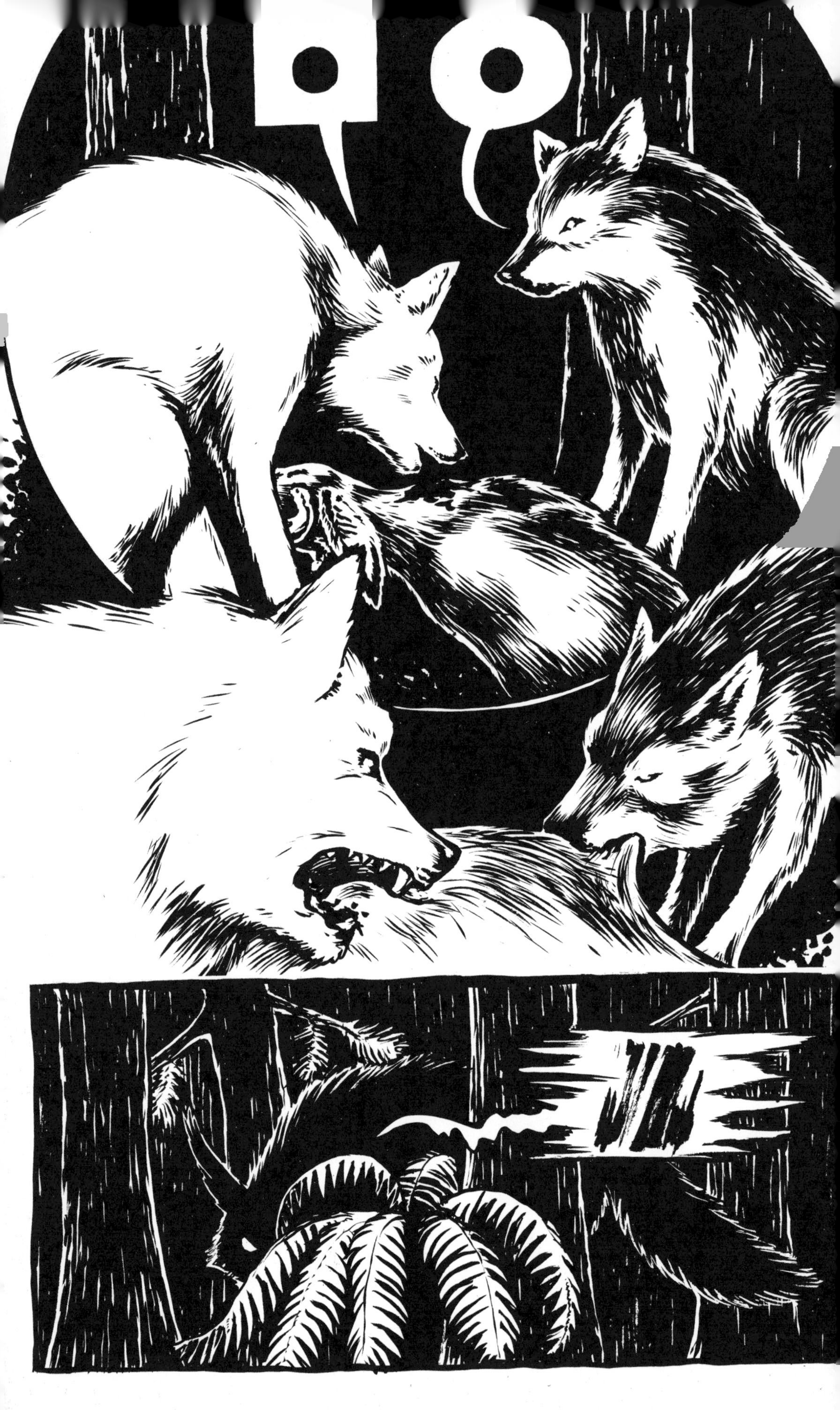

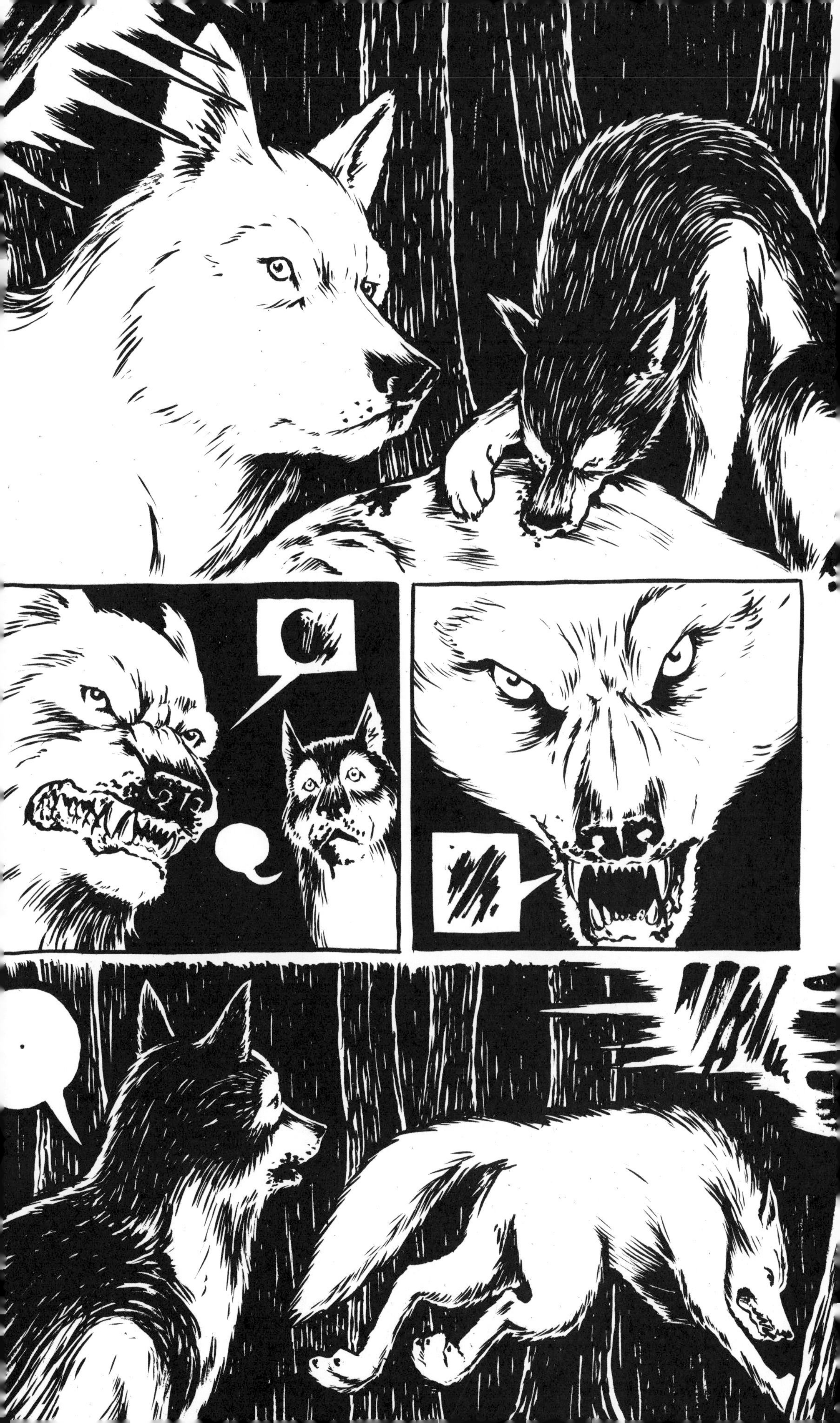

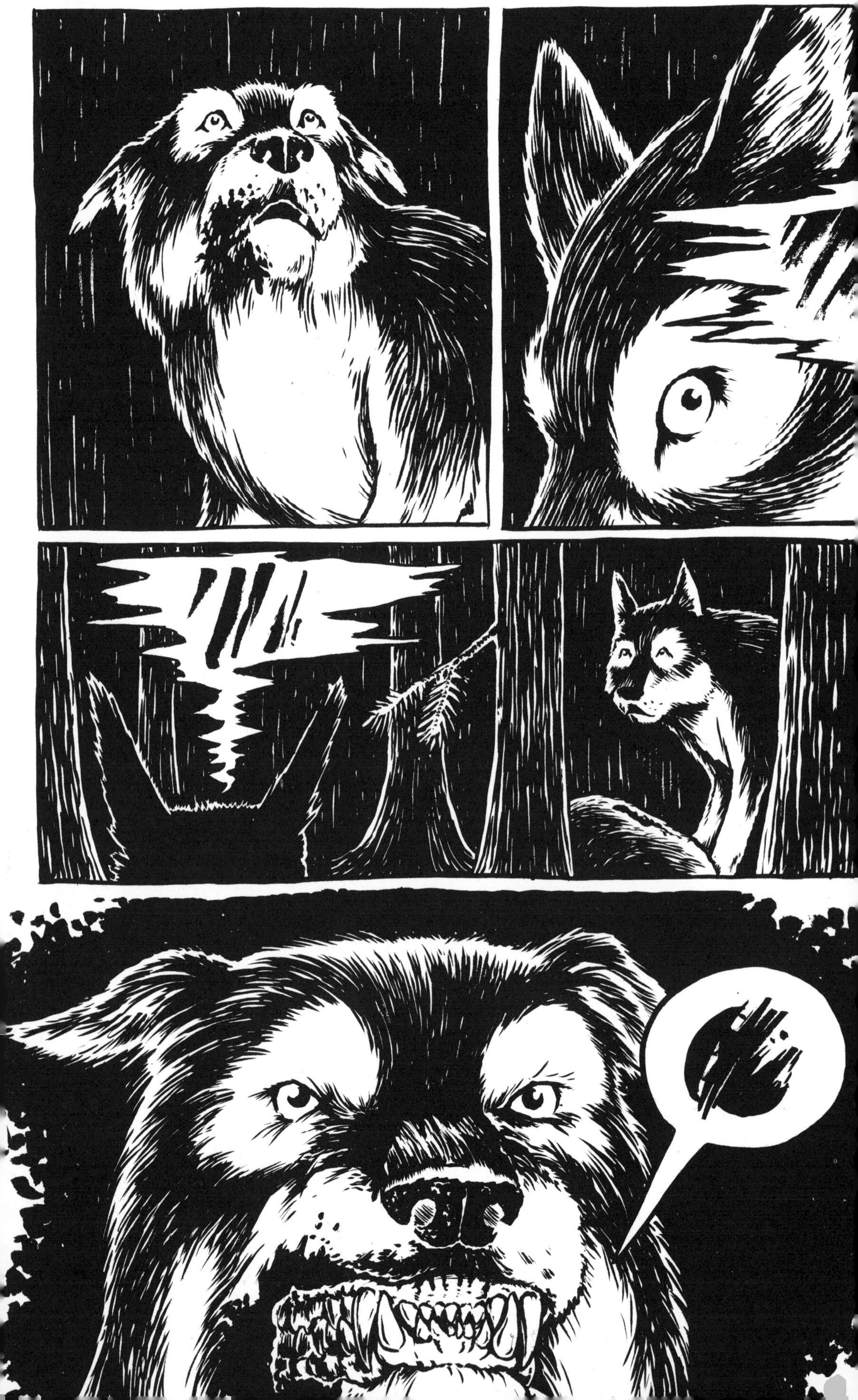

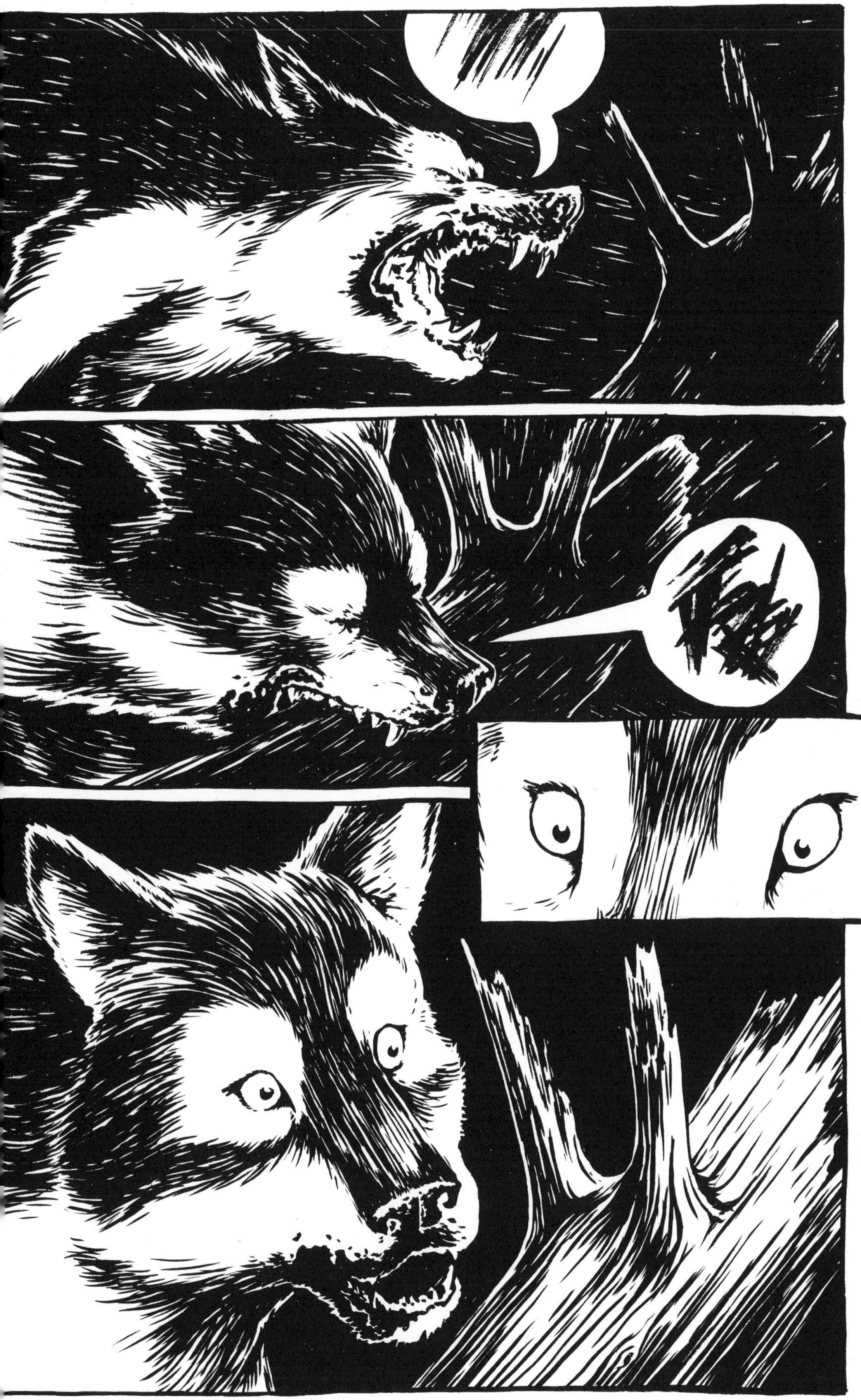

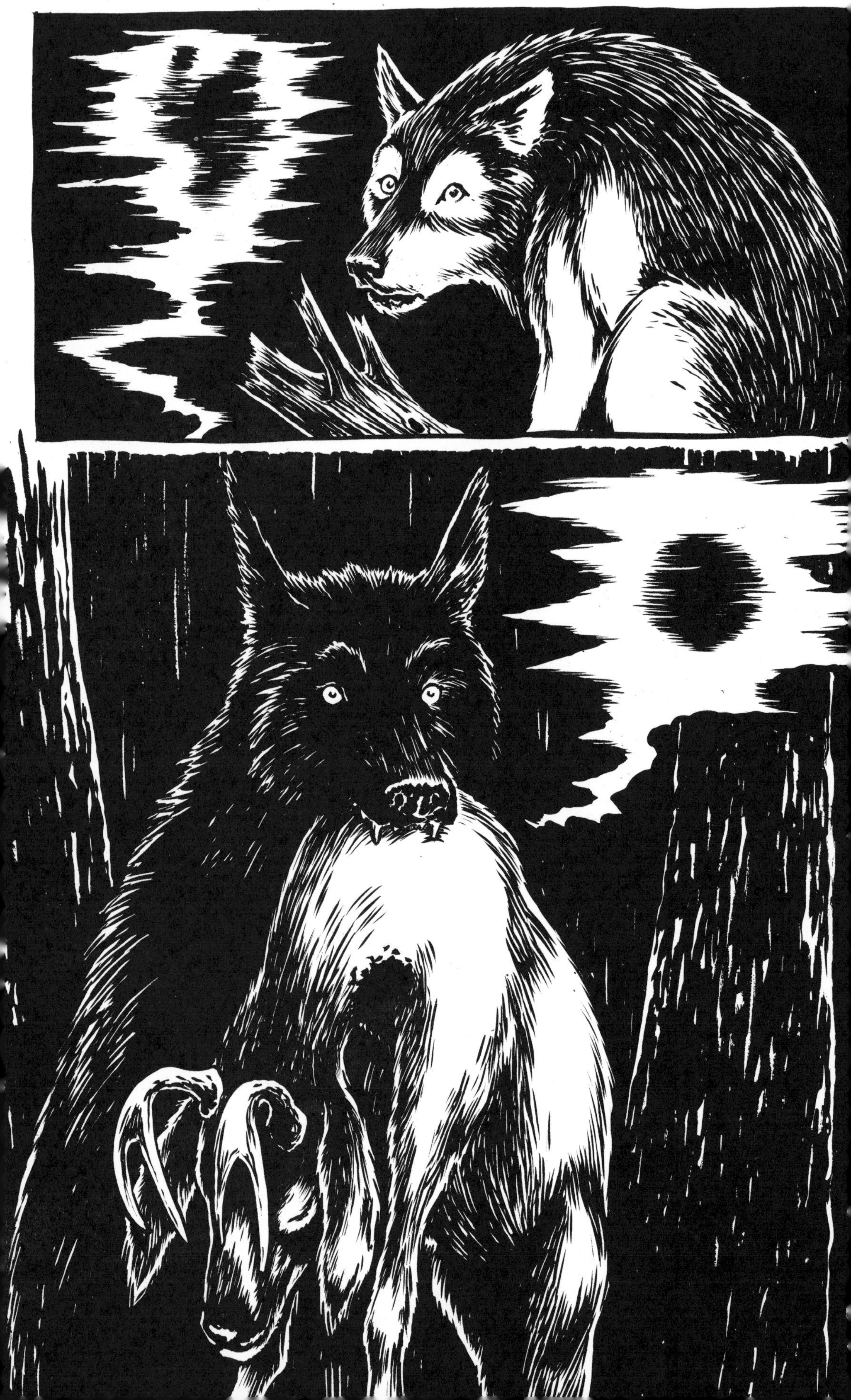

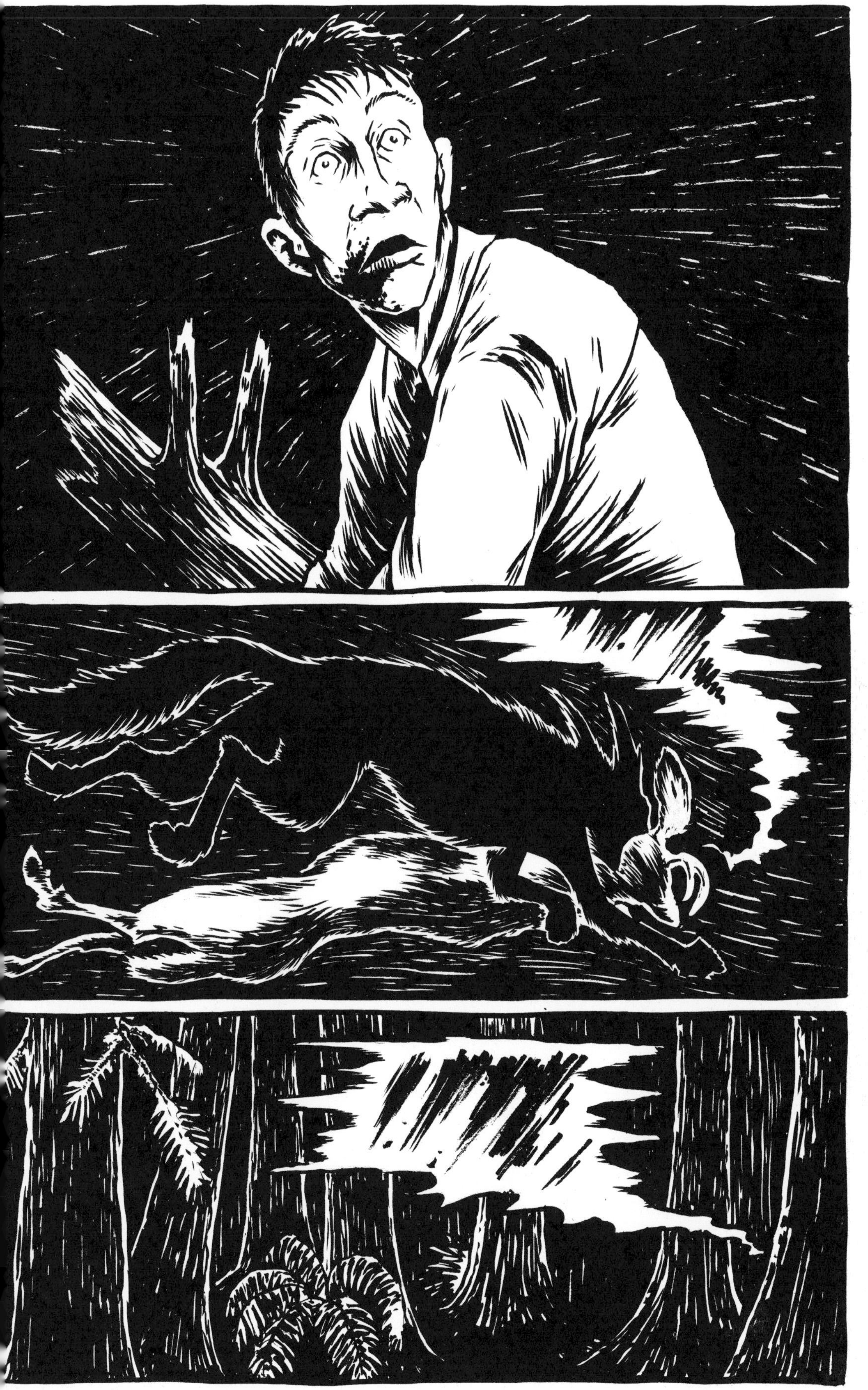

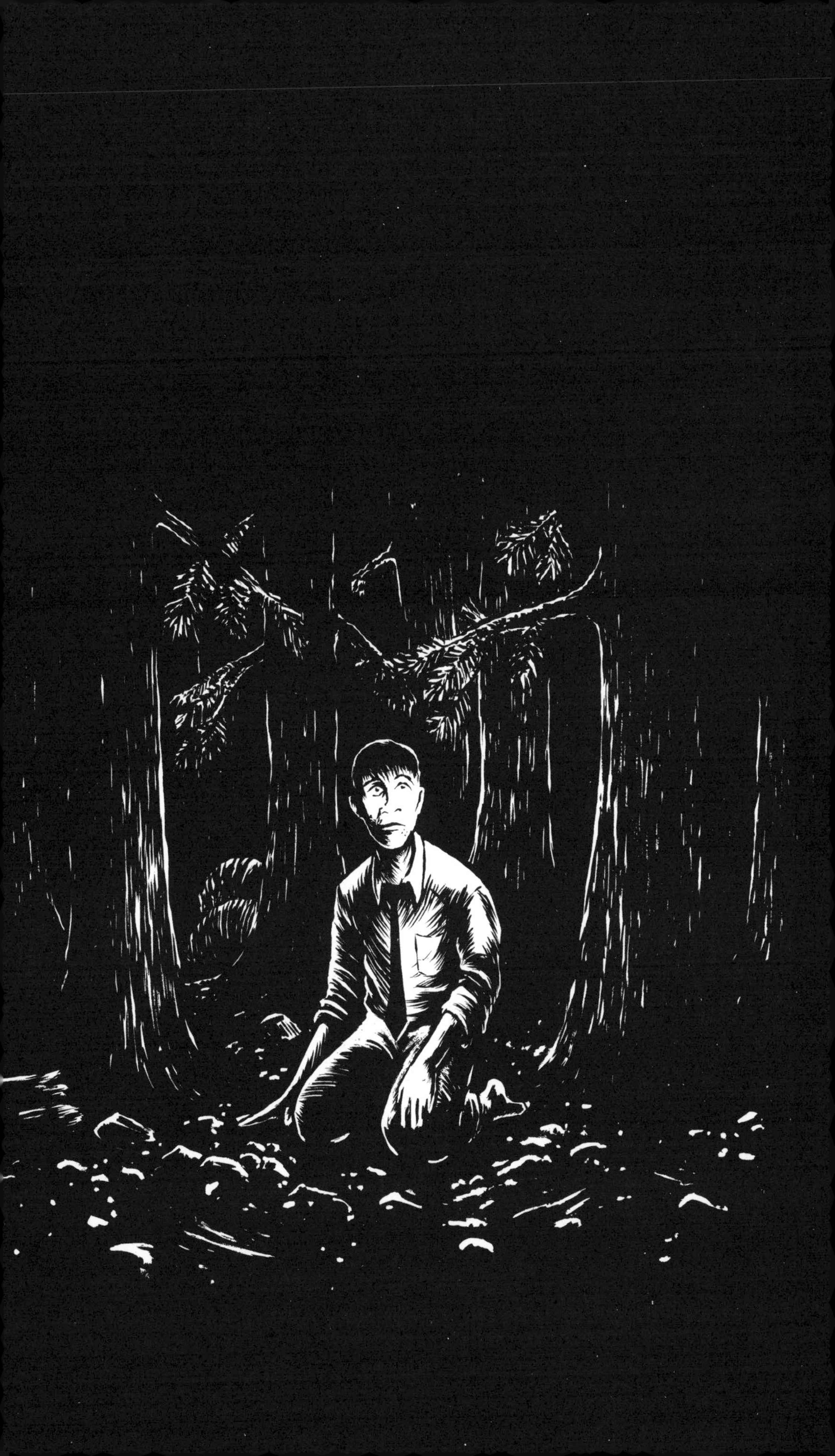

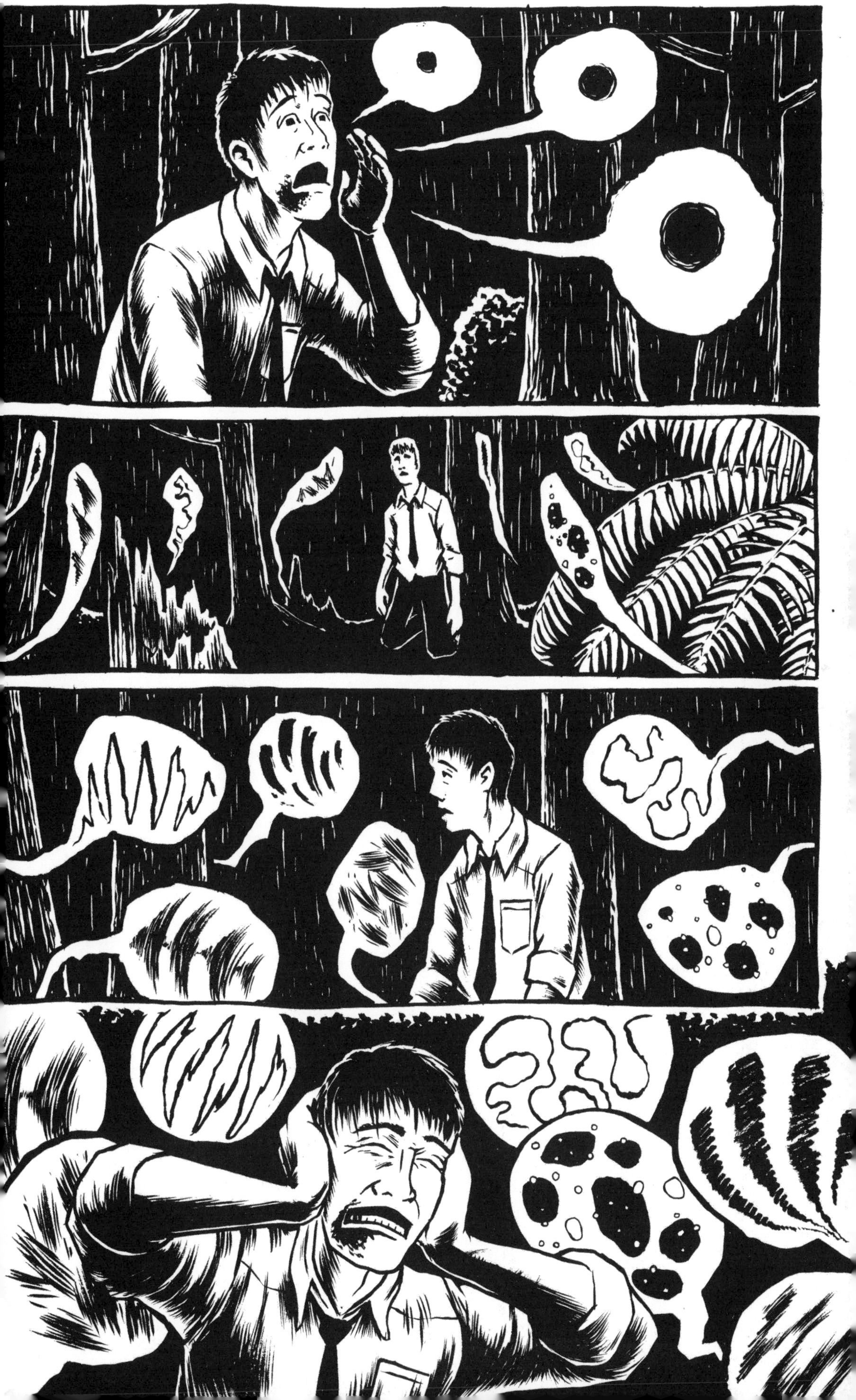

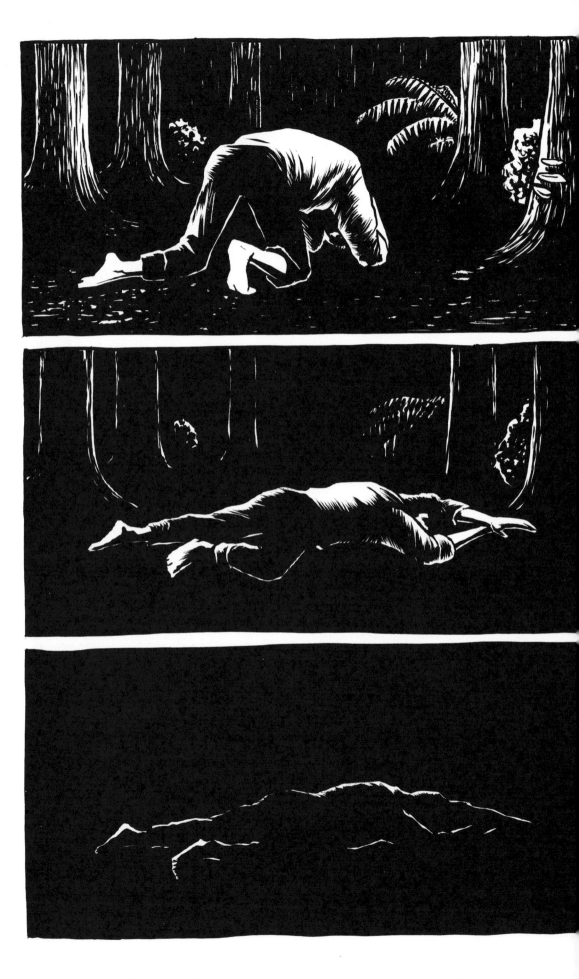

[redacted]

[redacted]

[redacted]

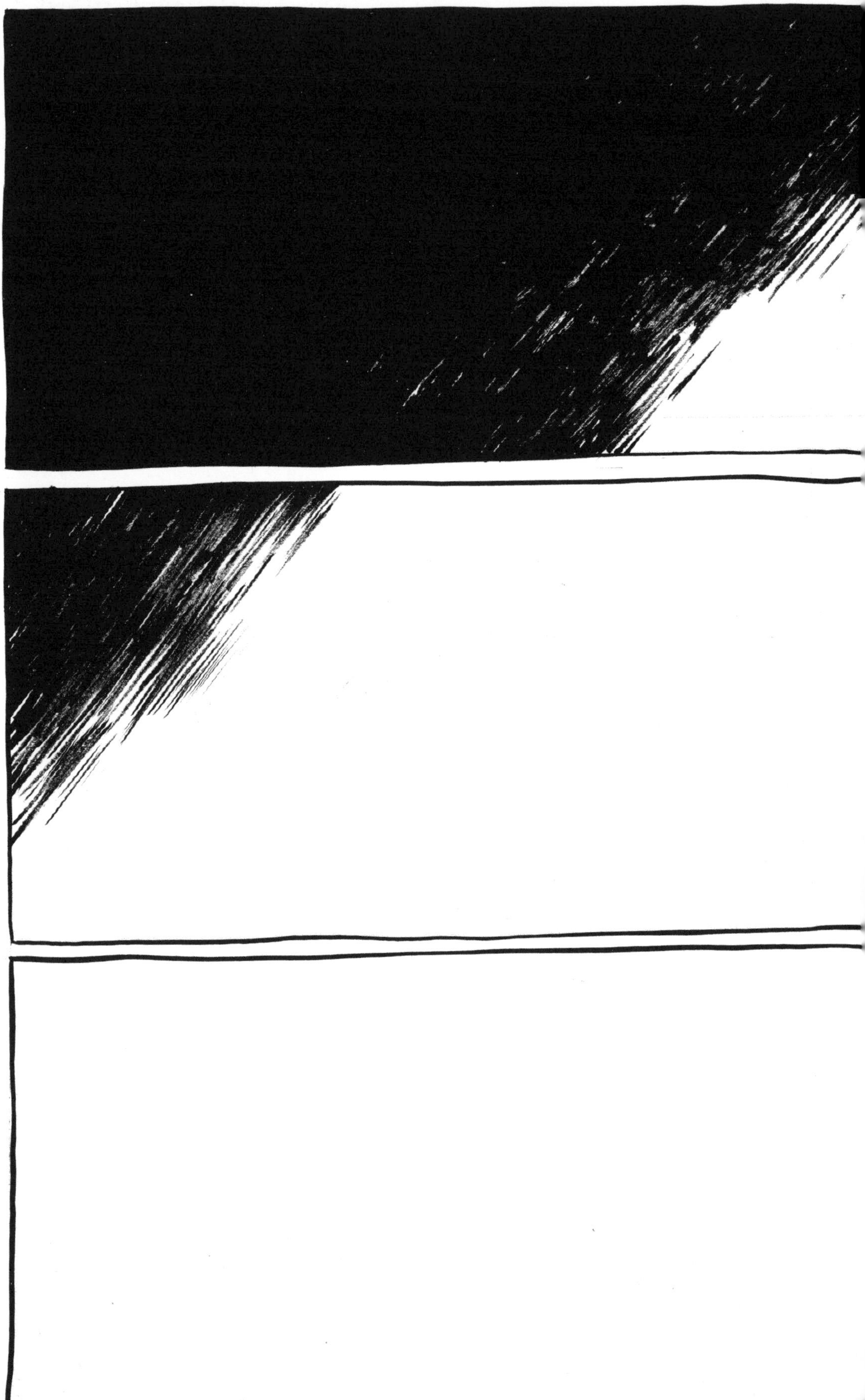

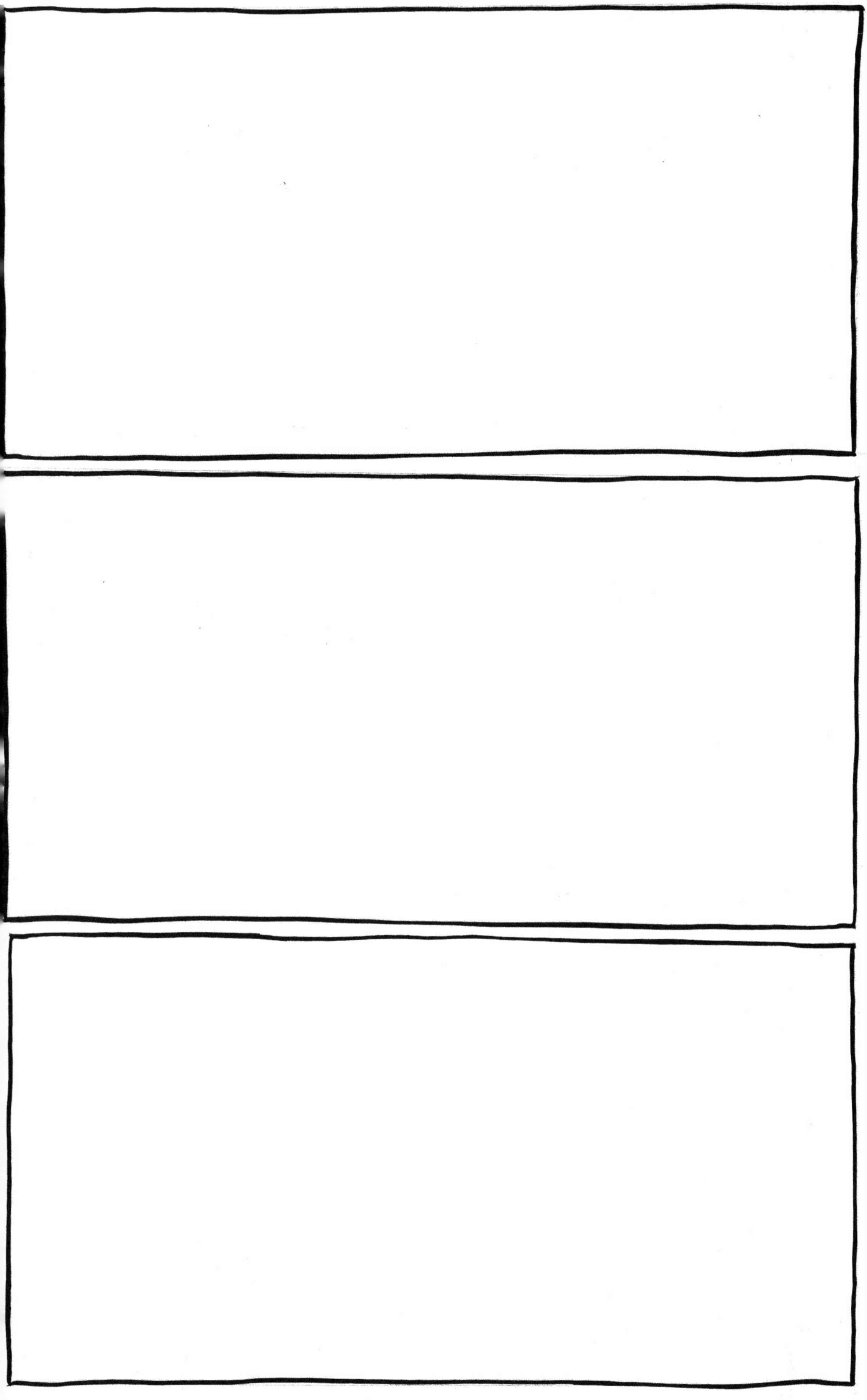

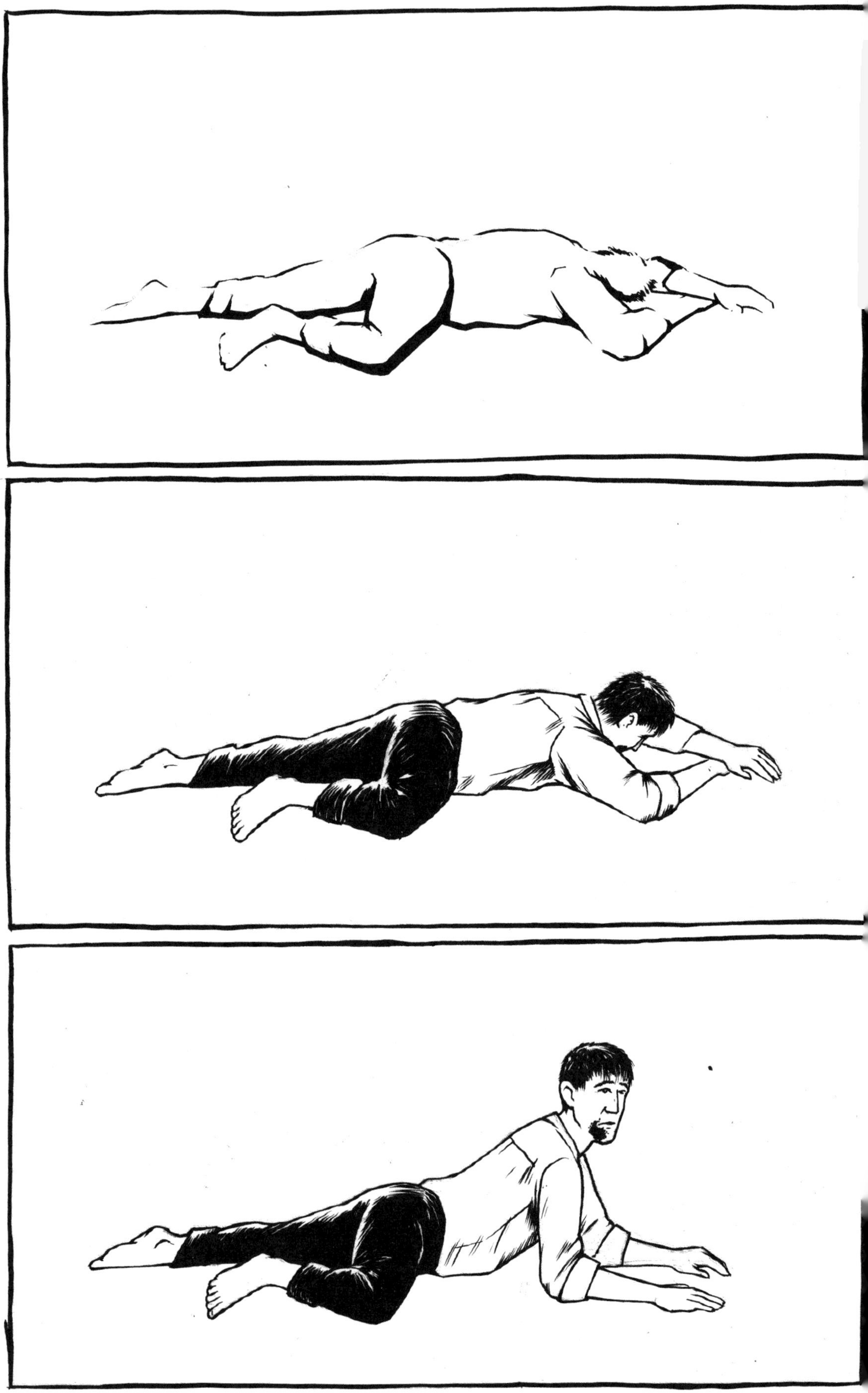

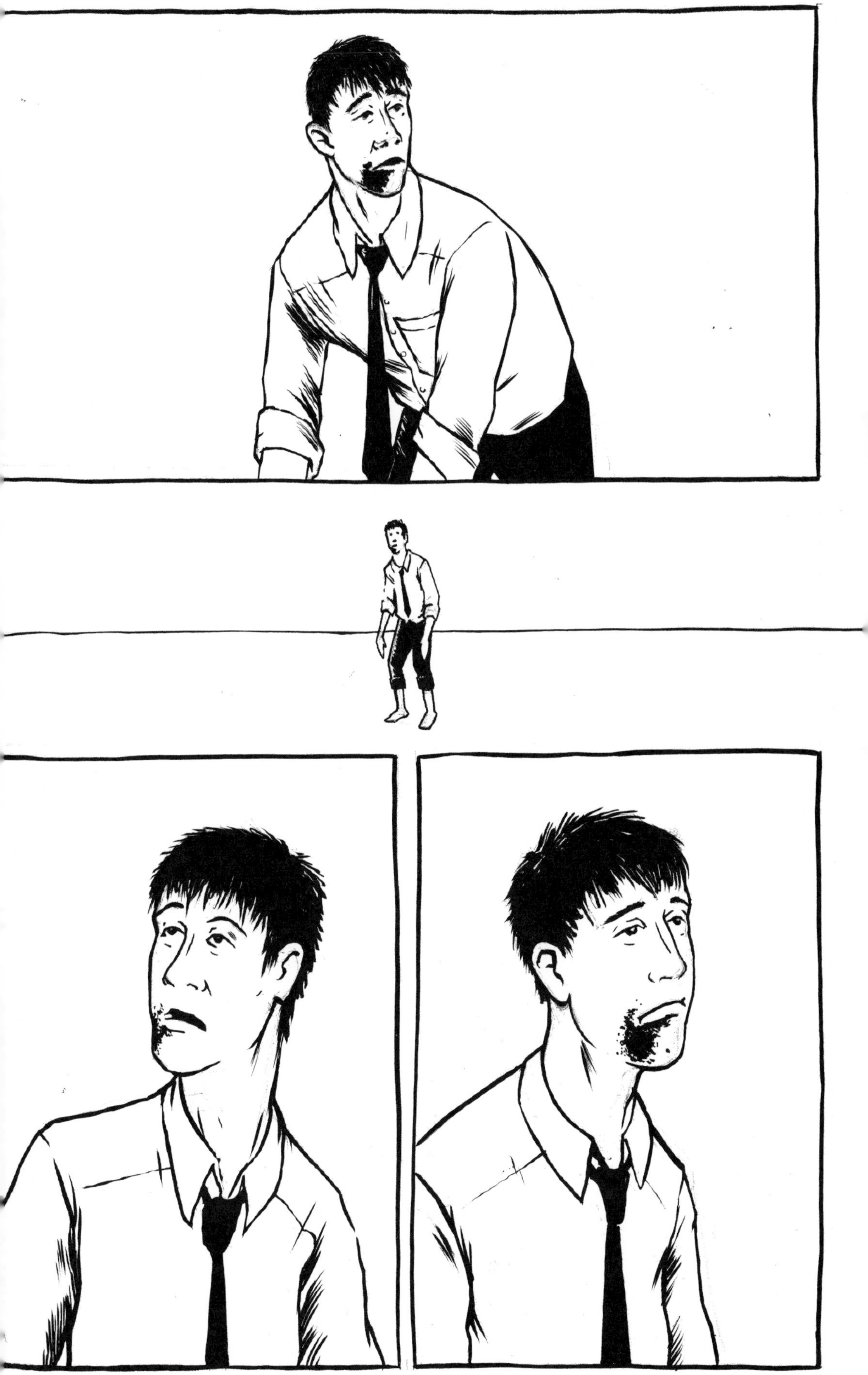

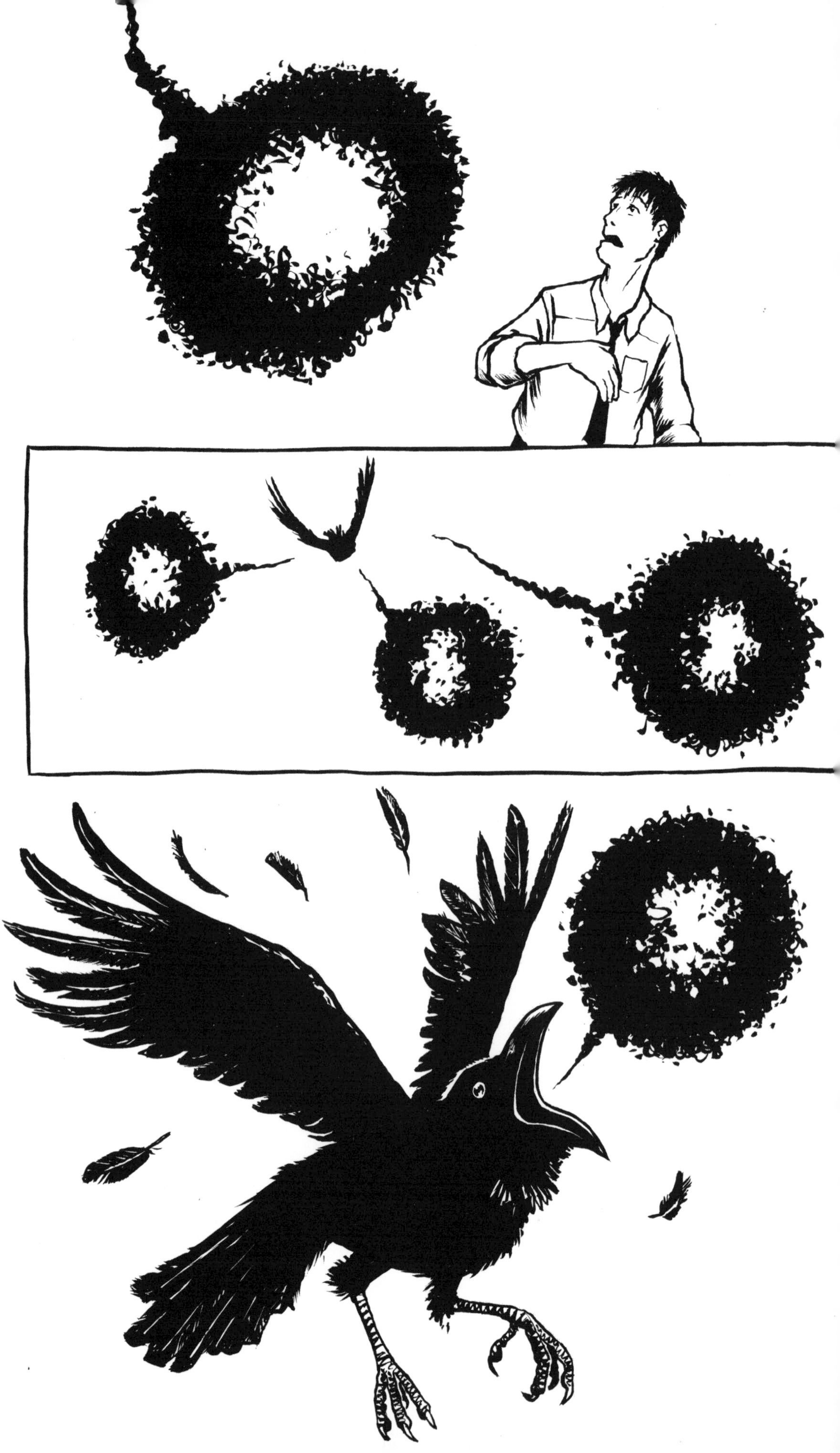

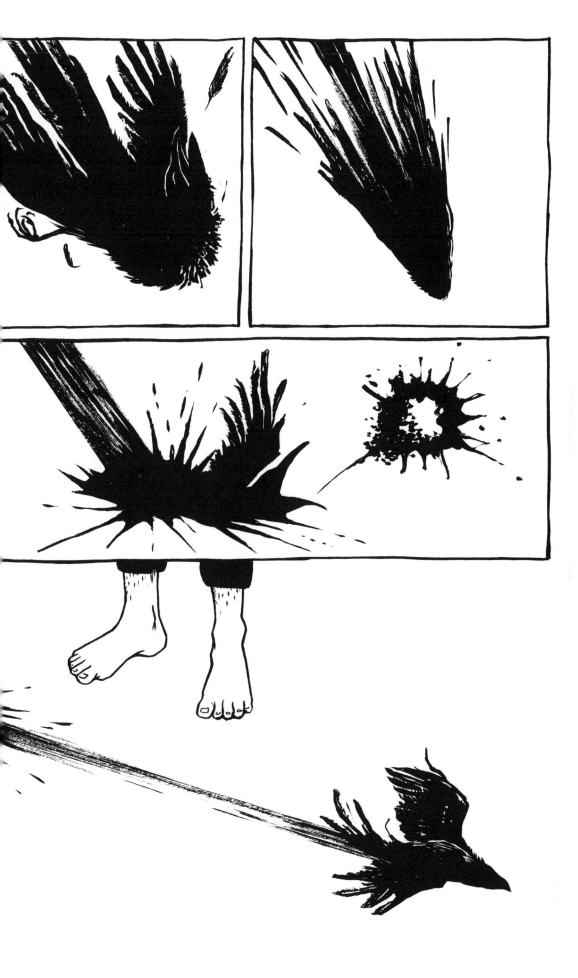

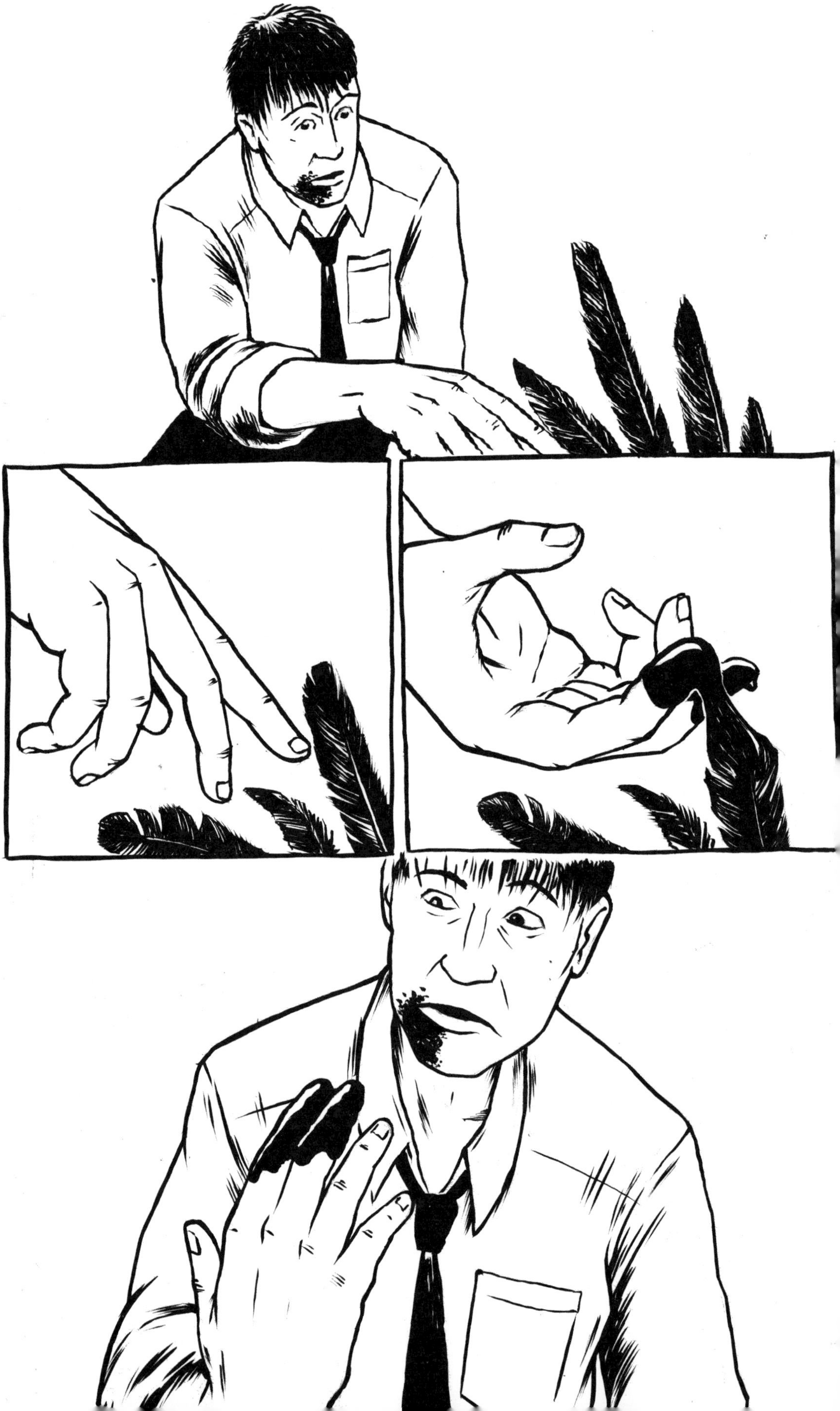

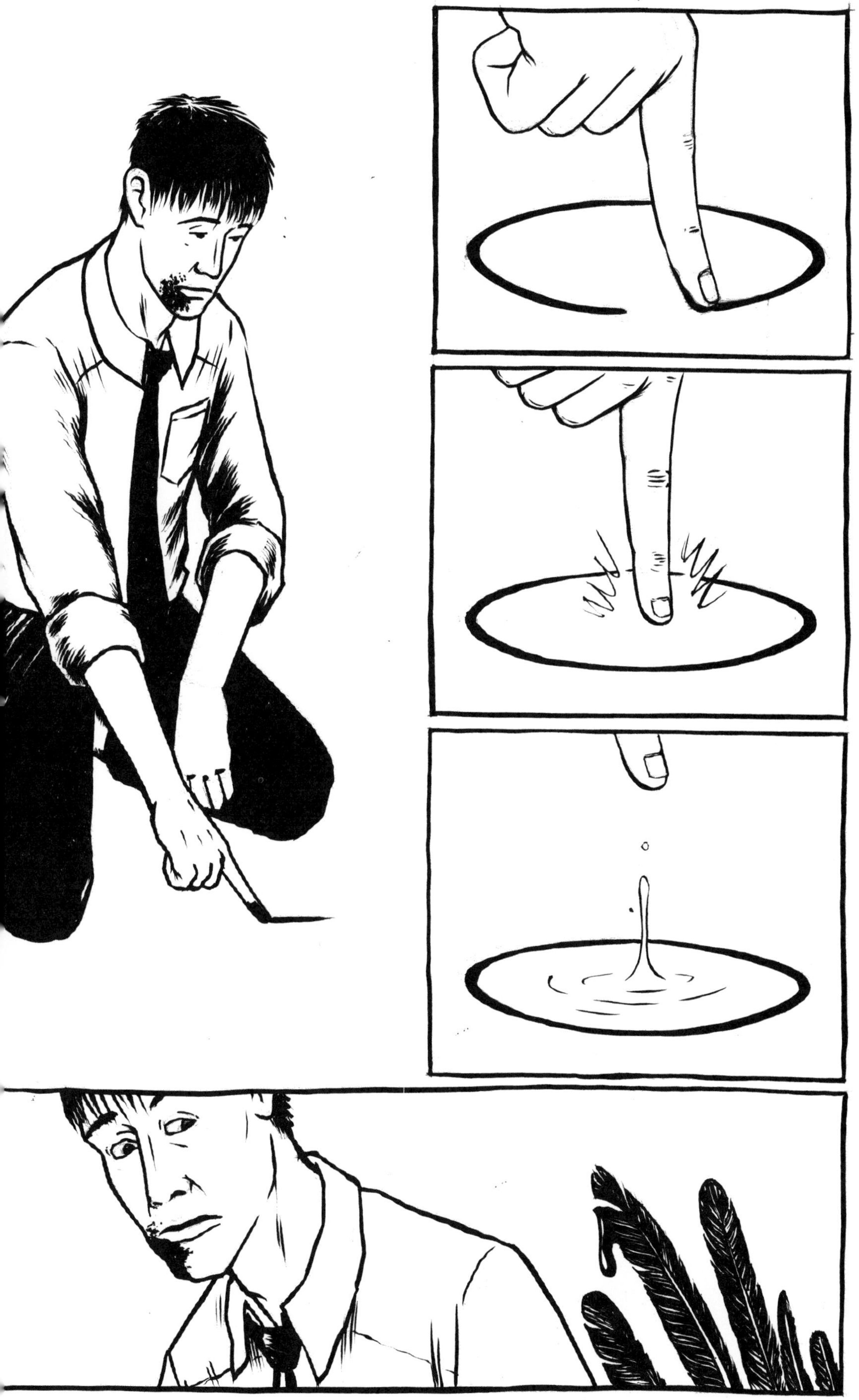

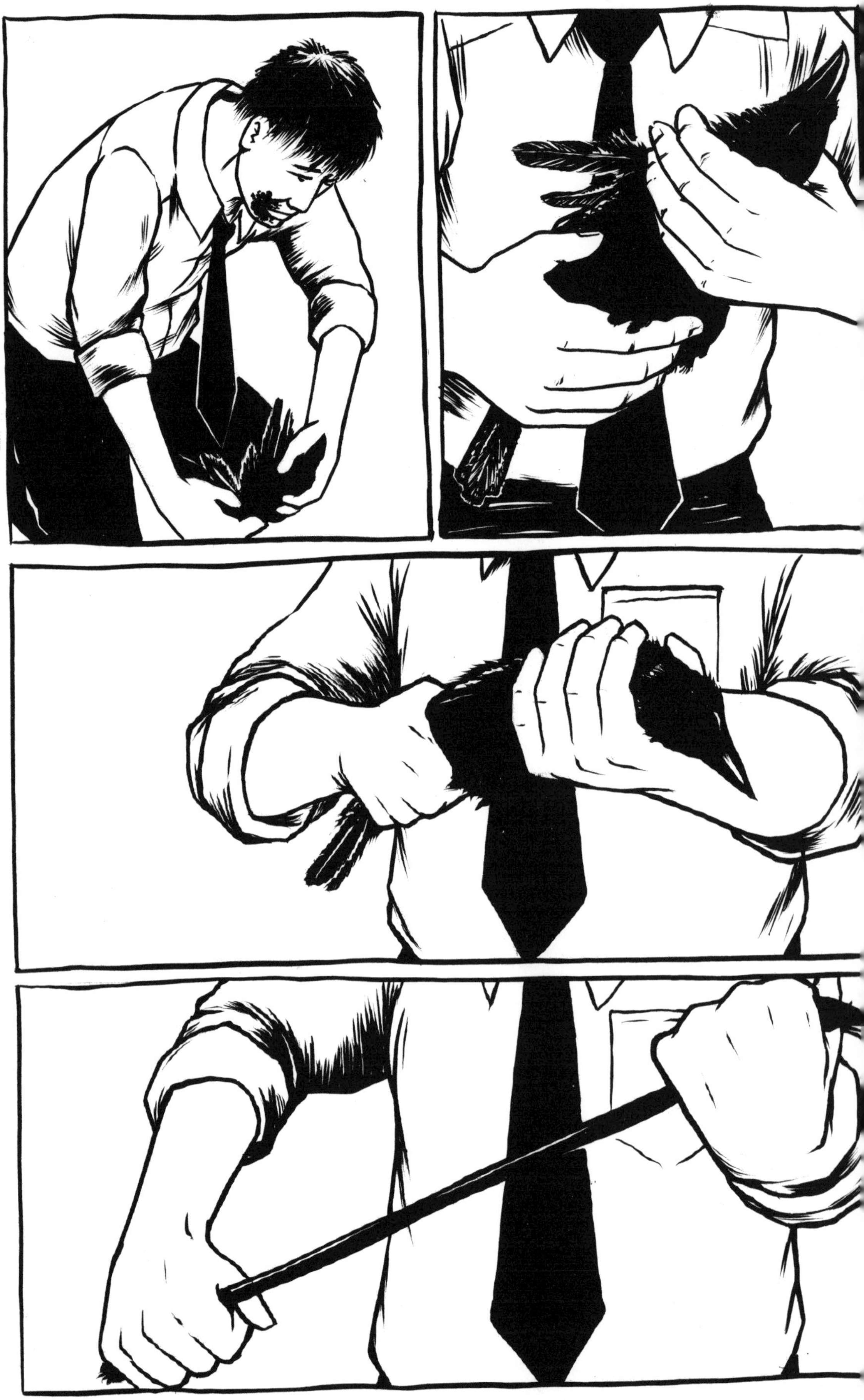

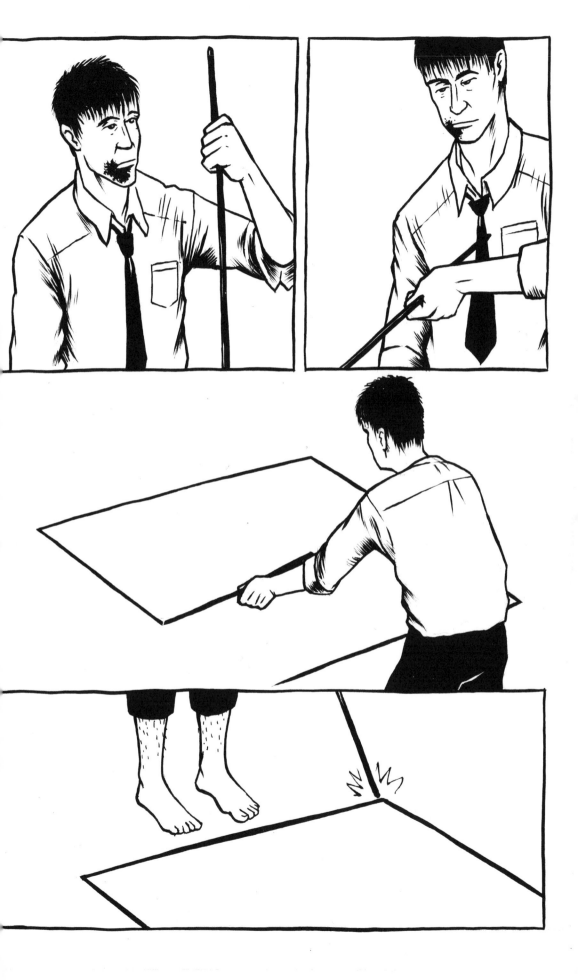

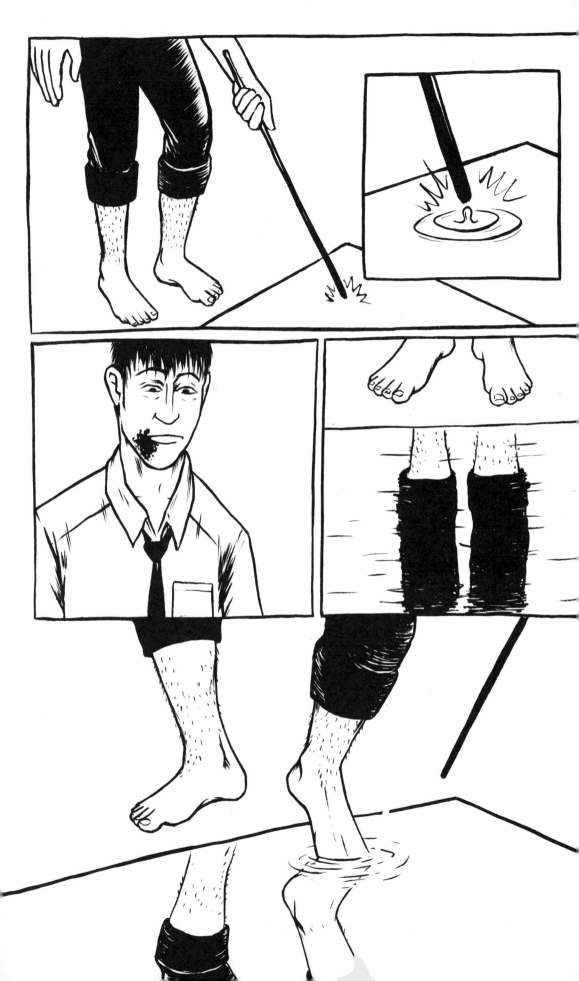

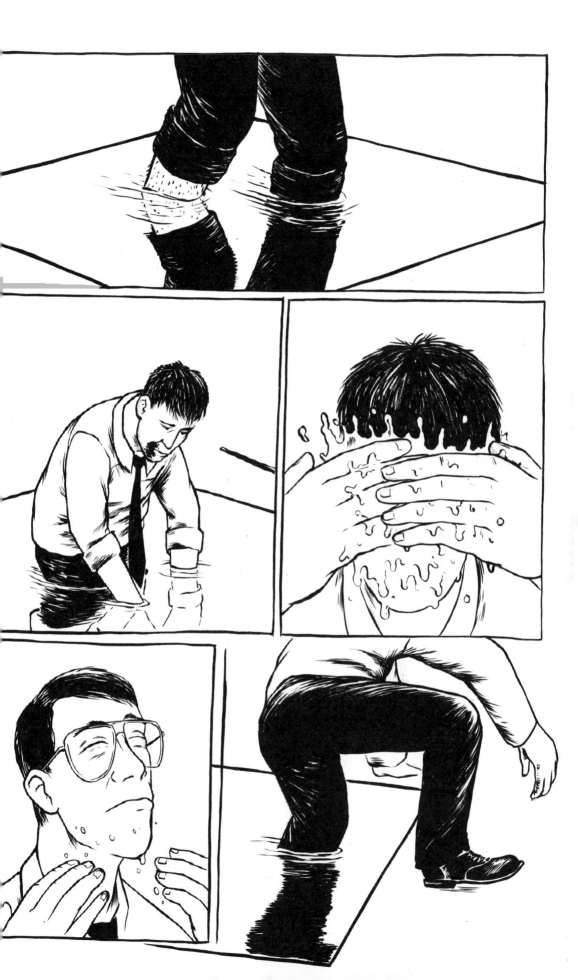

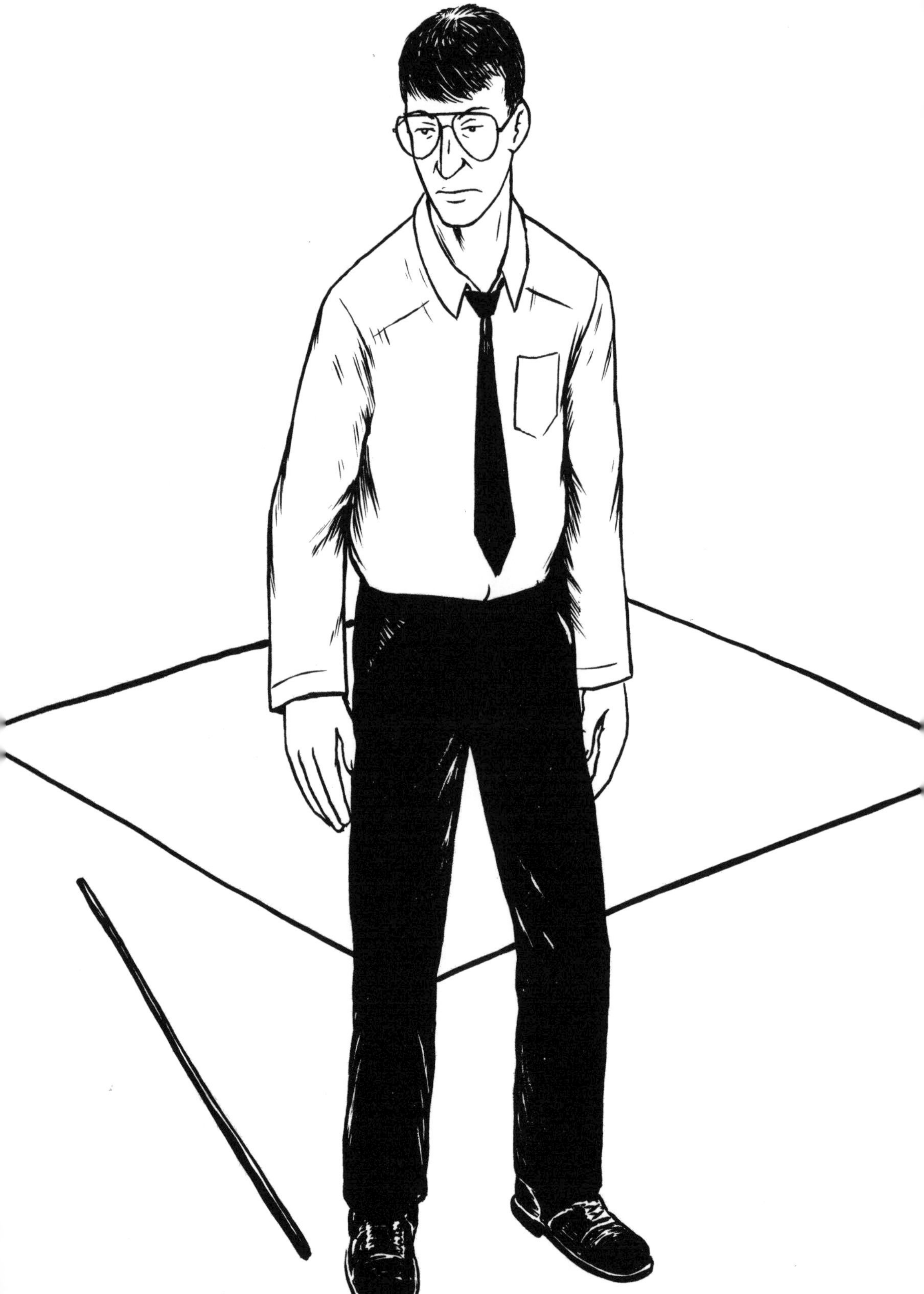

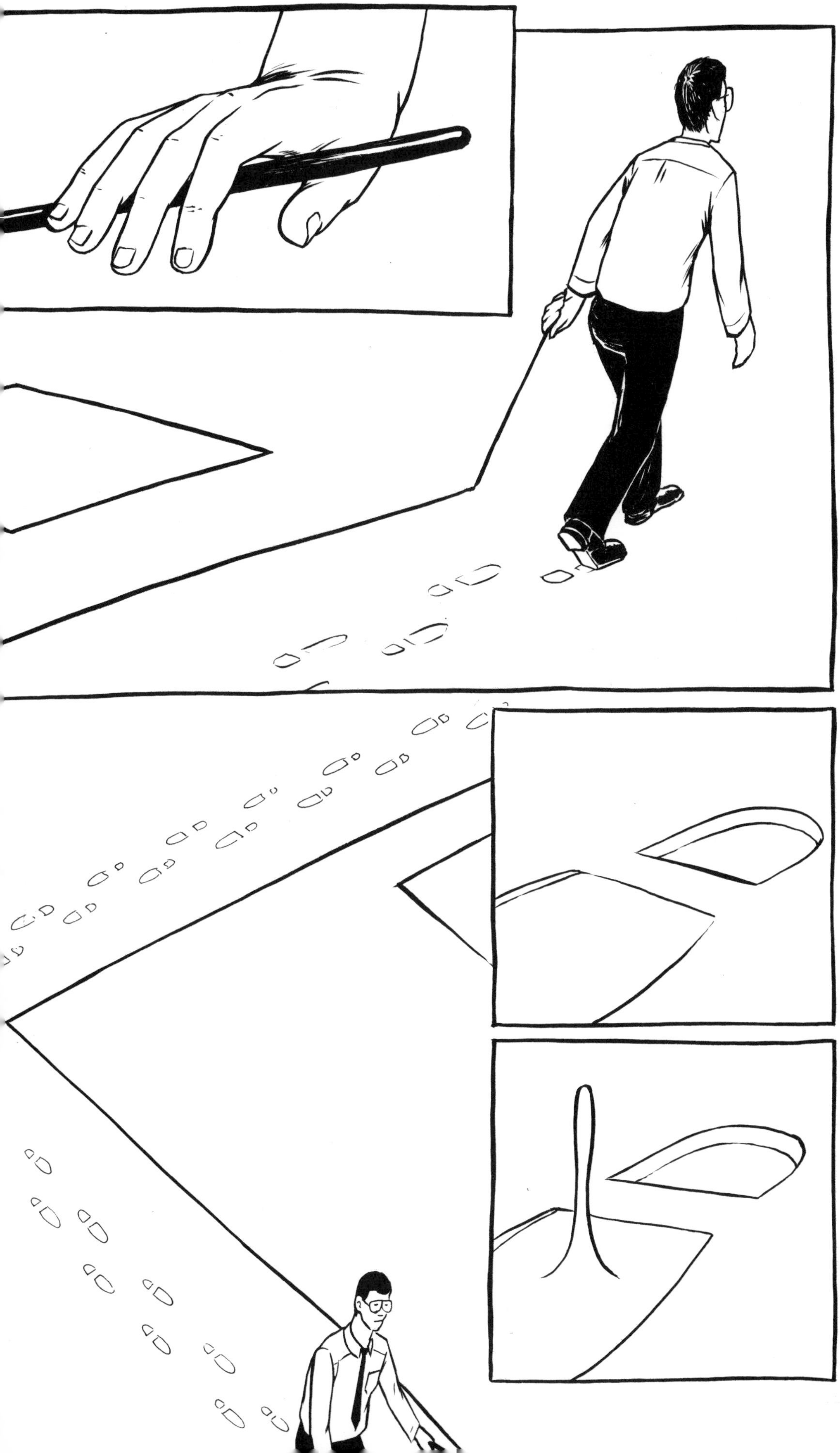

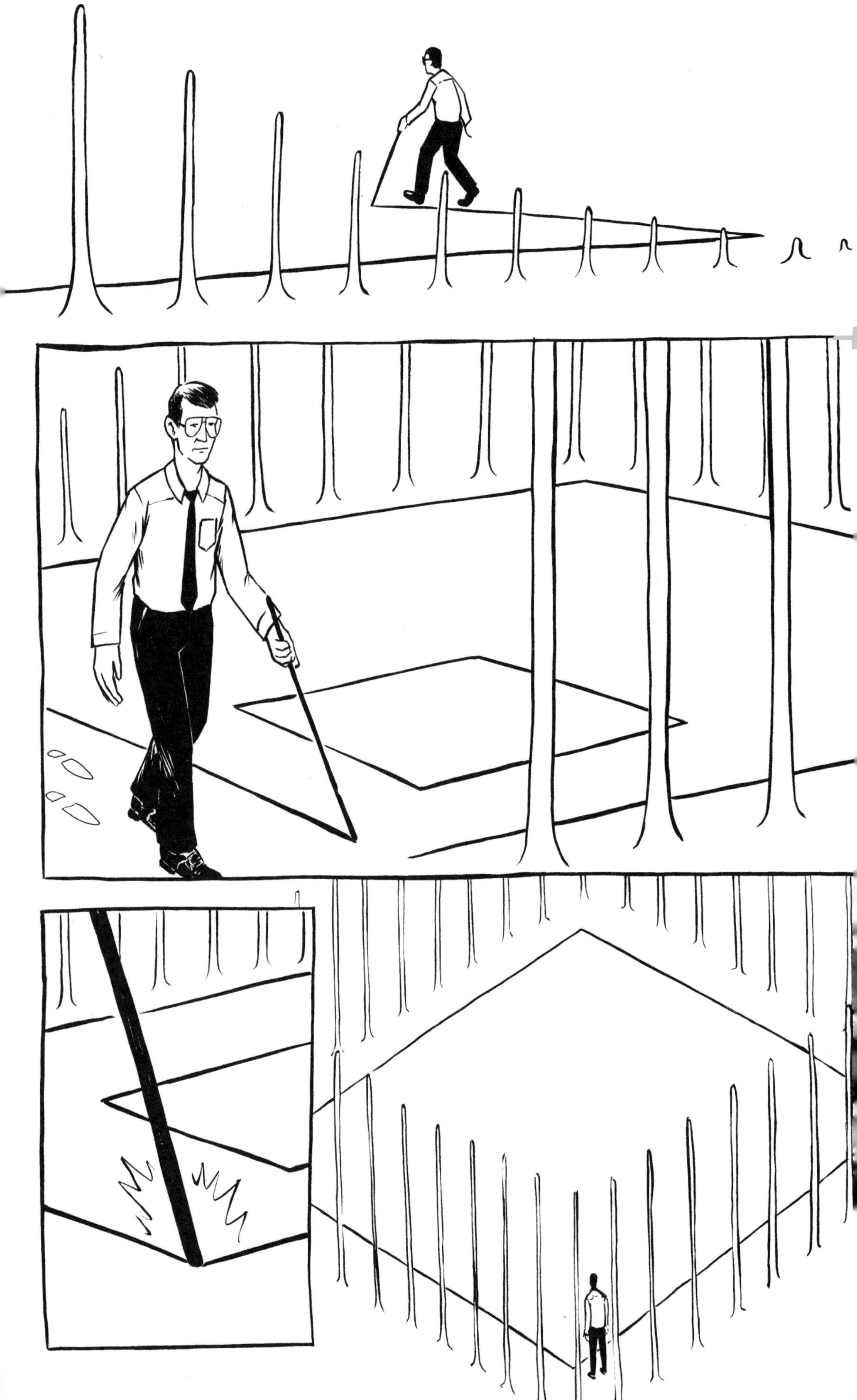

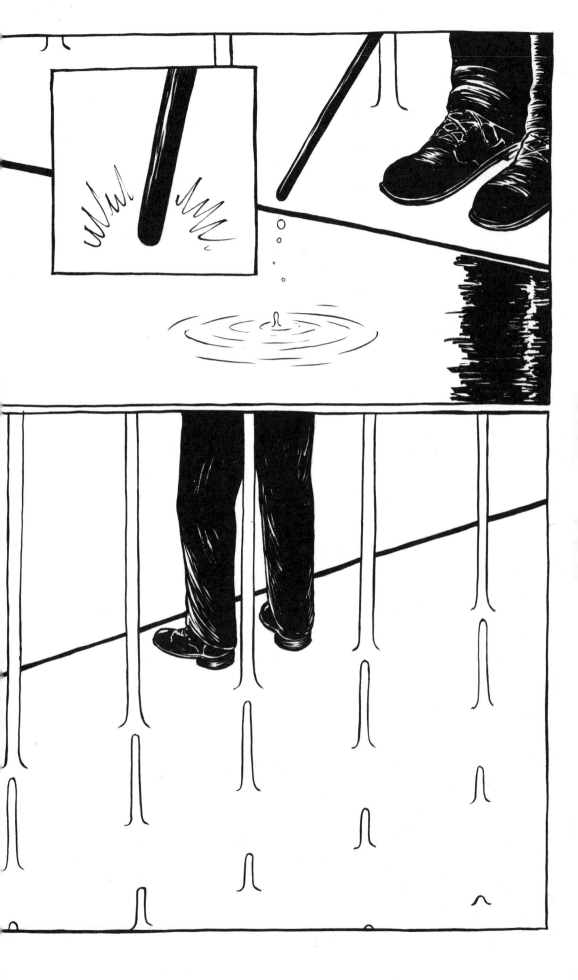

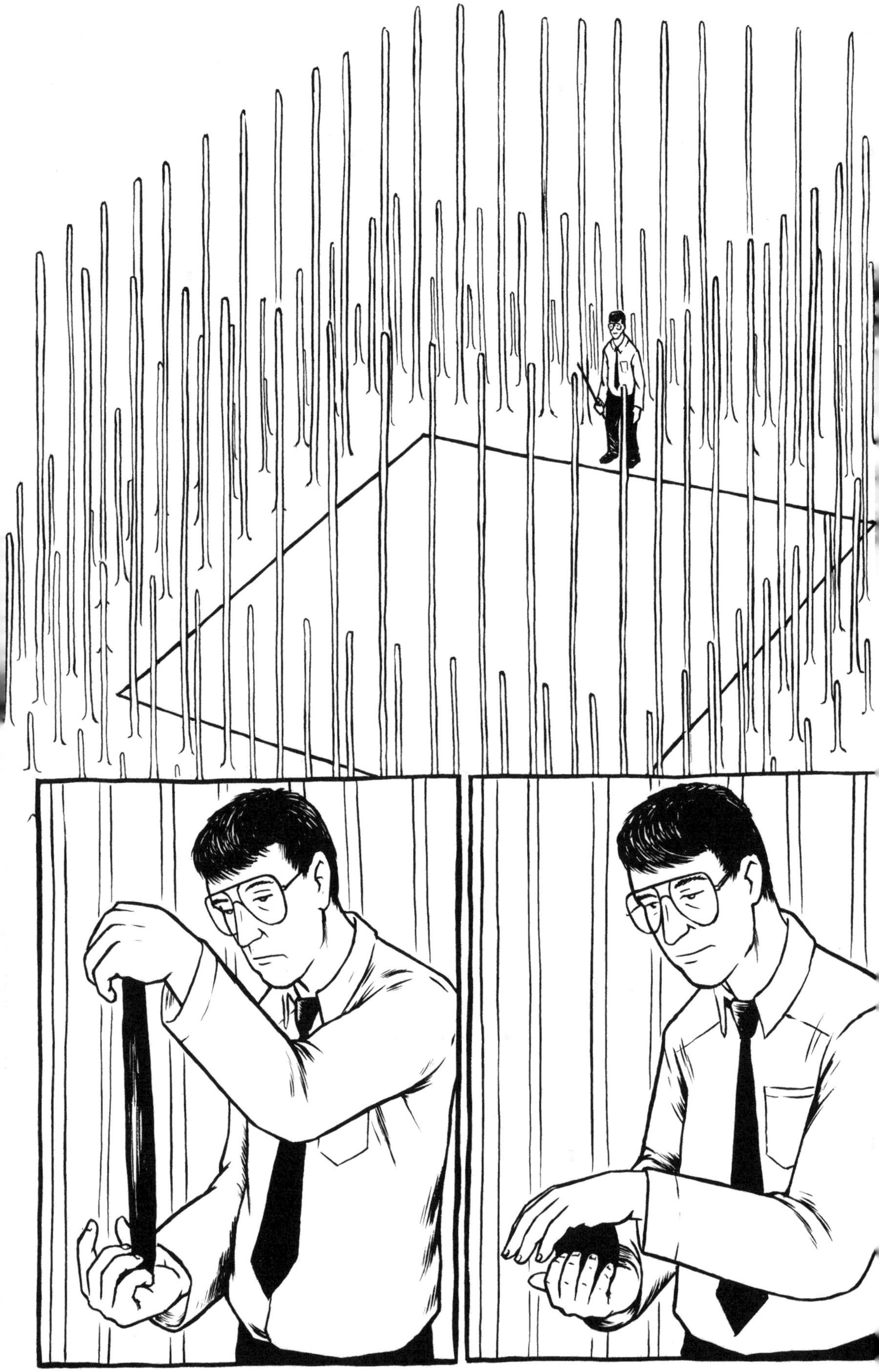

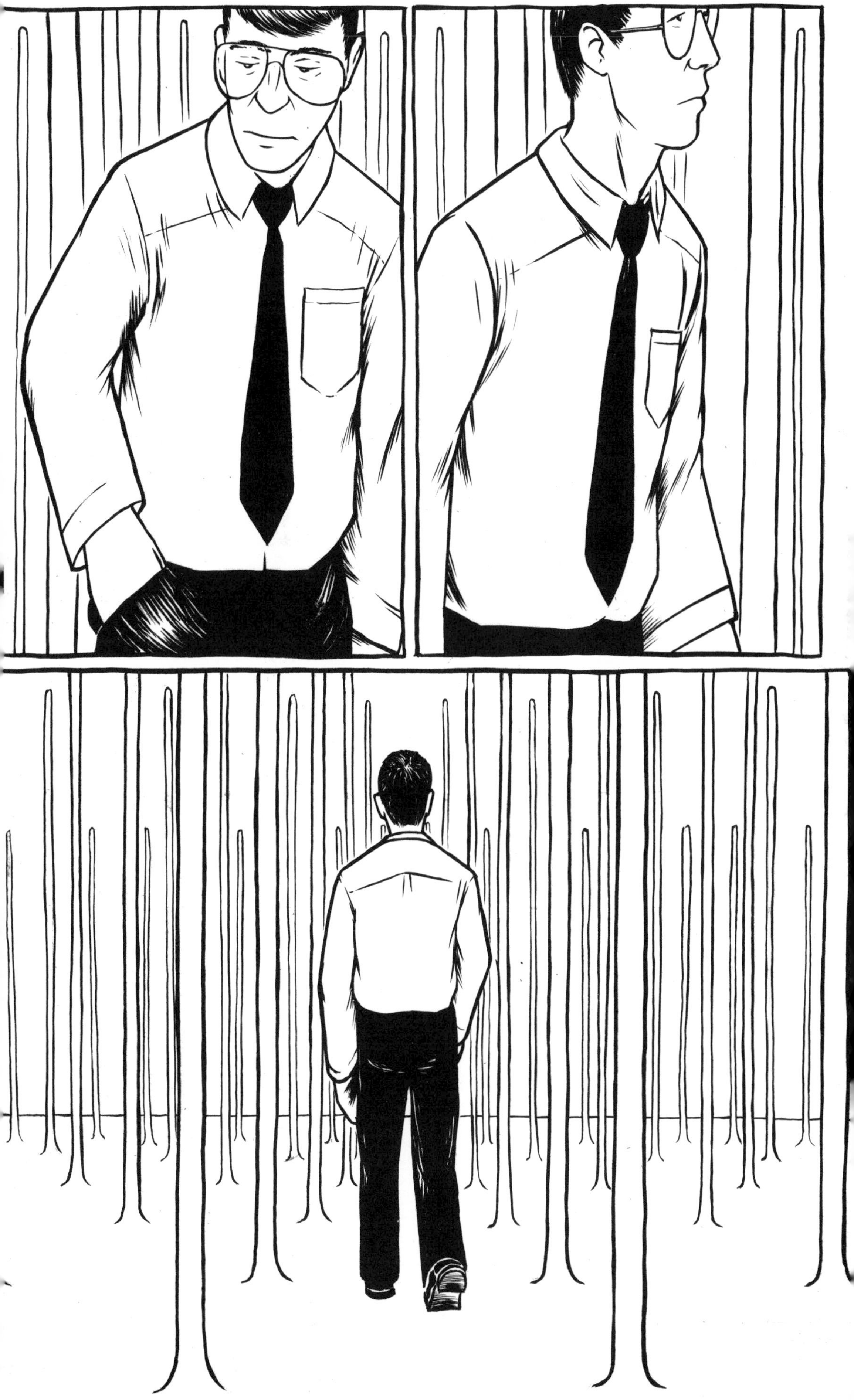

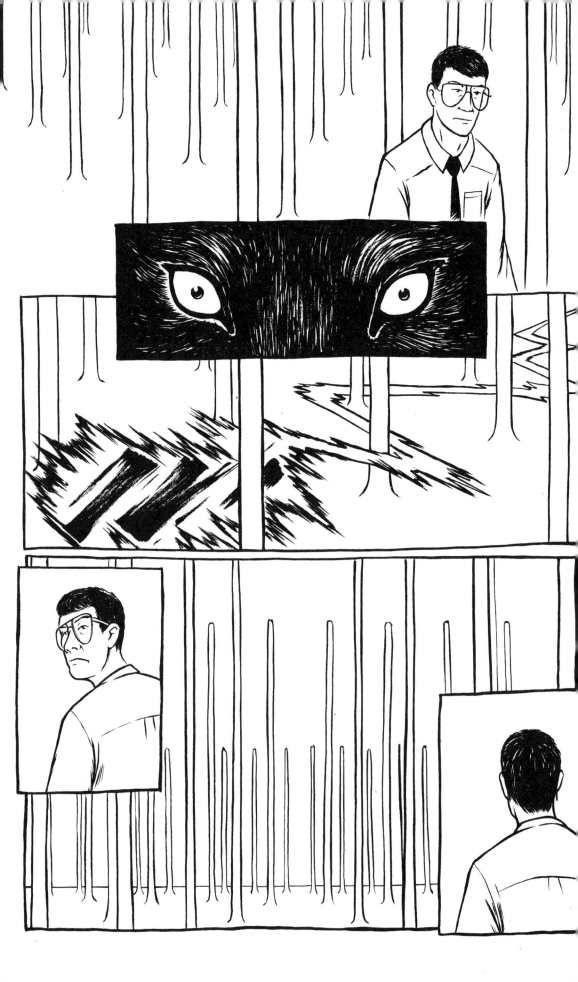

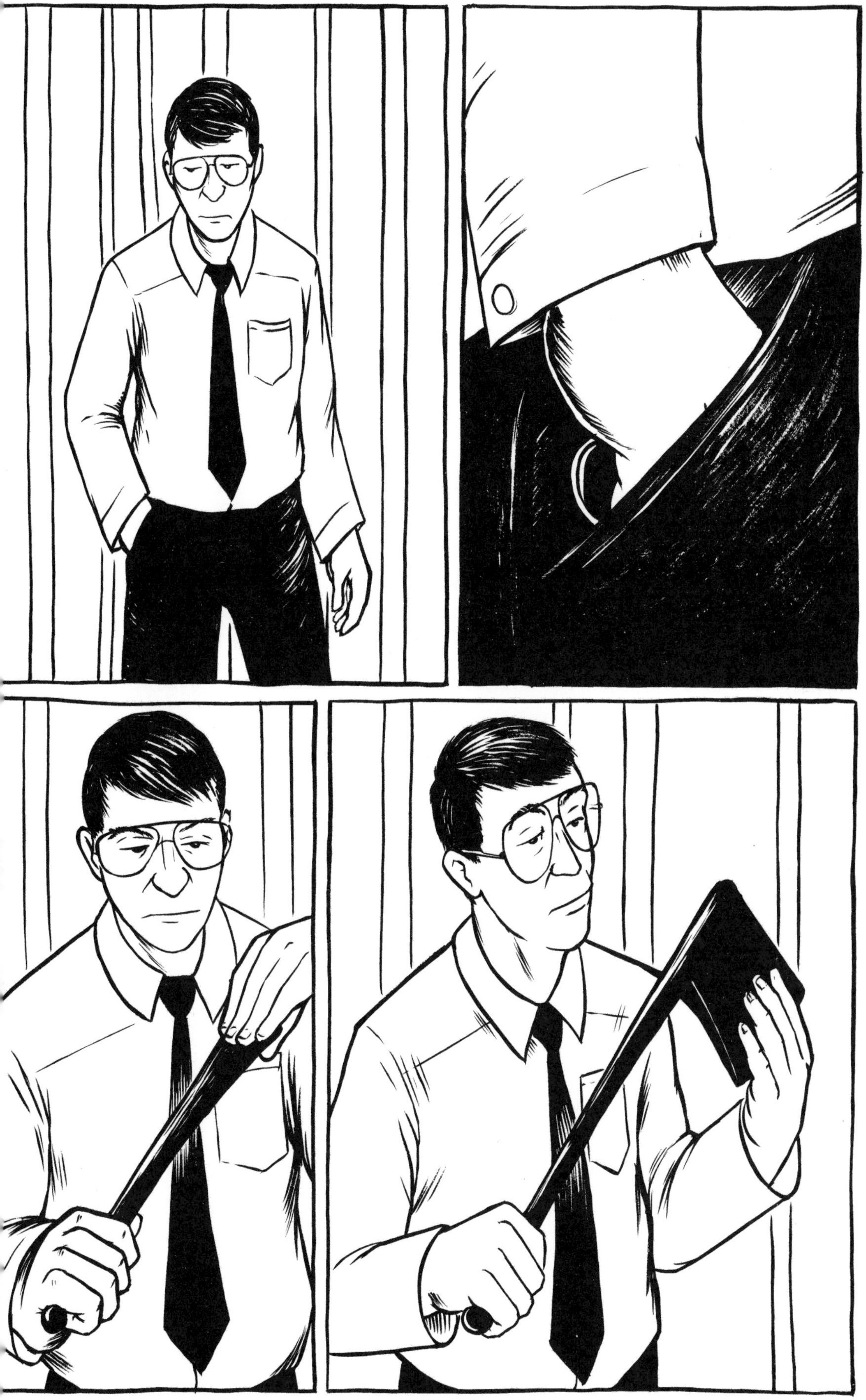

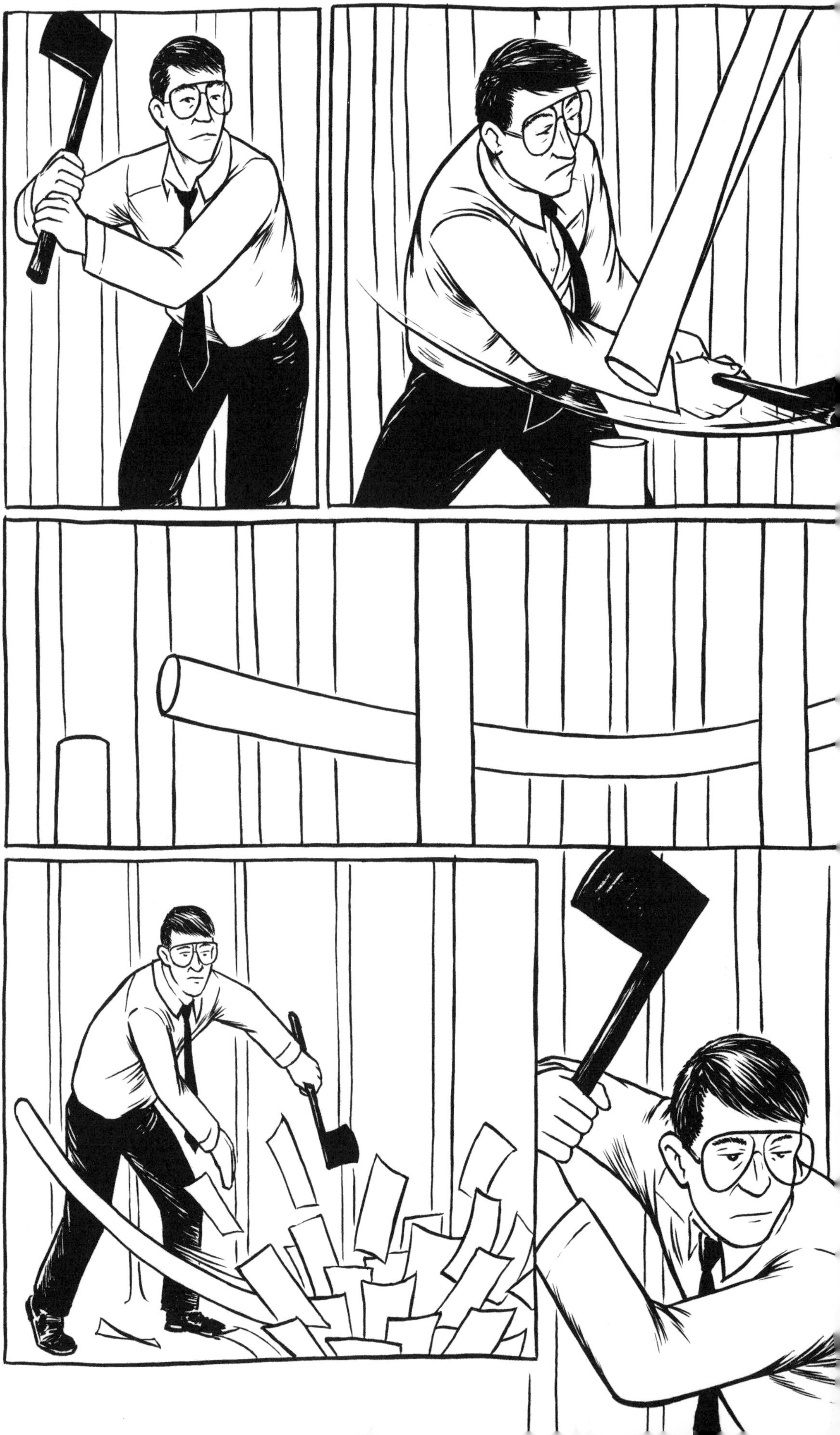

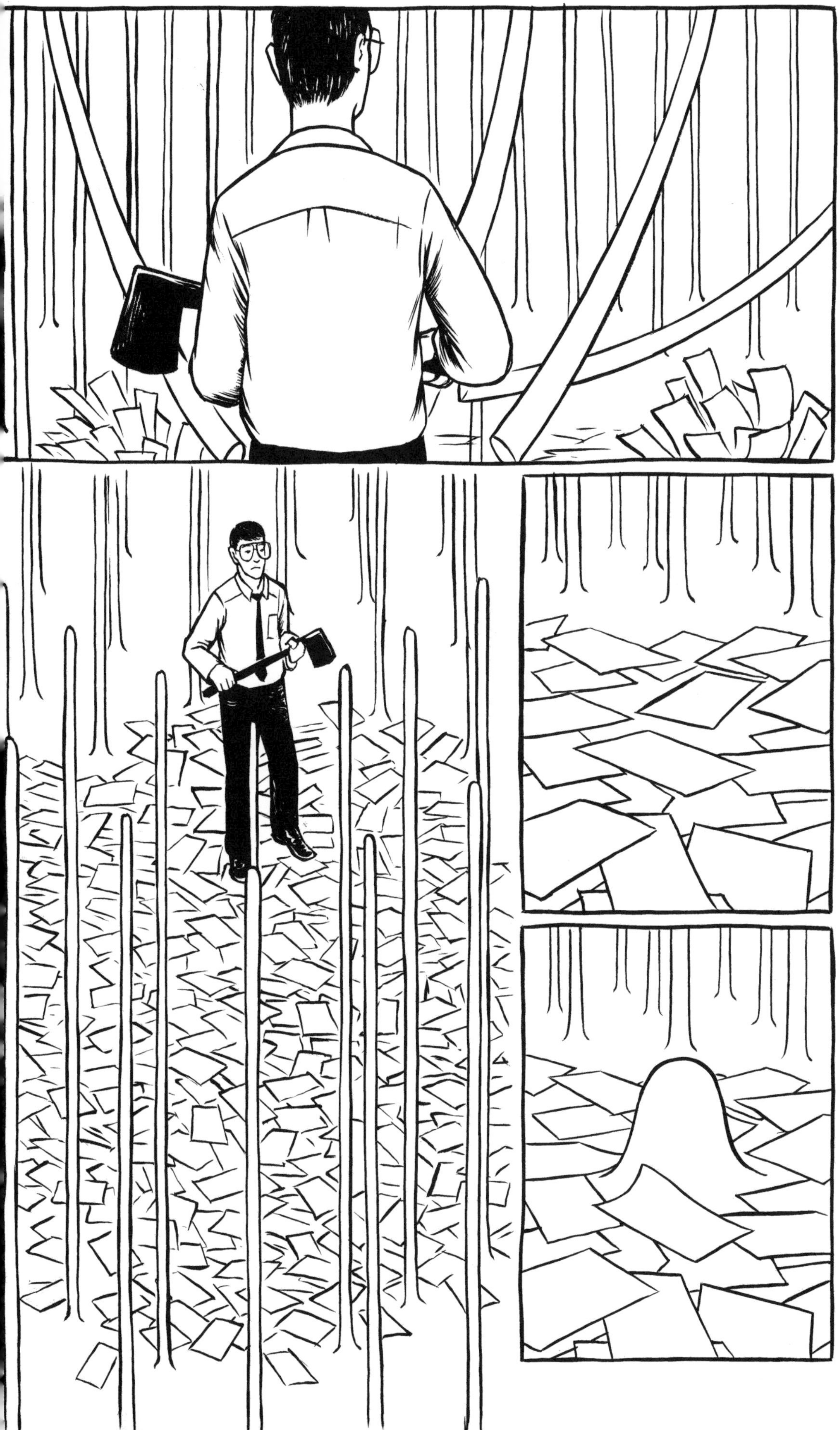

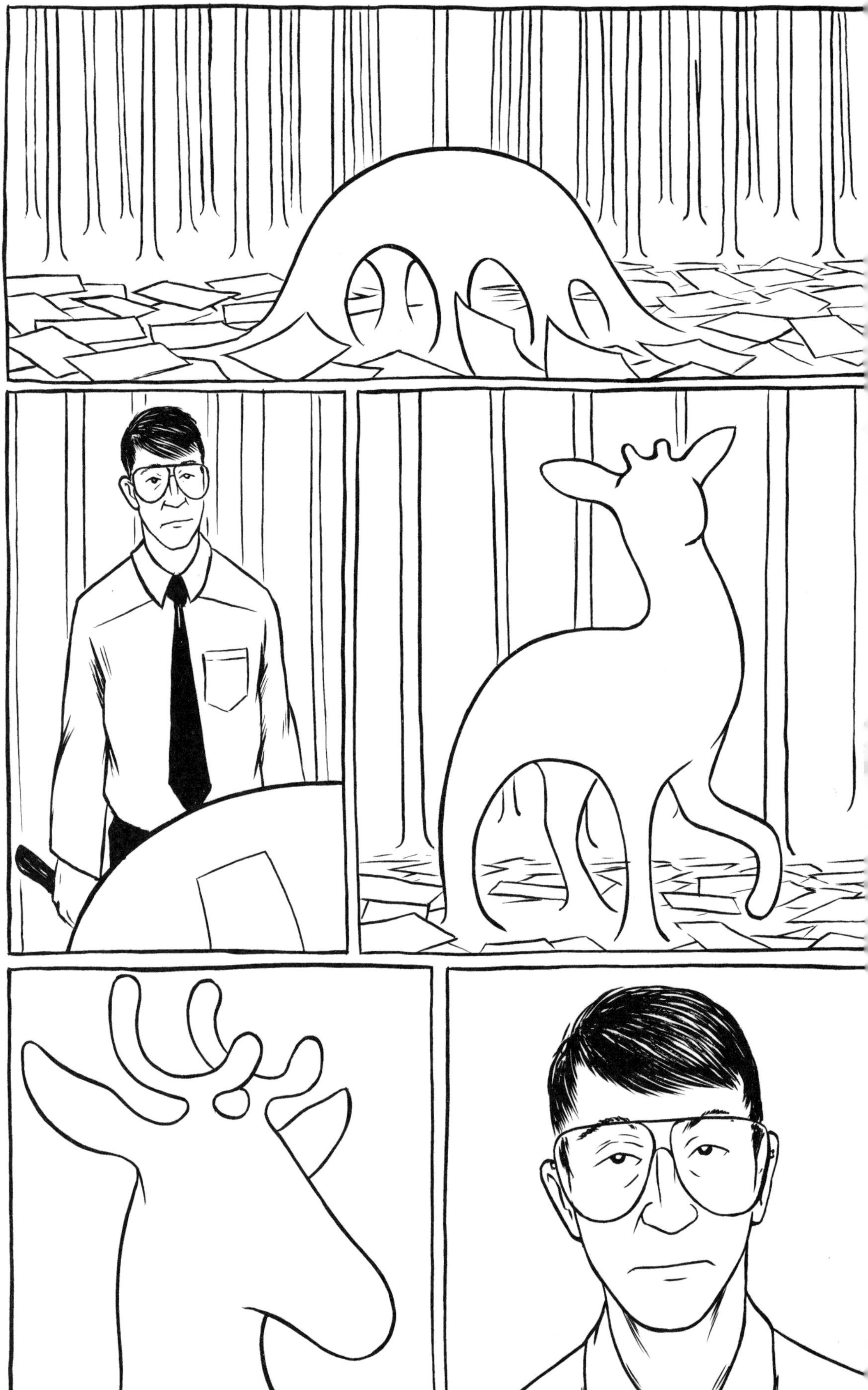

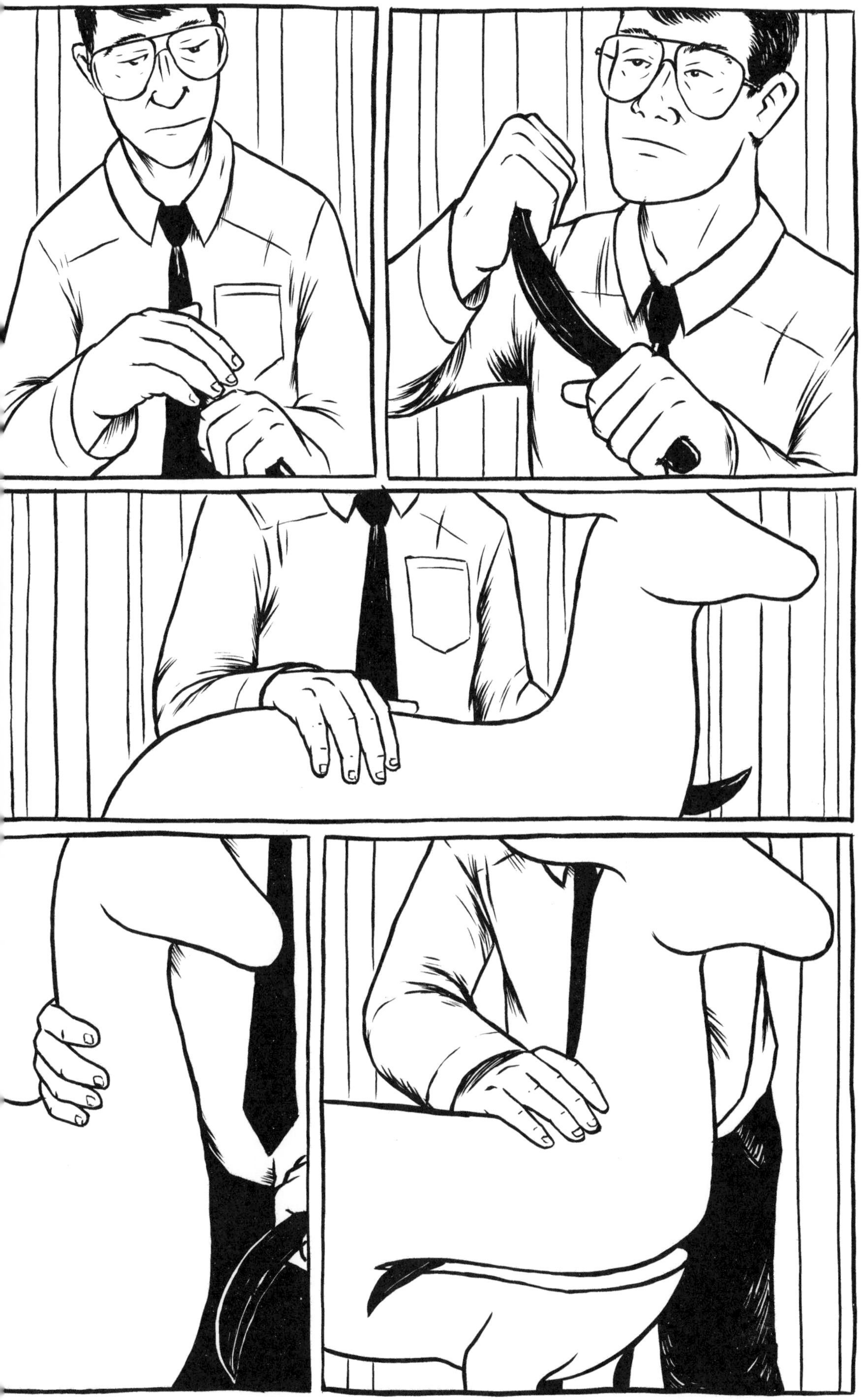

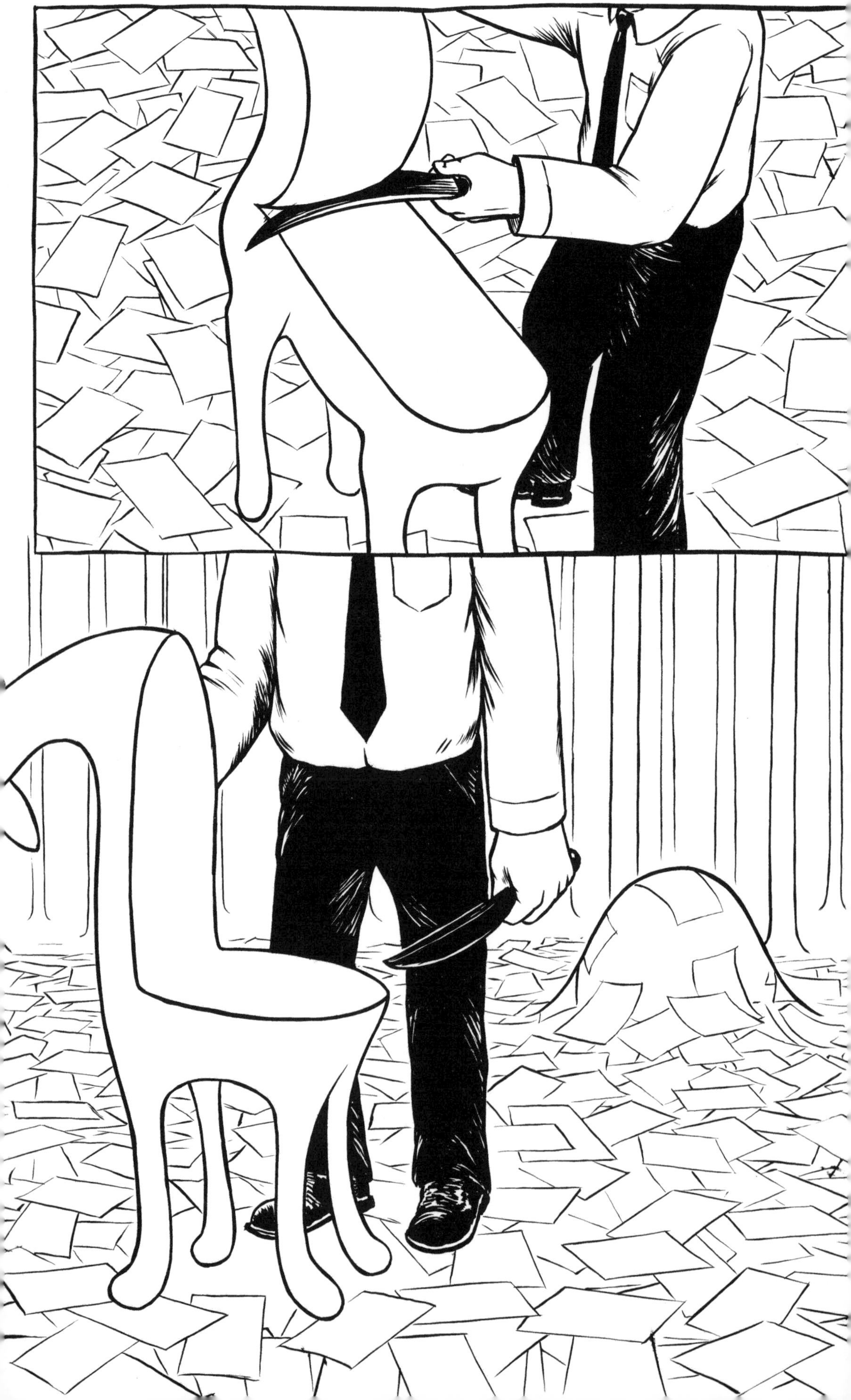

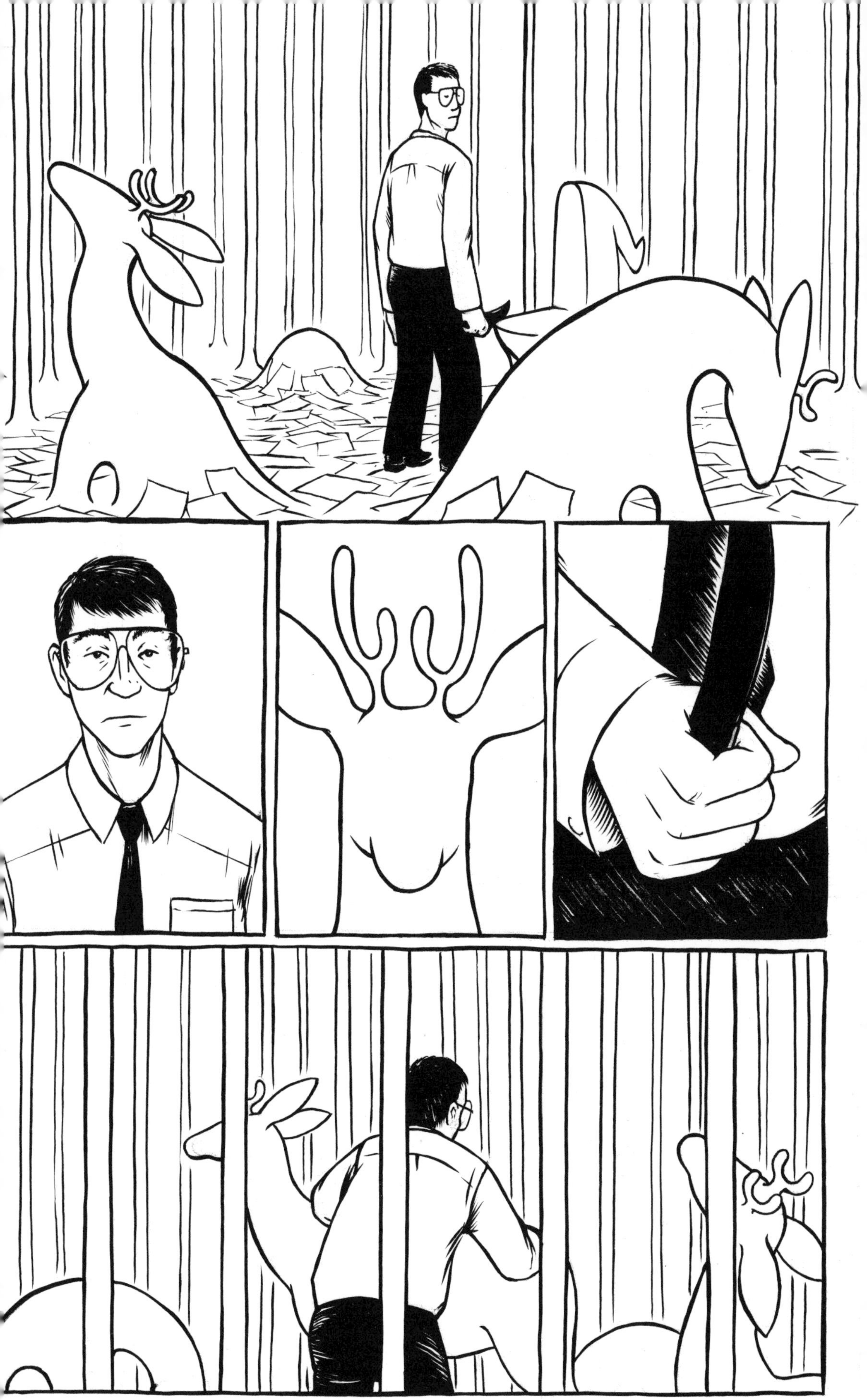

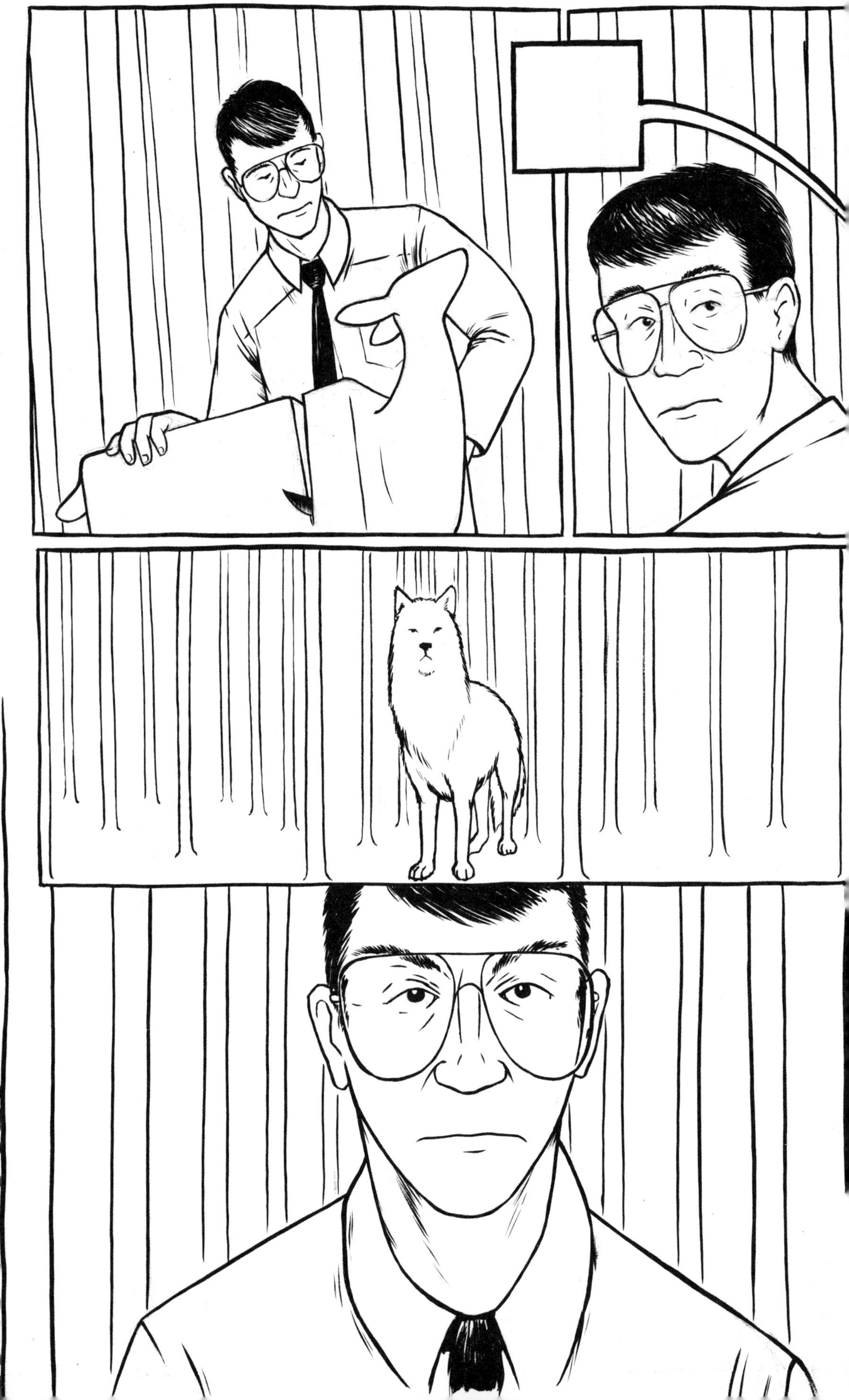

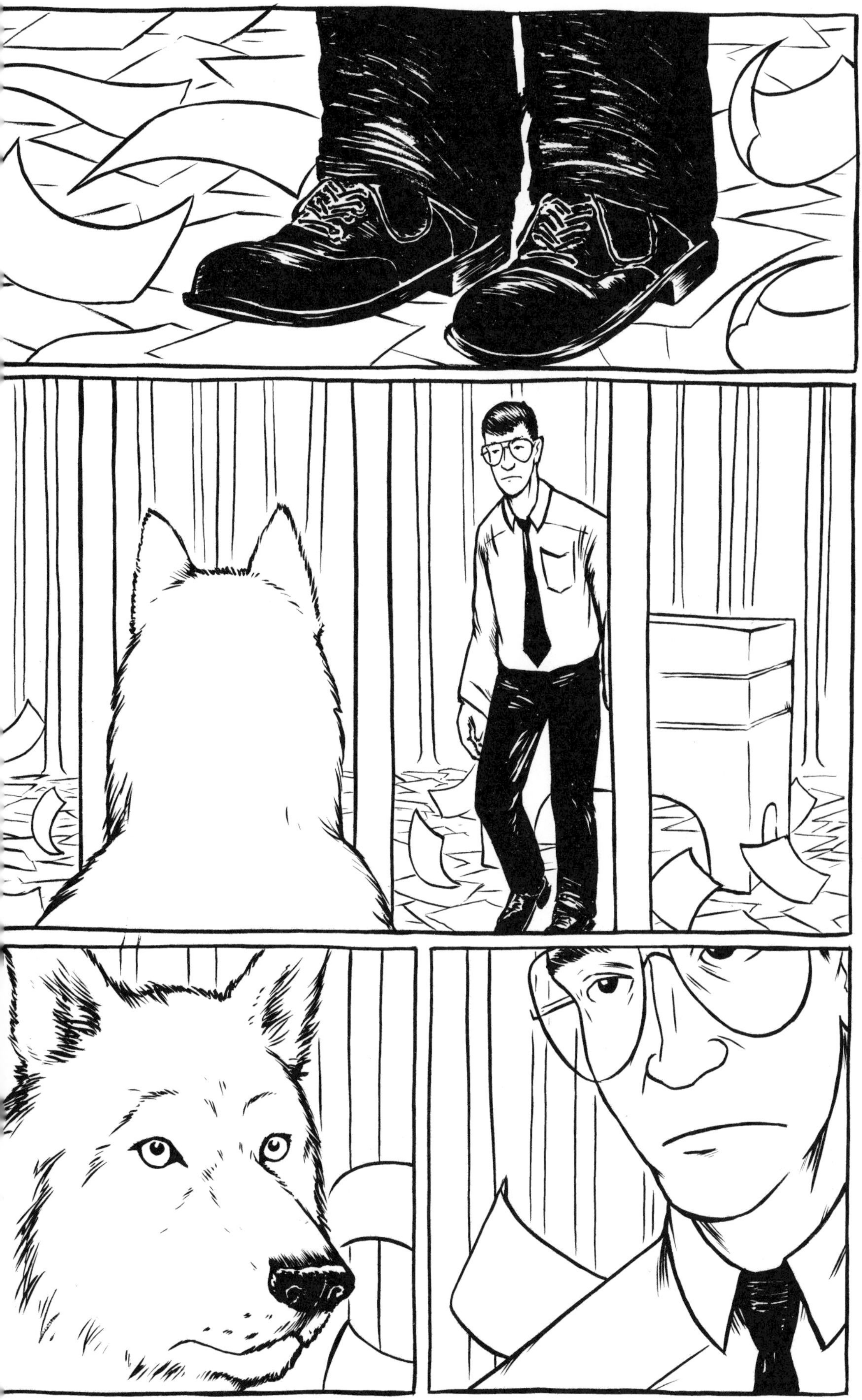

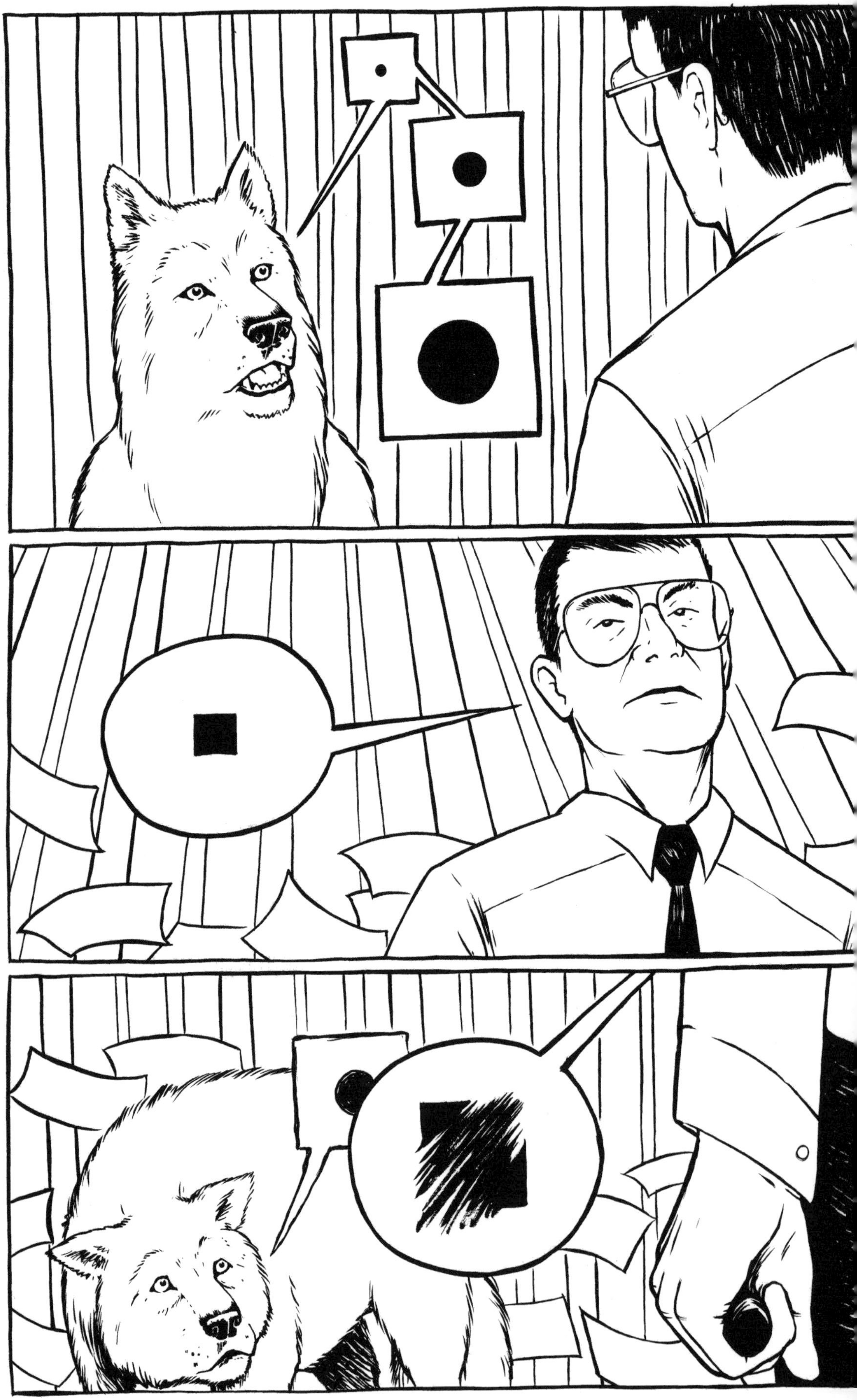

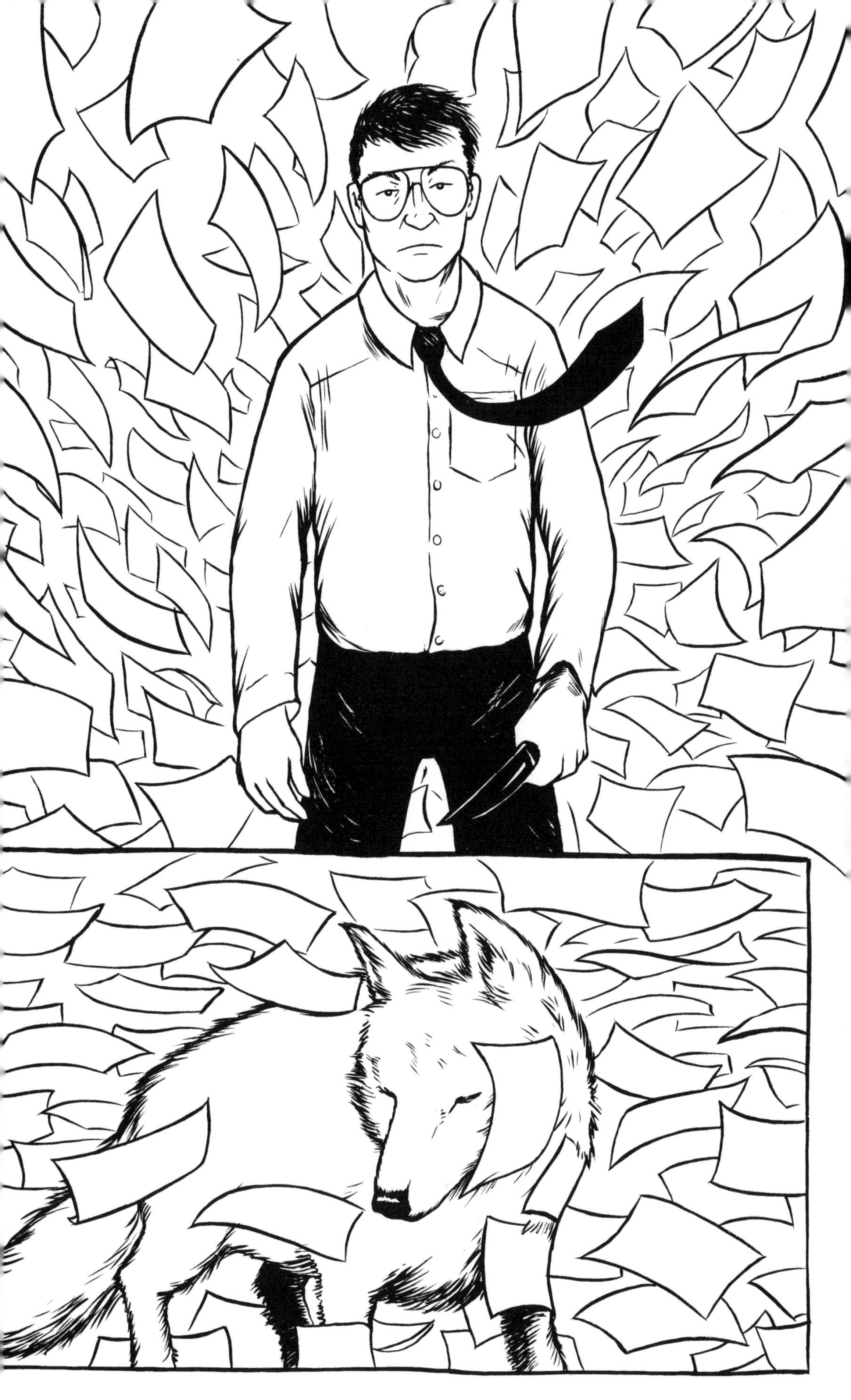

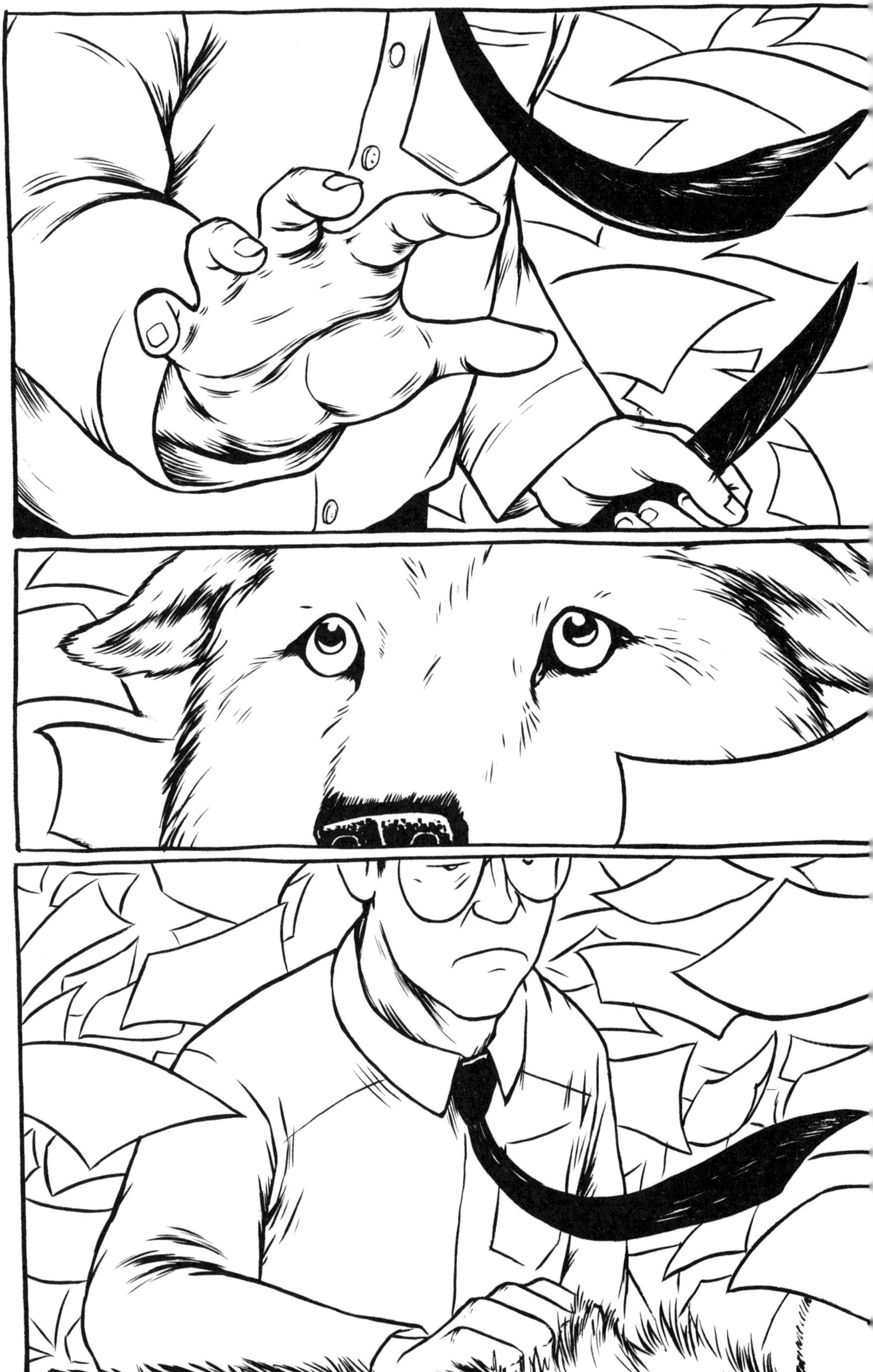

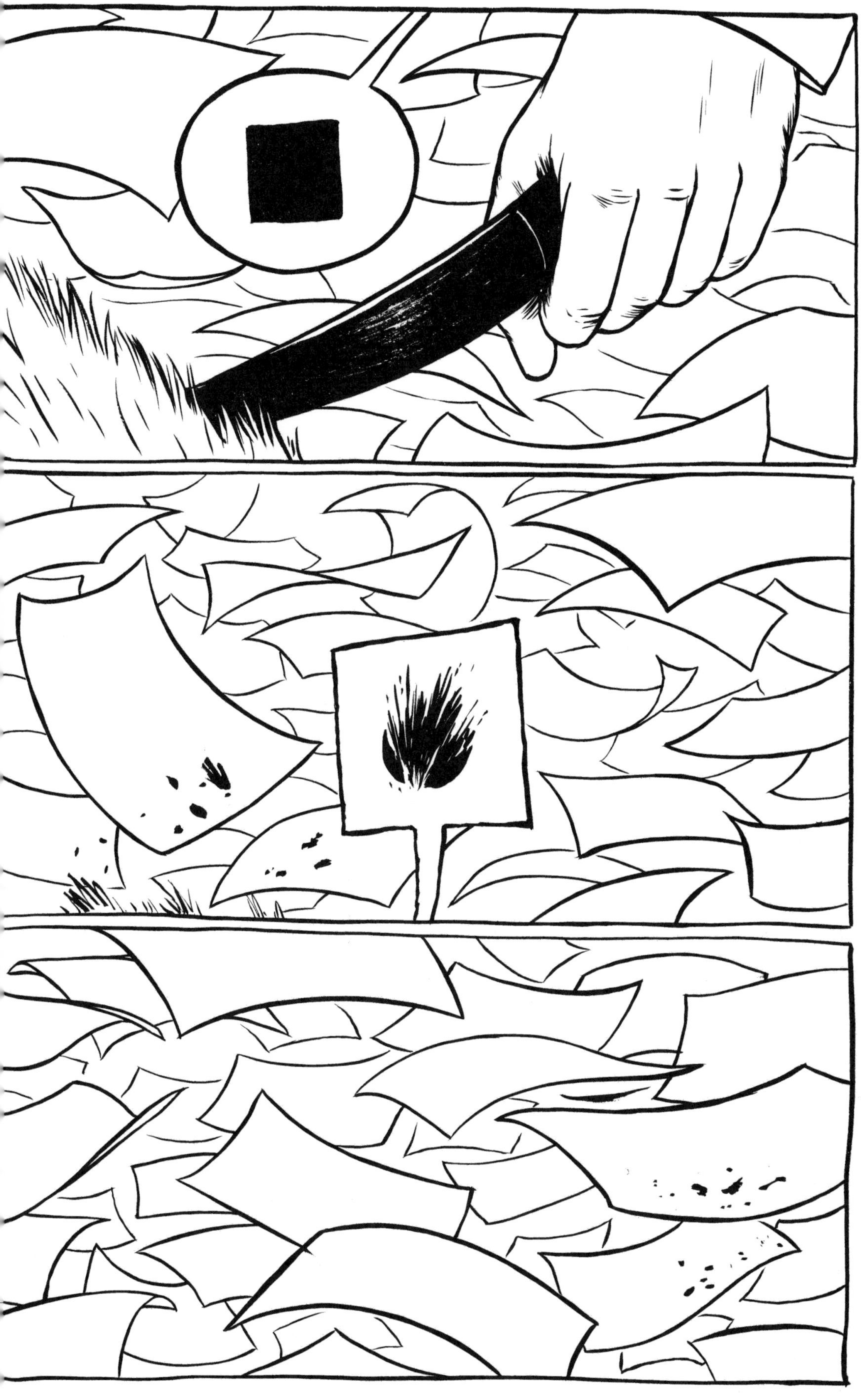

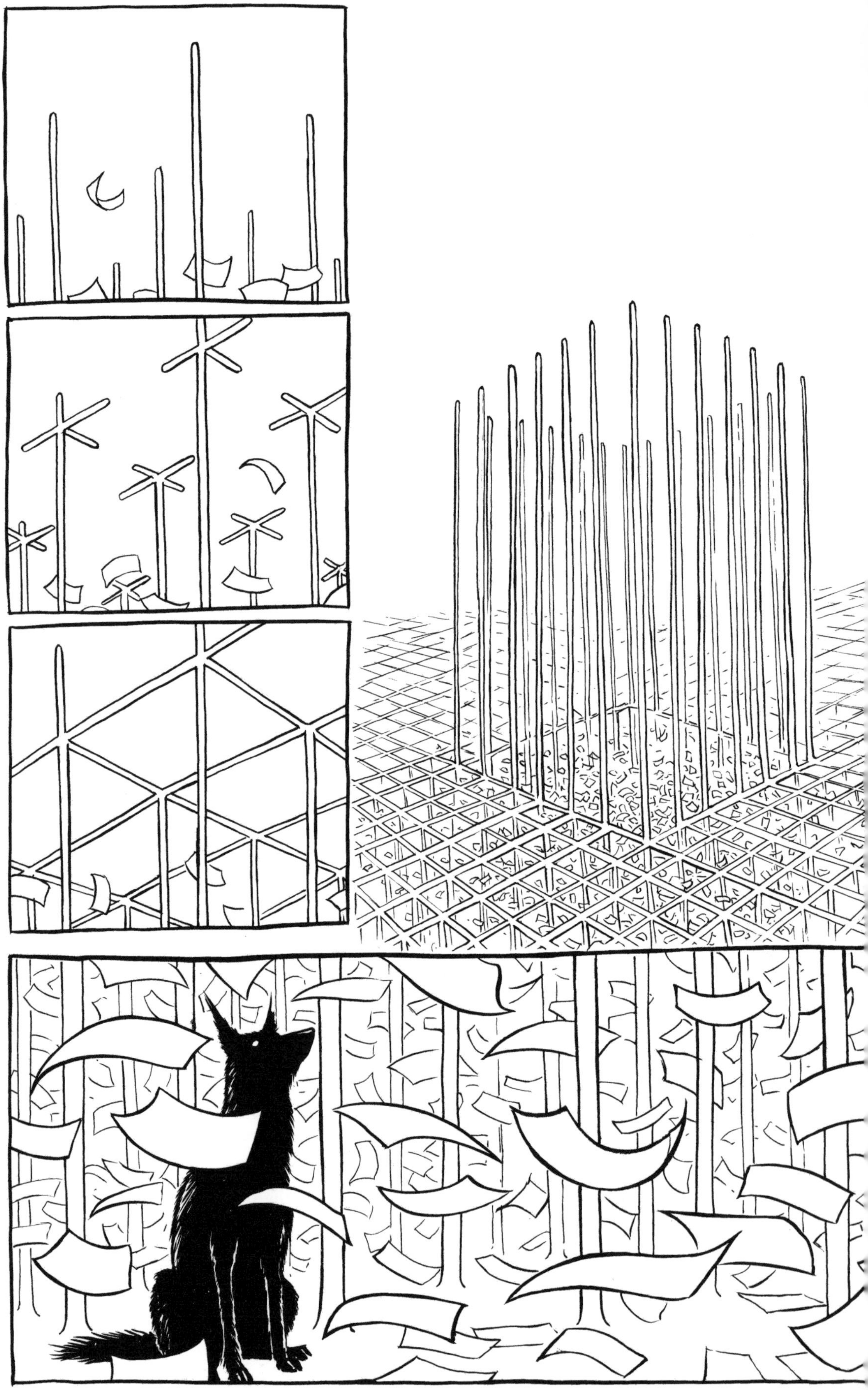

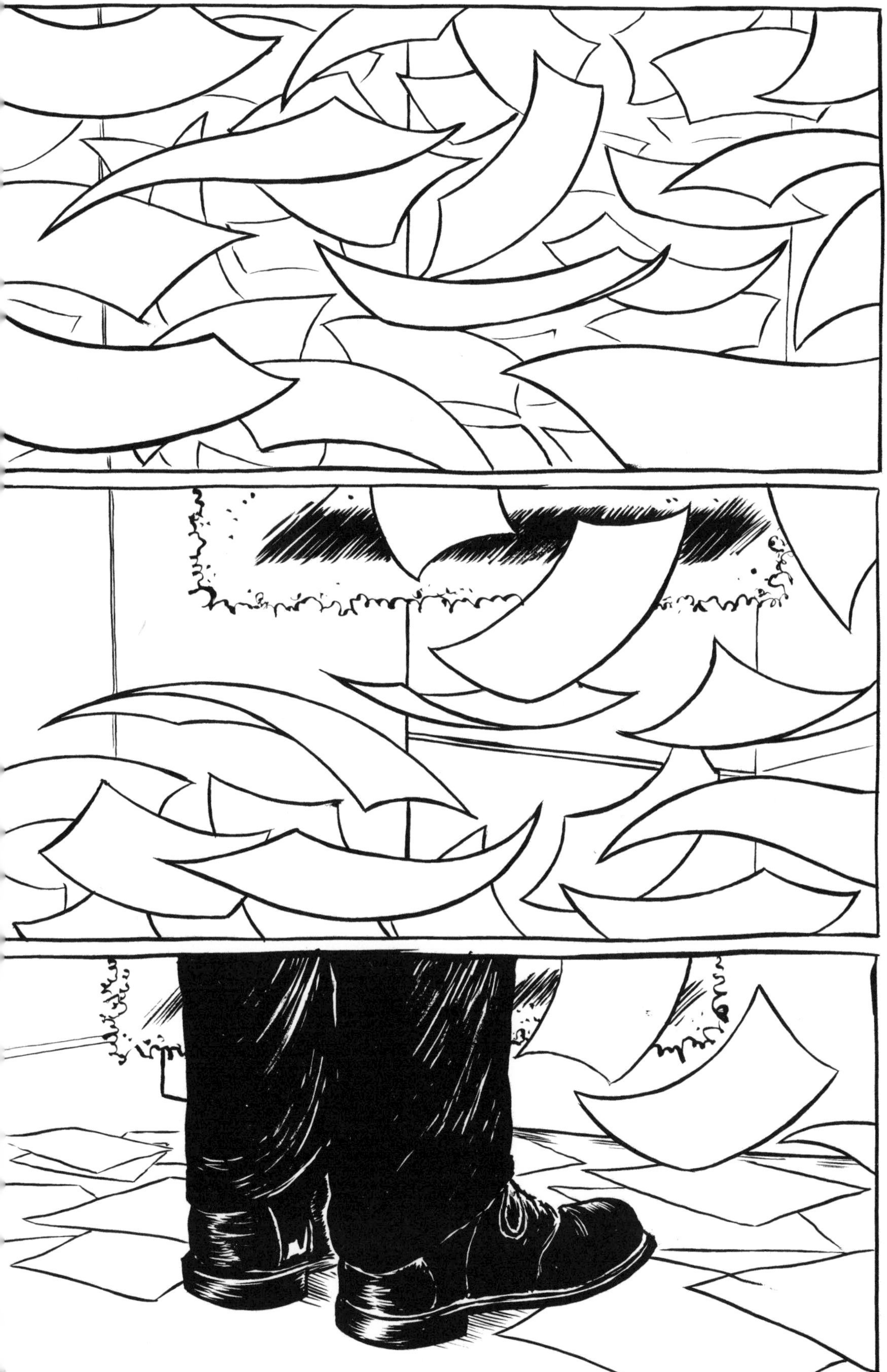

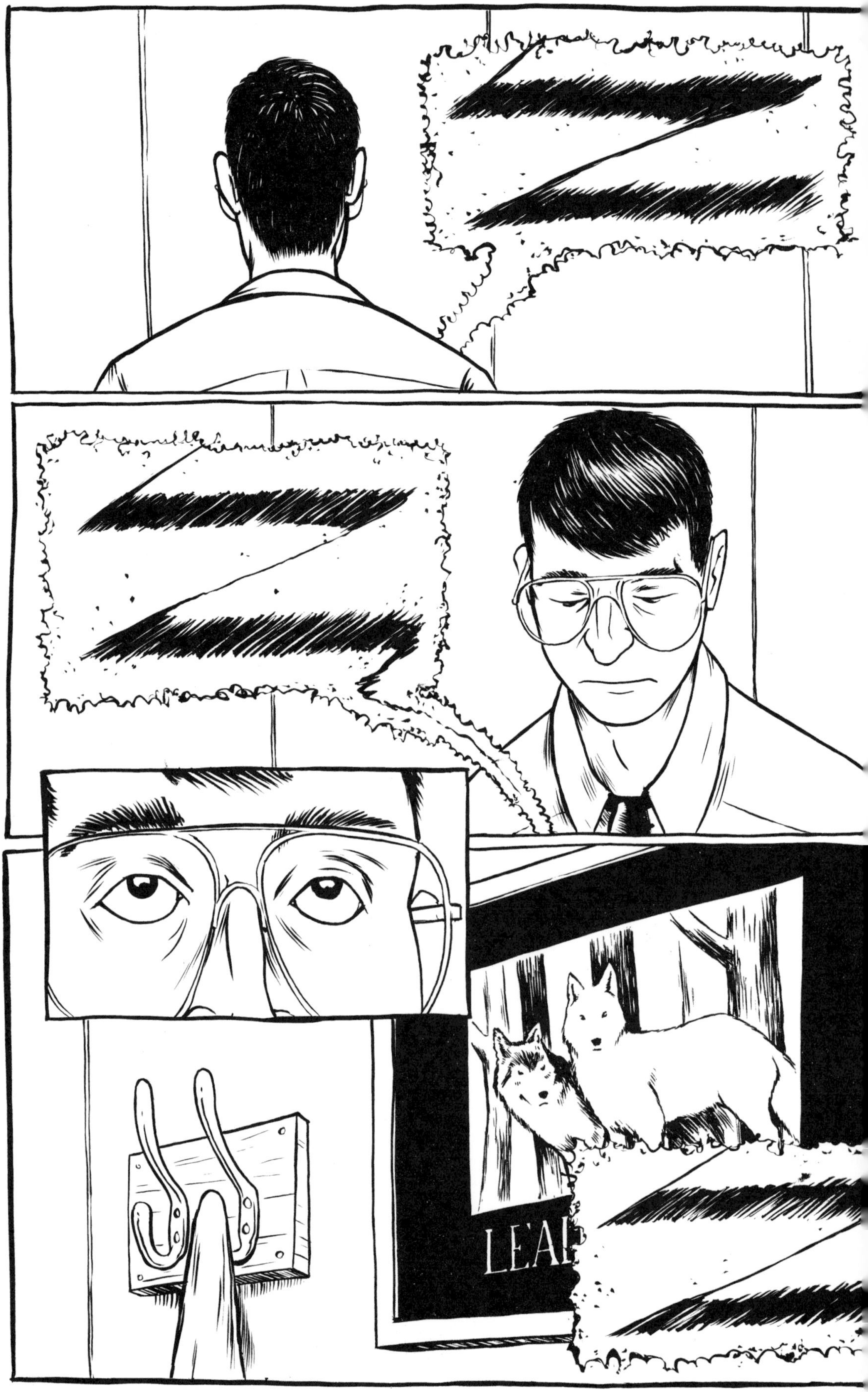
LEA

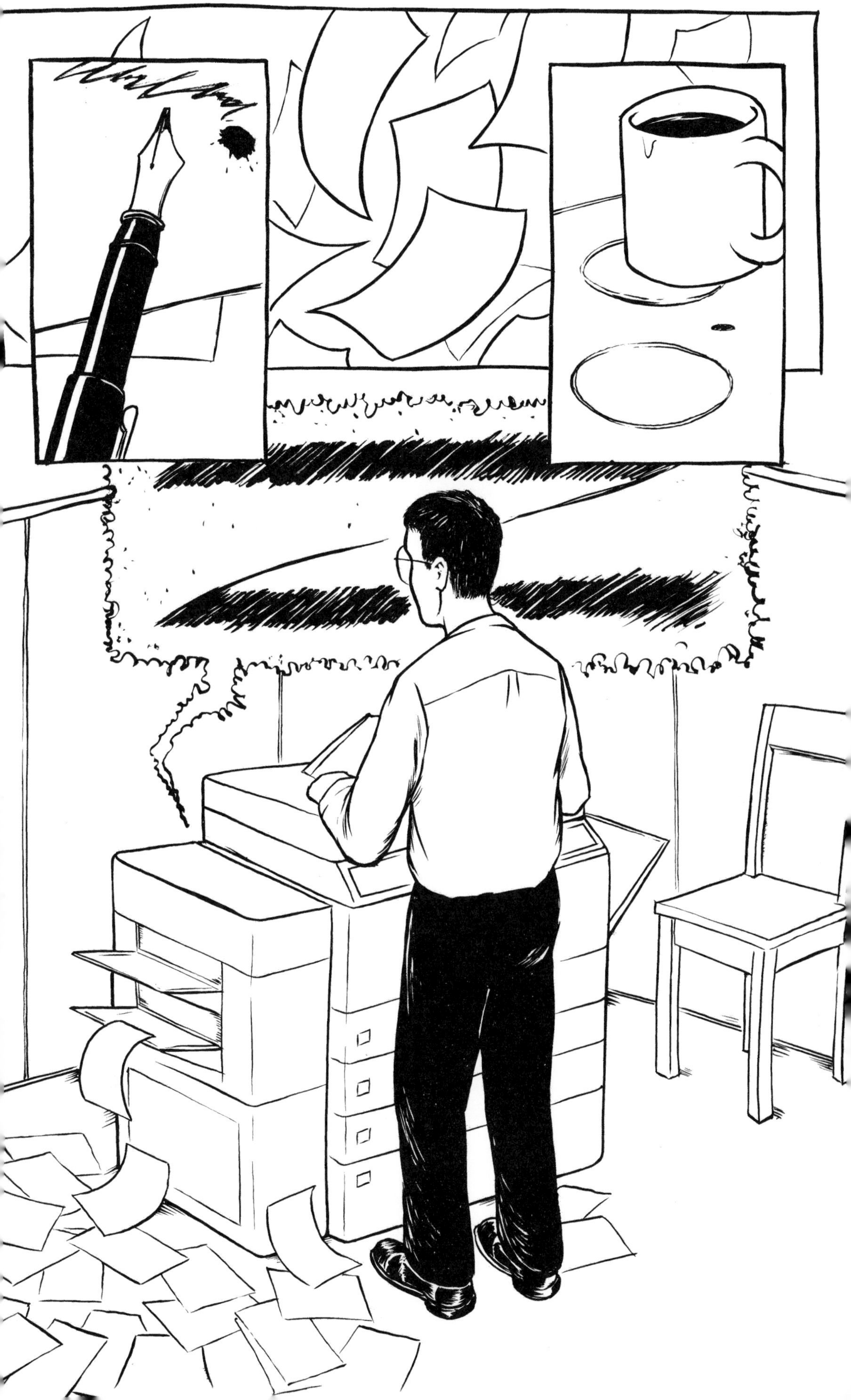

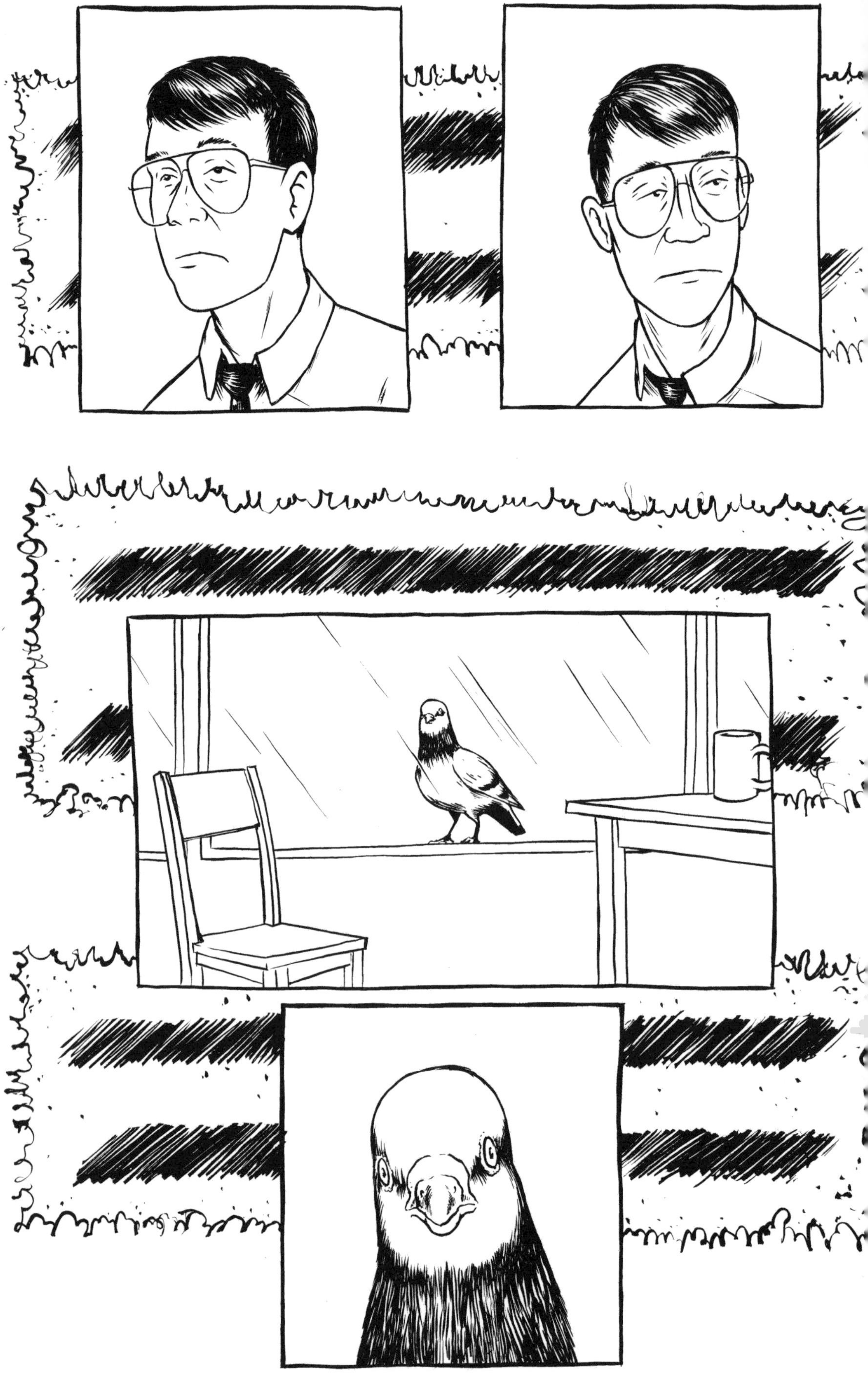

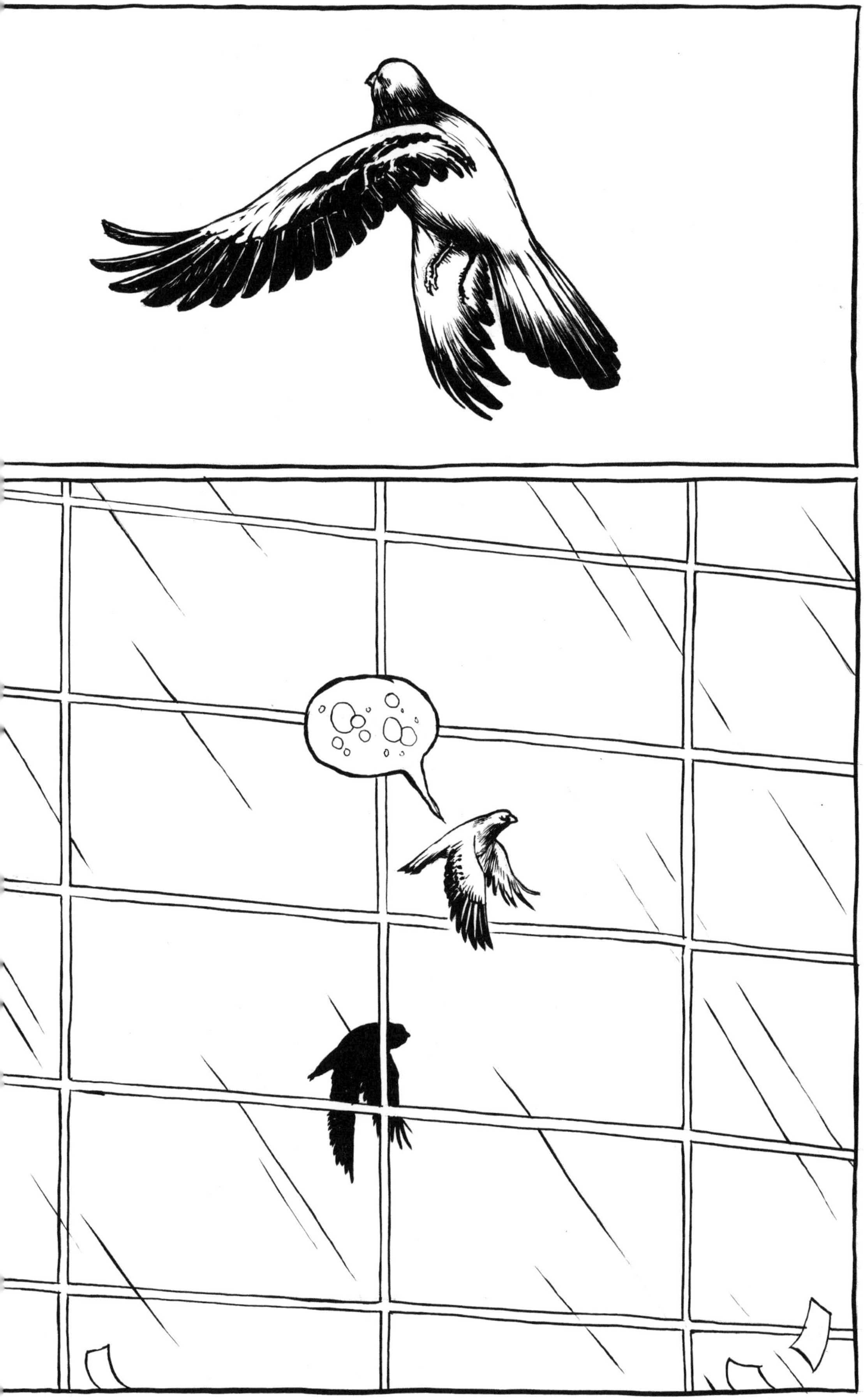

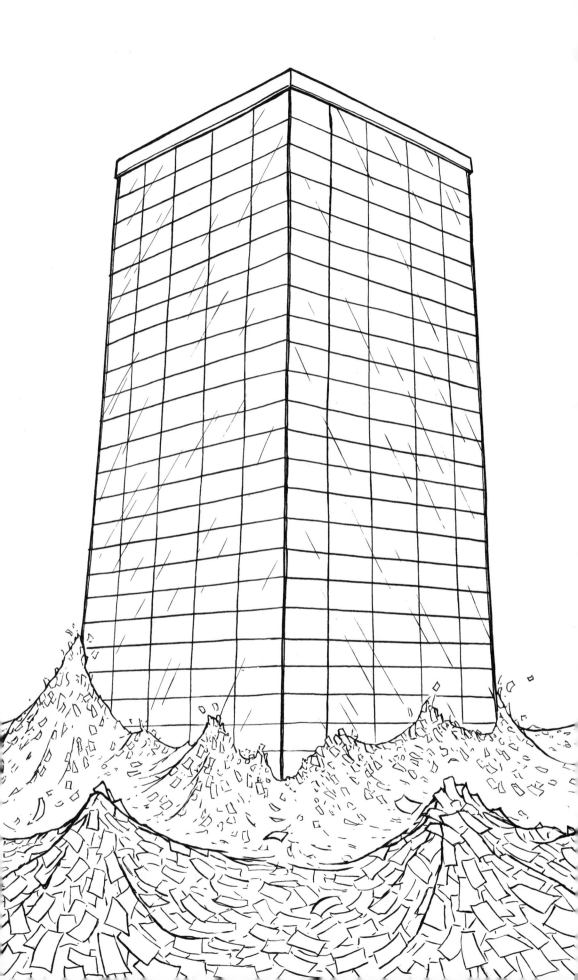

THANKS TO

LEON AVELINO, BARRY MATTHEWS, JOSH SHALEK, TYRELL CANNON,
MATTHEW OCASIO, NEIL BRIDEAU, KENAN RUBENSTEIN, MICHAEL
MANOMIVIBUL, ZACK SOTO, SHANNA MATUSZAK, FRANÇOIS
VIGNEAULT, MARC ARSENAULT, ERIK AUCOIN, FAREL DALRYMPLE,
NICK ABADZIS, MITA MAHATO, ARON NELS STEINKE, KINOKO EVANS,
BT LIVERMORE, EVAN DUMAS, PHILLIP STEWART, WALKER CAHALL,
RICHARD ROLFE, JAKE FRANCE, NAN ALLISON, ANDREA ISASI,
SARAH MIRK, CHAYA BOGORAD, JUSTIN HOCKING, SEAN PLISKA,
POLLYANNE BIRGE, MARY CAMPBELL, GREG PSALTIS,
MARYELLEN PSALTIS, BILL CAMPBELL, SHARON CHAIT,
BRYAN CAMPBELL, CAROLYN CAMPBELL, WILLIAM CAMPBELL,
KEVIN CAMPBELL, AND SYLVIA CAMPBELL